American Dietetic Association

Making Nutrition Your Business

Private Practice and Beyond

Faye Berger Mitchell, RD, and Ann M. Silver, MS, RD, CDE, CDN

Diana Faulhaber, Publisher
Laura Pelehach, Acquisitions and Development Manager
Elizabeth Nishiura, Production Manager
Krisan Matthews, Assistant Development Editor

10 9 8 7 6 5 4 3 2 1

Library of Congress Cataloging-in-Publication Data

Mitchell, Faye Berger.
Making nutrition your business: private practice and beyond / Faye Berger Mitchell and Ann M. Silver.
p. ; cm.
Includes bibliographical references and index.
ISBN 978-0-88091-440-6
1. Dietetics—Practice. I. Litt, Ann Selkowitz. American Dietetic Association guide to private practice.
II. American Dietetic Association. III. Title.
[DNLM: 1. Dietetics. 2. Entrepreneurship. 3. Practice Management—organization & administration. 4. Private Practice—organization & administration. WB 400 M6805m 2011]
RM218.5.M58 2011
613.2068—dc22
2010022044

Cover photograph: Gregor Schuster/Getty Images

Contents

Acknowledgments

This publication would not have been possible without the support of many individuals. We'd like to thank:

- Laura Pelehach and Krisan Matthews, our editors, who patiently worked with us and guided us through the challenges of revising the original book into a new and up-to-date book.
- Pam Michael and Tori Bender from ADA's Nutrition Services Coverage Team for their assistance in interpreting the technical HIPAA and third-party reimbursement information.
- Karen Post for her legal expertise.
- Our incredibly resourceful and generous colleagues from the Nutrition Entrepreneurs Listserv, who were willing to assist other aspiring entrepreneurs by sharing tips, marketing strategies, and personal experiences to make this publication come to life.

Special thanks to Dina Aronson, Jean Caton, Molly Kellogg, Cindy Heroux, Teresa Pangan, Rebecca Scritchfield, and Lisa Stollman for their willingness to answer questions and provide invaluable assistance as needed.

Thanks also to our husbands, Andy and Perry, and our children, Hannah, Jessica, Elan, and Dena, who saw less of us—and ate more "take out" then they care to remember—so that we could complete this project.

This book is in memory of our dear friend and colleague Ann Selkowitz Litt. You are always in our hearts and minds. Working on this project, reading and revising your words, we felt your presence every step of the way.

Reviewers

Blair Giles, MS, RD, CDE
Owner, Atlanta Dietitian, LLC
Atlanta, GA

Cathy Leman, MA, RD
President/Owner, Nutrifit, Inc.
Glen Ellyn, IL

Christine M. Palumbo, MBA, RD
Nutrition Communications Consultant
Naperville, IL

Traci A. Thompson, MA, RD, CLT
Vice President of Nutrition Services, IMAGEplus Health Concepts
Littleton, CO

Therese S. Waterhous, PhD, RD
Owner, Willamette Nutrition Source, LLC
Corvallis, OR

Mandi Wong, RD
Co-owner, Feed Your Career, LLC
Allen, TX

Preface

This book is partly a revision of and partly an addition to the *American Dietetic Association Guide to Private Practice*. The original book, co-written by Ann S. Litt, MS, RD, who suddenly passed away in 2007, was geared toward registered dietitians (RDs) with aspirations of starting a private practice. Although it also provided advice on other types of consulting opportunities for those starting a nutrition-based business, the emphasis was on starting a practice.

The *American Dietetic Association Guide to Private Practice* was published in 2004, and at that time most of the RDs who owned their own businesses were in private practice. However, some entrepreneurial RDs were successfully branching out into other areas of consulting. Now, only six years later, the "face" of entrepreneurial dietitians has changed. Registered dietitians across the country have successful, thriving businesses in many arenas. From best-selling authors to media moguls, RDs have come a long way, and they continue to make in-roads into uncharted territory. With this in mind, we, along with our editor, decided to expand the focus of this publication beyond private practice. Therefore, we have written a book for aspiring nutrition entrepreneurs that provides information on the endless opportunities to begin a nutrition-based business.

This book is divided into three sections. Section 1: The Basics of Starting Your Business provides a wealth of information that can be applied to starting any type of nutrition business. Section 2: Everything You Need to Know About Private Practice takes the concepts discussed in Section 1 and applies them specifically to private practice. From marketing to setting up your counseling office to managing your money, the practical advice and examples in this section provide a step-by-step guide. Section 3: Beyond Private Practice explores alternate ways for RDs to capitalize on their unique qualifications as *the* food and nutrition experts.

Use this book as your roadmap. It contains the tools you need to get started but is not intended to replace the advice of accountants, lawyers, graphic designers, and other professionals. Nor does this book provide every detail of everything you need to know when starting your business. You will read sections or even sentences that leave you asking for more. This is your cue to consult further resources to satisfy your curiosity. Chapter 14 provides additional resources that can be helpful. Also seek the input of colleagues with more experience, as well as friends, family and other business people for their ideas and input.

We have both been fortunate to own our own businesses, and we are glad you have decided to make nutrition your business, too. We hope this book will save you from making some of the mistakes we made and provide you with the support you need to take the plunge. The work is hard, but the rewards are tremendous. We wish you good luck and a sense of humor as you set out to make nutrition your business.

Faye Berger Mitchell, RD
Ann M. Silver, MS, RD, CDE, CDN

Section 1

The Basics of Starting Your Business

Chapter 1

Going Solo: Is It for You?

If you are reading this book, you have given some thought to starting your own business. Many people dream about being their own boss—but it's not for everyone. Before you give up a steady paycheck to follow your dream, read on. Carefully evaluate yourself as a potential business owner, your motivation for being on your own, and the pros and cons of starting a business. Then, complete the self-evaluation in Box 1.1 (1) to help you determine whether this is an entertaining fantasy or a viable option.

Box 1.1 The Small Business Owner's Aptitude Test

After reading each question, note your numerical response on a scale from 1 to 5.

1. In the games that you play, do you play harder when you fall behind, or do you have a tendency to fold your cards and cut your losses? (5 if you play harder, 1 if you wilt under pressure)
2. When you go to a concert or sporting event, do you try to figure out the owner or promoter's revenues? (5 if you often do, 1 if you've never considered it)
3. When things take a turn for the worse, do you look for someone to blame or do you try to find alternatives or solutions? (5 if you look for alternatives/solutions and 1 if you complain or blame)

(continued)

Box 1.1 *(continued)*

4. Compared to friends and colleagues, how would you rate your energy level? (5 is high, 1 is low)
5. Do you daydream about being your own boss? (5 if you often do, 1 if you never do)
6. When you are faced with important life changes, do you worry and fret about them or do you look forward to them, do your research, and consider changes exciting? (5 if you make changes after research and thought, 1 if you are too worried to make a change)
7. Do you look at the upside of opportunities or consider the downside first? (5 if you always see the upside and recognize risks, 1 if you dwell on the downside)
8. Are you the happiest when you are busy or when you have nothing to do? (5 if you are happiest when busy, 1 if you are happiest when idle)
9. As an older child or young adult, were you scheming or have ideas about how to make money? (5 if always, 1 if never)
10. Did you work part-time or summers as a teenager, or did you head to the beach or pool over the summer? (5 if worked, 1 if beach)
11. Did your parents own a business? (5 if owned one for a long while, 1 if they never owned a business)
12. Have you worked for a small business for more than one year? (5 if you have, 1 if you haven't)
13. Do you like being in charge and the center of attention? (5 if you really crave those things, 1 if you detest those things)
14. Do you have a problem borrowing money? (5 if you don't have a problem, 1 if it's a huge problem)
15. How creative are you? (5 if extremely, 1 if not creative at all)
16. Do you have to balance your checkbook to the penny or is "close" good enough? (5 if "close" is good enough, 1 if to the penny)
17. When you fail at a project or task, does it scar you or does it inspire you to do better the next time? (5 if it inspires you, 1 if it scars you)
18. When you truly believe in something, are you able to sell it? (5 if almost always, 1 if never)
19. In your own circle, are you generally a leader or a follower? (5 if almost always a leader, 1 if almost always a follower)
20. How good are you at keeping New Year's resolutions? (5 if you almost always keep them, 1 if you never do)

Scoring the test:

80–100: Go for it . . . you should be a successful entrepreneur.

60–79: You probably have what it takes to be successful, but take some time to look over the questions where you scored low.

40–59: Too close to call.

0–39: Tests are sometimes wrong, but you are probably better off staying as an employee.

Source: Adapted from *Small Business For Dummies, 2nd Edition,* by Eric Tyson and Jim Schell.

What is your motivation for wanting to start your own business? Do you want to spend more time with your patients? Do you want to have a work schedule that accommodates your family life? Do you want to make more money? These are all valid reasons for wanting to be your own boss, and they are all realities of running your own business. However, not everyone is cut out to be an entrepreneur.

Before taking the giant leap out on your own, it is important to know what it takes to be a successful entrepreneur. There are personal and professional characteristics and traits typical of those who are successful (1–4). It is not necessary (or likely) that you naturally possess all these traits. What is important is the ability to evaluate your strengths and weaknesses and ask for help when you aren't capable of doing it all.

Personality Traits of Successful Entrepreneurs

Many registered dietitians (RDs) have mastered the necessary educational, clinical, and foodservice skills to be effective in their employed positions. Understanding what makes a successful RD provides insight into the traits of a successful entrepreneur. These skills must be expanded upon and new skills learned to become a successful business owner. The following traits are recommended for those going into their own business.

Being a Risk Taker

It is risky to leave a reliable job, regular paycheck, benefits package, and sense of performance expectations. Questions you never entertained as an employee will loom large when you are a business owner. How will you establish yourself in the community? How will you structure your day? How will you make money? You likely never considered these questions as an employee, but they will weigh heavily on you as a business owner.

Many entrepreneurs are not natural risk takers. You can take actions to hedge your bets that you will succeed, but no matter how you package it, there is an inherent risk in moving from employee to business owner. To take that first step requires courage.

The Small Business Association estimates that one-third of small businesses fail within the first two years (3). Minimize your risk and increase your chances for success by being prepared. Seek the advice of business advisers, RDs who have gone into private practice, and friends who are business owners. Create a business plan and assess the environment to determine whether your business is feasible.

To lessen the risk, investigate the possibility of part-time employment while you develop your business. If part-time employment isn't an option, perhaps you will find it easier to moonlight—and build your practice by seeing patients in the evening or on weekends. Eventually, you will need to leave the world as an employee and enter the world as a business owner, and that will feel risky no matter how you structure it.

An entrepreneur will encounter many risks in the business world. That first step is just the beginning. Risk taking is a quality that eventually becomes part of your job description. You will learn to tolerate risk and see it as energizing rather than frightening.

Being Disciplined

To be on your own, you need to be disciplined. You won't need to punch a clock, state where you are going in the middle of the day, or give an excuse for a day off. Without discipline, it may be tempting to not "go to work," since you aren't accountable to anyone but yourself and your clients.

By establishing workdays and hours when you will see patients or meet with clients, you will impose discipline and structure based on when you are most productive. Determine whether you will go into the office on days when you don't have patients scheduled, and when you will do paperwork, answer your phone, read your e-mail, and network. Creating a work schedule will force you to be more organized.

Disciplined practitioners will also need to plan events and schedule opportunities to stay current. As an employee, you may have been able to attend grand rounds, join journal clubs, or benefit from professional dialogue with colleagues. On your own, you will need to make the effort to keep your skills current. You may have to carve time out of your workweek to attend a meeting. You will need to set aside time to stay current by tracking issues online or subscribing to and reading many different publications. You might also want to make it a point to meet with colleagues on a regular basis just to "stay in the loop."

Plan your schedule to include free time, too. You need to be disciplined enough to take time off to attend a child's field trip, go on a family vacation, or just give yourself a mental health day. If you're not disciplined, you might find yourself doing paperwork in your office long after the traditional workday has ended. All work and no play will not make a productive entrepreneur.

Having Confidence

Some individuals are born confident, and others need to find their confidence. If you are going to be successful, you will need to develop confidence and act as if it was always there. The more successful experiences you have in practice, the easier this becomes.

Confidence is being able to promote yourself 24 hours a day, 7 days a week. According to James Stephenson of Entrepreneur.com, self-promotion is one of the most beneficial, yet most underutilized, marketing tools that the majority of home business owners have at their immediate disposal (5). No one really feels comfortable relentlessly self-promoting. Be sure to assess the environment and determine when it is appropriate and when it just doesn't feel right to sell yourself. Refer to Box 1.2 for more tips on self-promotion.

Box 1.2 Selling Yourself

- Tell people what you do in a way they can fully understand. Keep this pitch brief, interesting, and to the point.
- Exude confidence to persuade people to respect and trust you and the services you provide.
- Ask people for what you want—a raise, a promotion, or a contract.
- Be passionate about your business—passion sells.

Confidence also means you are able to admit deficiencies and look for ways to correct them. A confident RD will readily refer a patient to someone more skilled in another area, send a reporter to an RD who might have more expertise in a particular subject, or call upon a Web designer to construct a Web site. Assessing your skills and determining what you are capable of handling and what should be delegated are also signs of confidence.

Being Adaptable

Being in business requires you to be a visionary. You must be able to spot nutrition trends in the marketplace. You don't need to be a trendsetter or compromise your beliefs. You do need to be open-minded enough to see the existing trends and recognize that your clients may want information on topics you don't agree with.

Being adaptable means knowing when to drop an idea that isn't going to fly, regardless of how much you like that idea. Moving on and getting over a failed project is part of being an adaptable entrepreneur.

You will meet many personality types in business. Although you are not required to become best friends with your business acquaintances, a flexible personality will enable you to keep many people on your side—an important asset in the business world.

Another important aspect of adaptability is having a back-up plan for days that do not go as scheduled. If you have a cancelled appointment or meeting, you can still be productive.

Being Tenacious

Entrepreneurs need to be driven self-starters who never give up. They tend to grab an opportunity and take advantage of it, without acting impulsively (6). An entrepreneur will always see the glass as half full instead of half empty. You will make many mistakes. Benefiting from those mistakes rather than feeling defeated, and learning how to turn disappointments into learning experiences are important lessons for anyone in business.

Owning a business is demanding, exhausting, and of course exhilarating. To realize the exhilaration, you will need to be strong to endure the emotional and physical demands placed on a business owner. It may be difficult at times to remember why you even wanted to be your own boss. Tenacity and drive are needed to energize and recharge—even when you think you've made it.

Professional Skills of Successful Entrepreneurs

Unless you had a successful business career before you became an RD, you need to develop a new set of professional skills. Most dietetics programs provide very little business training. Although many RDs are very comfortable with their clinical expertise, professional skills beyond clinical training are needed to run a business. Gaining real-world experience, whether or not it is clinical, will be helpful before you go out on your own. Most important will be your ability to assess what you can and can't manage on your own as a business owner.

Business Savvy

Being a businessperson requires a transition in thinking. RDs are in the profession to help people. You will never leave that helping profession, and you will need to expand your thinking to include how to reach out to your target market and provide quality goods and services that offer consumer value. This expansion in thinking helps you become a more skilled businessperson. What counts in business is the bottom line.

How you price your services is only one factor in determining your bottom line. Learning how to control costs, when to cut corners, and where to sink valuable dollars requires a business mind. If you are unsure, solicit input from colleagues established in the field already, other allied health professionals in practice in the community, and business organizations such as the Small Business Association and others listed in Chapter 14.

A unique aspect about providing nutrition services is that the public views nutrition and diet as familiar topics. Some may find it surprising that you charge for your services. Organizations, community groups, and even friends may assume this is a hobby, not a profession. It is easy to run into situations where you might be expected to give away your services.

Providing free lectures, volunteering at health fairs, or doing pro bono work at a local health clinic may be opportunities you view as important to promote your services. In business, however, you need to charge for the services you provide to earn a living. You need to determine how much charity or volunteer work you want to provide and where you draw the line.

If you expect payment for your work, keep your rates and policies intact. Practice saying, "My fee for this will be," so that when opportunities present themselves, you will feel comfortable asking for a fee. Alternatively, if you are not sure what rate to quote, you can ask, "What is the honorarium?" or "What is your budget?"

A savvy business owner learns to make decisions under pressure. In dietetics, you make decisions about patient care, so the foundation for decision making is in your training. Business situations may be unfamiliar, and you might have only your gut instincts to guide you at times. Thinking like a businessperson is a work in progress.

Organizational Skills

Knowing how to delegate, organize, and multitask are tremendous business skills. A small business owner will be required to plan, organize, and implement everything related to the business. You may not have the luxury of a technology person to help you create a presentation, an assistant to schedule your appointments, or a custodian to clean your office. You will need to determine what you can do and delegate what you can't do.

Planning is an important aspect of organization. When submitting proposals for consulting jobs, it is important that you have the ability to provide accurate time estimates and completion dates. In private practice, be sure to plan for administrative tasks such as scheduling appointments, contacting other health care providers on the treatment team by phone, sending follow-up letters, billing, and accounting.

You will need to multitask but be careful when doing so. In some cases, work performed while multitasking may not be as effective as work done individually. Make sure the quality of your work does not suffer when trying to multitask (7). Carefully evaluate the tasks at hand and determine whether you can do them simultaneously. For example, tasks that lend themselves well to multitasking are sending a fax while checking e-mails and holding on the phone with an insurance company.

Communication

Excellent communication skills are important in everything you do in life. In business, you must be able to communicate in a firm, positive way. You need to put a positive spin on your business as you communicate to the public. Being a good communicator means being a good listener, too. Whether you are communicating with a patient, a reporter, or an audience, you need to be comfortable with the give-and-take of conversation.

The first introduction to your services may be the initial telephone call to schedule an appointment or hook a client. You need to be persuasive without making promises that can't be kept. Learn how to speak succinctly and effectively. It is also quite possible that the first introduction to your services is a written inquiry via e-mail. Make sure your written communication skills are polished, and consider having a few blurbs available to explain your services to a potential client.

There are many excellent resources available on communication (8–10). Chapter 12 provides tips on communication and public speaking, as well as suggestions for ways to gain experience. If you are not a natural communicator, effective communication is one business skill you will need to acquire to be successful.

Professionalism

Remember that first impressions do count. Your appearance makes a statement about you and the quality of your work. Putting your best foot forward completes your marketing package. It is particularly important to dress for success if you are calling on clients, speaking in public, or working with the media. Avoid jeans, rumpled clothes, or excess makeup and jewelry. Dress conservatively in clothes that fit well. You may even dress differently depending on the situation. For example, if you are giving a talk to a group of high school athletes, you may dress a bit more casually than you would if presenting a lunch-and-learn session to a group of attorneys.

It is also important to treat others with respect and maintain diplomacy when dealing with difficult situations. Also be sure to return phone calls in a timely manner and answer calls in a professional way. Being prepared and on time for all meetings and appointments completes the package (6).

Clinical Expertise

Experience in clinical practice is a good foundation for any type of nutrition-related business. A clinical position in a hospital, clinic, or corporation can be a stepping-stone to opening your own business.

If you plan to have a medical nutrition therapy (MNT) practice, it's essential to have a strong clinical background and hospital-based work experience. The experience you gain and contacts you make while practicing in a traditional role are irreplaceable. If you plan to practice primarily in the areas not commonly classified as MNT—such as weight management, wellness, or general nutrition—you might find your clinical skills less important. Even if you do not plan to see patients at all, a basic knowledge of food, clinical nutrition, and possibly food service set the groundwork for you to branch into other aspects of consulting.

The Advantages of Going Solo

Starting a business is appealing for many reasons. You may be excited to leave employment and be your own boss. There's a thrill and prestige of being on your own. The following sections highlight some of the specific benefits an entrepreneur can enjoy.

Ability to Control Your Schedule

One of the biggest draws to owning your own business is the ability to control your schedule. When you set your office hours, the days you work and when you take vacation are your choice. Take advantage of this flexibility by structuring your day around when you are most productive. If you are a morning person, set up early office hours or do most of your work at that time. If you want to take vacation time during the busy holiday season, don't schedule patients or work during that time.

Private practice and writing offer the luxury of flexibility. A private practice should allow you to practice when, where, and how much you want. You might be able to choose the hours you see patients and select an office location convenient for you. Similarly, writing can be done at anytime night or day, as long as you are mindful of your deadline. If you are consulting to the media or providing corporate seminars, you may have less flexibility but can still choose times you are not available. Be prepared to work more than you did as an employee. The difference is you will decide when you will put in those long hours to have a profitable business.

Balanced Life

Going solo appeals to many people looking to find the perfect balance between work and parenting. The image of a home-based office, close to the family, seems like an ideal solution. The reality is that starting a business and having a family are both extremely demanding. They are not mutually exclusive, but both create stress and require you to learn new skills. In an ideal world, you might want to have one or the other in place rather than embarking on both at the same time (11). The flexibility and ability to "call the shots" is an appealing advantage to anyone seeking more control over their personal life.

Potential Earnings

An RD entrepreneur can earn more than an RD working as an employee (12). However, starting a practice, like starting any other business, is not a get-rich-quick scheme. Financial rewards take time. It is estimated that a new business takes three to five years to realize a profit (3). Starting your own business carries risks, but the benefits should include making more money than when you were an employee. Keep in mind that some of the income boost can come from the many potential tax advantages small business owners are afforded.

The earning power of a private practice is not limitless. Money is made by billing patients and there are only so many billable hours in a week. You may increase your earning potential by branching into other types of consulting. Often, you can realize more profits by writing, public speaking, consulting with the media, or developing and selling a product.

Expressing Your Own Style

Your business will be a personal extension of you. What you say, how you say it, and to whom you say it should reflect your style. You are the boss. You only have to answer to your professional code of ethics, not the party line of the hospital or facility that employs you.

Regardless of where you work, you need to maintain a professional image. Think about your work setting. If you are in private practice and renting space from a group of physicians, you may feel most comfortable wearing a lab coat. If you are working with a professional population, wearing a suit may make sense. In a health club, you may prefer to be more casual. Even when speaking, consider your audience. If you are presenting to a group of preschoolers, consider wearing something with brightly colored fruits or vegetables on it. If presenting a lunch-and-learn at a law firm, pull out the suit. Regardless of the setting, you will want to present a professional image.

Professional Pride

One of the most gratifying aspects of business ownership is pride in knowing you work hard for your personal and professional fulfillment. Success will be self-perpetuating. You need to be passionate about what you do . . . and sell that passion.

The Disadvantages of Going Solo

Of course, you need to think about the disadvantages as well as the advantages of your new potential venture. Anyone in business can speak to the pros and cons of going solo. Listen carefully. There are risks and struggles involved in being an entrepreneur. For those of us who are successful entrepreneurs, we can see the cons, but the pros far outweigh them.

Doing It All

Nutrition counseling or consulting will be just one small part of your business. The challenges of learning many new things will seem overwhelming at times. You will be wearing all the hats to make a business work. When the fax machine breaks, the scale needs calibration, or bills need to be sent out, you will be the one responsible.

One of the downsides to having your own business is the pull to always be working. Work demands can put strains on personal relationships. Try to focus on the flexibility you have as a business owner. Be careful not to overextend yourself. There are times you will have to say no, and that can be frustrating. Remember your priorities when it comes to outside obligations, such as family versus work. You must prioritize the demands on your time. To accomplish this, keep in mind that you will often feel there is still work to be done.

You will carry all the responsibilities on your shoulders. You will take all the blame when things don't work out. This can be draining, both emotionally and physically. Recognizing you can't make everyone happy is a reality of business ownership.

Financial Concerns

There will always be financial risk involved in owning a business. Cash flow may be a problem. To keep your business alive, you might need to invest your own savings, moonlight to have a steady income, or borrow money to stay solvent. In any situation, the financial arrangements may create stress in your life.

Financial issues ultimately affect those dependent on you, as well. It is important to have the moral support of your family when you take on the risk of being in your own business. They may need to feel the sacrifice is worth it for you to succeed.

Financial concerns can become more intense should you become ill or need to take time off for other reasons. Whether you are ill, want to take a day off to attend a conference, or have to cancel patients due to inclement weather—these are all situations that will impact your bottom line.

Your income will be erratic. You eventually will come to know the normal fluctuations and patterns. Pace yourself by learning which months are busy and which are slow. Try to schedule vacations when your patient population seems more likely to be taking time off too or when your workload is a bit lighter.

Professional Isolation

Going solo means just that. You are on your own. You must make an effort to network with others. There are ways to avoid feeling isolated, but it is up to you to make that happen. Make a point to connect with other professionals regularly. Join relevant Listservs, meet for lunch dates with colleagues, or just go out for an afternoon with a friend. You will need to recharge to stay motivated.

Going Solo? A Summary

Here are the key points you should take away from this chapter:

- Personal traits of successful entrepreneurs include being a risk taker, being disciplined, having confidence, being adaptable, and being tenacious. You may not possess all these traits, but you need to identify your weaknesses and supplement with professional help as needed.
- Professional skills for stepping out on your own include business savvy, good organizational skills, being an effective communicator, and possessing expertise in some area of nutrition.
- There are pros and cons to being your own boss. Be honest in looking at the whole picture before you jump into your own business.

- As RDs consider private practice or consulting, they must carefully assess the environment and their own commitment. There is nothing more gratifying if it works. Being a successful entrepreneur should be financially rewarding and professionally and personally fulfilling.

References

1. Tyson E, Schell J. *Small Business for Dummies*. New York, NY: John Wiley and Sons Publishing; 2008.
2. Pinson L, Jinnett J. *Steps to Small Business Start-Up: Everything You Need to Know to Turn Your Idea into a Successful Business*. Chicago, IL: Dearborn Publishing; 2006.
3. US Small Business Association. FAQs: Frequently Asked Questions. http://web.sba.gov/faqs/faqindexAll.cfm?areaid=24. Accessed March 23, 2009.
4. Harrington J. *The Everything Start Your Own Business Book*. Avon, MA: Adams Media; 2006.
5. Stephenson J. 25 Common Characteristics of Successful Entrepreneurs. http://www.entrepreneur.com/homebasedbiz/article200730.html. Accessed August 10, 2009.
6. Ezine Articles. Traits of the Successful Entrepreneur. http://ezinearticles.com/?Traits-of-The-Successful-Entrepreneur&id=3991&opt=print. Accessed March 13, 2009.
7. What to Know About Multitasking for Business. Available at: http://whattoknow.org/23-what-to-know-about-multitasking-for-business. Accessed August 11, 2009.
8. Boothman N. *How to Connect in Business in 90 Seconds or Less*. New York, NY: Workman Publishing; 2002.
9. Halli B, Calabrese R, O'Sullivan MJ, O'Sullivan MK. *Communication and Education Skills for Dietetics Professionals*. New York, NY: Lippincott Williams & Wilkins; 2008.
10. Carnegie D. *How to Win Friends and Influence People*. New York, NY: Pocket Books; 1998.
11. Stevenson L. A mother in private practice. *Today's Dietitian*. 2003;5:58.
12. Rogers D. Compensation and benefits survey 2007: above average pay gains seen for registered dietitians. *J Am Diet Assoc*. 2008;108:416–427.

Chapter 2

First Steps: Business Essentials

Whether you are striking out entirely on your own or accepting one small independent project, the information provided in this chapter will help you understand the first steps you need to take to build a nutrition business. Choosing good advisers, setting up the structure of your business, and writing a business plan will build a foundation for your success. In addition, your success as an entrepreneur will depend on how well you meet your legal obligations and insure yourself and your business.

Who Are You? The Difference Between Employment and Self-Employment

As you move from being an employee to self-employment, you need to determine what you will call yourself. Are you a nutrition consultant, a registered dietitian (RD) in private practice, a writer, or an entrepreneur? Possibly you will use all of those titles and more—sometimes simultaneously.

In important ways, the Internal Revenue Service (IRS) may determine what you ultimately call yourself. The IRS provides guidelines for determining whether you are an independent contractor or an employee. These distinctions are critical to determine your federal tax obligations, your Social Security and Medicare payments, and how and when to file your tax returns (1). See Chapter 13 for more information on IRS criteria for independent contractor status.

As you launch your business, you may decide to maintain your status as an employee but take on other projects as an independent contractor. This is an important decision to make from the onset, because having a steady stream of income can be crucial during your transition to self-employment.

Business Advisers

There are many types of business advisers available to help you do what you cannot do, do not want to do, or should not do. As most of us have been trained as registered dietitians (RDs) and not entrepreneurs, it is important to know when to ask for help. Spending money on an adviser who knows about small businesses will be a wise investment in your future. Following is a list of people and a brief explanation of how they might assist you in the business world.

Accountants

An accountant can advise you on your taxes, legitimate business deductions, suitable business structure, and overall record keeping. As your business grows, an accountant can also advise you on investments. It is best to work with an accountant who is familiar with small businesses. Be aware, however, that fees vary tremendously. Ask around for recommendations for an accountant from colleagues, friends, and family.

Attorneys

It is advisable to consult an attorney before making any decision with legal implications, such as deciding your business structure, drawing up a partnership agreement, and drafting or signing a contract. You might also consult an attorney before signing a lease, negotiating a bank loan, or copyrighting written material. Be sure to hire an attorney who is familiar with small businesses and has fees in line with what you can afford (2,3).

Bankers

Establish a relationship with a friendly banker. Even if you don't plan to take out a loan, a banker can often advise you on the best accounts for your business, lead you to credit cards with the most attractive interest rates, and even help guide you about accepting credit cards in your practice. Open a checking account and obtain a credit card to be used only for your business. This will make it easier to track your business and keep it separate from your personal expenses. A banker can also provide you with information on setting up individual retirement accounts (IRAs) and Keogh plans for small businesses. Best of all, the advice from bankers is free.

Business Consultants

A business consultant can serve as an overall adviser to your business. He or she may be able to guide you to an ideal office location, help you to project a professional image in the community, or offer ideas for establishing your business priorities. The best way to find an adviser is by speaking to others who have started a business. The Small Business Administration (SBA) may also keep lists of people who are available in your community; this information can be accessed through the SBA Web site (4). Valuable business services are also available through the Service Corps of Retired Executives (SCORE). SCORE services are free. You can find out more about SCORE at its Web site (5).

Marketing Consultants and Public Relations Advisers

As your business grows, consulting with a marketing person or a public relations adviser might take you to the next level. These consultants can help you name your business; design your logo; develop business cards, stationery, and a Web site; identify media contacts; or create marketing and social media campaigns. They are probably more helpful once you are off the ground and running. Fees vary tremendously. Shop around and be sure to get references from individuals with similar business goals.

Information Technology Consultants

A computer will be an essential tool in your nutrition business. The advice of an information technology consultant or computer specialist can assist in identifying your computer needs and can help when you have computer problems. Chapter 4 discusses the selection of computer equipment and office software. Chapter 6 explores Internet and social media technology. See Chapter 7 for information on nutrition-related software and databases.

Coaches

A coach—also referred to as a life coach, executive coach, or career coach—can empower you to understand the right business path for you. The coaching process focuses on helping you to discover the gap between where you are now in your business and life and where you want to be, and how to close the gap. A coach will ask powerful questions and listen rather than simply giving advice. Coaching can help you find what you thought was impossible. Many RDs work with a coach when starting out or transitioning their businesses. There are RDs who specialize as coaches and can help you in your business endeavor. You can find a coach by asking colleagues, posting on a dietetic practice group (DPG) Listserv, or checking on the Nutrition Entrepreneurs DPG Web site.

Choosing an Appropriate Business Structure

Business structure is not a static concept. You might operate under more than one type of structure at the same time. What you may find to be an appropriate structure when you start your business may change as your business develops. How you structure your business will determine what you are entitled to deduct as business expenses, how and when to file your taxes, how to protect your assets, and which, if any, business licenses you are required to have.

There are essentially two business structures to choose from: "incorporated" and "unincorporated." Sole proprietorships and partnerships are unincorporated businesses. Corporations, S corporations, and limited liability corporations (LLCs) are examples of incorporated business options. The difference in the business structure determines how you will file and pay your taxes, the amount of legal paperwork you are required to complete to operate your business, how you will be able to raise money if needed for your business, and your personal liability (6–8).

Sole Proprietorships: Going It Alone

Sole proprietorship is the most common type of business structure in this country. Most businesses start out as a sole proprietorship (7). There is a good reason for this. It is the easiest and least costly way to operate a business. Should you decide to open your business tomorrow, you could essentially do so as a sole proprietor.

As a sole proprietor, you can operate under your own name or choose a fictitious name. (See "Naming Your Business" later in this chapter.) When you are a sole proprietor, you are the boss. You make all decisions about your business. You pay for all your expenses, you are responsible for all your debt, and you reap all the profits. Should you choose to stop practicing and close your doors, you can quite literally shut the door behind you and call yourself retired (or out of business).

Your business is not a taxable entity as a sole proprietor. However, you are responsible for paying a self-employment tax. Your business expenses, profits, or losses are recorded on either Schedule C, Profit and Loss from a Business, or Schedule C-EZ, Net Profit from Business. They are then included with your annual individual tax return, Form 1040, and filed annually with your personal taxes. Depending on your profitability and your total household income, this structure could benefit you because your business losses can offset the income you have from other sources, allowing your net taxes to be lessened. For further information on tax forms, see Box 2.1 (8).

Box 2.1 Sample Internal Revenue Service Forms

Federal tax forms for sole proprietorship:

- Form 1040: Individual Income Tax Return
- Schedule C: Profit or Loss from Business (or Schedule C-EZ)
- Schedule SE: Self-Employment Tax
- Form 1040-ES: Estimated Tax for Individuals
- Form 8829: Expenses for Business Use of Your Home

Federal tax forms for partnerships:

- Form 1065: Partnership Return of Income
- Form 1065 K-1: Partner's Share of Income, Credit, Deductions
- Form 1040: Individual Income Tax Return
- Schedule E: Supplemental Income and Loss
- Schedule SE: Self-Employment Tax
- Form 1040-ES: Estimated Tax for Individuals

Federal tax forms for C corporations:

- Form 1120 or 1120-A: Corporation Income Tax Return
- Form 1120-W: Estimated Tax for Corporation
- Form 8109-B: Deposit Coupon

Federal tax forms for S corporations:

- Form 1120S: Income Tax Return for S Corporation
- Form 1040: Individual Income Tax Return
- Form 1040ES: Estimated Tax for Individuals
- Schedule E: Supplemental Income and Loss
- Schedule SE: Self-Employment Tax

Federal tax forms for an LLC are generally similar to partnership forms.

Note: This is only a partial listing. Depending on your business, some forms may not apply. Forms are subject to change.

Source: United States Small Business Administration. http://www.sba.gov/smallbusinessplanner/start/chooseastructure/START_FORMS_OWNERSHIP.html. Accessed March 23, 2009.

Being a sole proprietor has some disadvantages. If you need to raise money to operate your business, banks may be reluctant to issue you a loan. You are responsible for debt incurred by your business. If you are sued, it is possible that your personal assets will be at risk. Finally, unless you sell your business, it may end in the event of illness, injury, or death. For more advantages and disadvantages of sole proprietorship, see Box 2.2.

Box 2.2 Advantages and Disadvantages of Sole Proprietorship

Advantages:

- Sole proprietorships are easy to form and dissolve. Few if any legal documents are required to set up shop. When you are ready to close the business, you simply cease to operate.
- This is the least expensive form of business to start.
- Paperwork is minimal. Your state may or may not require you to register your business and obtain a business license.
- You are taxed as an individual.[a] Your business expenses and profit or losses from your business are recorded on a Schedule C and filed annually with your personal tax form. Depending on your profitability and your total household income, this could be a benefit, because your business losses can offset the income you have from other sources, which decreases your net taxes.
- You are the boss. You make all the decisions related to your business. You don't answer to anyone else. You retain total control.
- The big bucks are yours. Once your business is profitable, you are entitled to all the profits!

Disadvantages:

- Personal liability is unlimited. You and your business are viewed as one entity by the legal system. If your business incurs debts or if you are sued, your personal assets, such as your car or your house, may be seized to satisfy a legal claim or business debt. You should have insurance to protect your assets, but it may not be enough to completely protect you.
- Funding your business can be difficult. Banks may be less likely to lend to sole proprietorships than they are to corporations. Funding may depend on your personal credit history.
- It gets lonely at the top. Being a sole proprietor can be isolating. You need to make an effort to interact with and get input from others.
- Your business will lack of continuity. When you stop practicing, your business ends unless it is sold.

[a]Note that as a sole proprietor, you must file a schedule SE and pay self-employment tax.

Partnerships: A Match Made in Heaven?

A general partnership is an arrangement in which two or more people own and operate an unincorporated business. A partnership, like a sole proprietorship, is relatively easy to start. There are no required legal documents, although your state may require a business license. Partnerships appear very attractive and can be beneficial to RDs starting a new business. Partnerships allow you to pool your resources, talents, and expenses. If you are just starting out, that means one scale, one set of food models, and one rented office.

With a partnership, you can bring your talents together in a cooperative way. Perhaps one RD is a diabetes expert and the other has strong organizational skills because of her work as a chief clinical dietitian at a large teaching hospital. Combining these strengths can be very effective.

Reporting your income as a partnership is not as straightforward as reporting it as a sole proprietor. The partnership is not taxed, but each partner is required to report their share of the partnership income and deductions on IRS Form 1065, Schedule K-1. Many new entrepreneurs may require the assistance of an accountant to compile this information.

As with all business structures, there is a downside to partnerships. Partners expect much from each other. It is important to honestly assess and evaluate your partner as a business partner, not as a friend. You must understand each other's work ethic and share common goals and visions for the partnership. You must be explicit in determining what you expect from one another. If those expectations are not clearly stated, someone is going to be disappointed and the partnership will suffer.

Although you are not governed by legal documents, when forming a partnership (even with a close friend) it is highly recommended that you spell out all details pertaining to the partnership in writing (7). A partnership agreement should address the following:

- Name of partnership
- The purpose of the partnership
- Expectations of each partner
- How you will make business decisions
- How profits and losses will be distributed
- How money and time will be contributed
- How disputes will be resolved
- How new partners will be added, if needed
- How you will terminate the business in the event of a partner's death, disability, illness, or desire to leave

Like a sole proprietor, a partnership faces unlimited legal and financial liability. That means each partner is responsible for 100 percent of the debts. If one partner incurs debt, the other partner's assets can be used to cover the joint debt. And regardless of your partnership agreement, a creditor may collect from the partner from whom it is easiest to collect. If one partner is sued, both are vulnerable.

When a partnership is terminated, as when a marriage fails, you must clearly identify who is entitled to what. This can get very sticky if an agreement has not been developed and put in writing. For more information, see Box 2.3.

Box 2.3 Advantages and Disadvantages of Partnerships

Advantages:

- Partnerships are easy to form. Some states may require a business license to operate.
- You will have pooled resources and talent. Two heads are better than one.
- Little capital is required to start a partnership and your borrowing ability is greater than in a sole proprietorship.
- Partners are taxed as individuals rather than as a business.
- Partners have a broader management base than sole proprietors.

Disadvantages:

- When you decide to split the partnership, it can be difficult to dissolve. Assets and debts must be divided. (Think divorce.)
- Like a sole proprietor, partners are personally responsible for all debts. If one partner is sued, both are responsible. The partner with more assets stands to lose more.

The Limited Partnership

Limited partnerships are formed when there are two or more general partners owning and operating a business and two or more "limited partners." A limited partner is an investor and is not involved in managing or operating the business. The partner is liable for the investment but not for the entire company. According to the SBA, this partnership is not commonly used for retail or service businesses (8). It is best to have a business adviser help you determine which type of partnership is most appropriate for you to form.

Corporations: Not Just for McDonald's

When small business owners think about corporations, visions of McDonald's, General Motors, or Kraft Foods may come to mind. However, even a single

RD may become a corporation! In fact, many individual RDs do incorporate because of the distinct advantages.

A regular corporation is known as a C corporation. Corporations are legal business structures. Although they involve more complex and potentially expensive documentation and rules for operating, many RDs think that the advantages far outweigh the complexities. Unlike the sole proprietorship and the partnership, a corporation is legally separate from the people who own it. That means that your personal assets may be protected from your business assets in the event you are sued.

As a legal business entity, state laws govern a corporation. To be in accordance with such laws, paperwork must be filed and fees paid in order to conduct business. Generally, it is best to hire an attorney to assist you in complying with the paperwork needed to incorporate.

Once you incorporate, you will pay yourself a salary from the revenue you bring into the business. As with any business structure, this means you will need to establish a business account to keep your personal and business funds separate. Corporations pay taxes separate from the individuals who run the business. For these reasons, corporate finances may become time consuming. Such business matters can also be costly, especially if you pay an accountant to handle them.

There are options available that make incorporating feasible for small businesses. The S corporation and LLC are two examples suitable for smaller businesses. These types of entities protect the individual's personal assets, but their taxing structures are similar to that of a sole proprietor or partnership.

An LLC is a relatively new business structure and is available in all 50 states. An LLC is a hybrid entity that brings the best of partnership and corporation into one business structure (6). It provides the business owner with protection from personal liability similar to a corporation, but it can offer a taxing structure similar to a partnership. Many states allow you to complete the LLC forms online on your own, which can save money. Have a lawyer review the application before your file the form.

Some states also allow professionals to form a professional corporation (PC) or a professional association (PA). PCs and PAs were created for lawyers, doctors, and other professionals and may be appropriate for RDs in some states. The main advantage of PCs or PAs is that the professionals in the corporation are not liable for malpractice committed by others in the corporation.

There are no simple answers about who should or should not incorporate or what type of corporation is appropriate. This is an important business issue to discuss with your accountant, attorney, or business adviser. For further information on incorporating, see Box 2.4.

Box 2.4 Advantages and Disadvantages of Incorporation

Advantages:
- The corporation is a separate legal entity, so shareholders are generally protected from corporate liability.
- Ownership can be transferable.
- A corporation may be considered more legitimate than a sole proprietorship and has greater ability to raise or borrow money.

Disadvantages:
- Corporations can be difficult and more complex to manage because they are highly regulated by government. The paperwork adds to your workload.
- Corporations can be expensive and time consuming to form.
- Incorporating may result in higher overall taxes.

The Business Plan: Planning for Success

Purpose

Whether you are driving from Miami to Dallas, cooking a Thanksgiving dinner, or planting your vegetable garden, you have a map, recipe, or plan to guide you. Without a plan, you don't know where you are going or how to get to the finish line. The same is true with your business.

Your business plan is a blueprint for success. Writing your vision on paper doesn't make it a reality, but it does force you to focus on the essential information needed to run a business: who your target market is, what your philosophy is, how you will fund your business, what you will charge, and how you will market your business.

It is not only a good idea to write a business plan; it is essential if you hope to seek a loan from the bank. To obtain a loan from a bank, you must describe your business, your plans for managing the business, and your plans for how the money will be used.

Don't be intimidated. Writing a business plan should not be an obstacle to starting a practice. It does not need to be a 400-page tome. It may be a simple document that helps you formulate your vision and pave the way to making this vision a reality. There are many models and guides available, so it is not necessary to start from scratch (7,9,10).

What to Include

What you choose to include in your business plan is not mandated, but most business plans include the following information:

- **Cover sheet:** The cover sheet is a title page or cover sheet including the business name, address, telephone number(s), and contact information. A simple promotional description of your business should appear here, too.
- **Executive summary:** The executive summary appears at the beginning of the plan, but it will probably be the last thing you write because it will be an overview of the business plan. It should be no more than one page in length and succinctly describe your business structure, the goals of your business, what makes your business special or unique, your expertise, and your financial needs. It should translate the excitement you have for your business and encourage the reader to read on, especially if you are presenting your plan in an effort to borrow money.
- **Table of contents:** Like the table of contents in a book, this table of contents lists the information contained in your business plan and the corresponding page numbers. It is included to aid the reader.
- **Organizational plan:** This section outlines your business structure, where your business is located, and the equipment and resources needed to run the business. It also details what your services are, who will use your services, and why your services are important to the user. You might include an overview of your business that identifies your goals and objectives and explains why you are or want to be in business.
- **Marketing plan and analysis:** The marketing plan and analysis is where you evaluate and define your market. (Marketing plans are discussed in detail in Chapter 5.) You should include information about trends in the marketplace and how your services are impacted by those trends. Pricing of your services should be included in this section. You will assess the competition, detailing who they are, how you are different, and why consumers should choose you. You will also include your marketing strategy, which outlines the tools, resources, and techniques you plan to use for making the consumer aware of your services.
- **Financial plan:** This section is critical to the business plan. It is here that you determine the cash requirements for your business, such as what equipment is essential for starting out. You will also project income and create a cash flow analysis. If you are just starting out, this section is based on projected costs and income. It will be important to speak to other RDs in practice to get data for compiling this information.
- **Supporting documents:** The final section of a business plan should include supporting documents such as your resume, contracts or leases, articles of incorporation, partnership agreements, and personal financial statements.

Basic Requirements for Conducting Business

The requirements for running a business vary from state to state. Following is a summary of the general considerations and questions you will need answered before opening your practice. Your city hall, county court house, or state revenue department may have a comprehensive listing of requirements in your area. The local office of the SBA or the public library may have information and offer classes specific to doing business in your area.

Naming Your Business

If you are operating as a sole proprietor or partnership, you can use your own name(s) or choose a fictitious business name. Fictitious business names are referred to as DBA, or "doing business as." The process for naming your business varies from state to state.

Naming your business protects your name locally, but it does not prevent someone in another locale from using the same name. It is necessary to file your business name to both protect that name from others using it and use that name legally on your bank account (11).

Generally, if you are going to name your business, you must file that name with the county clerk or other local government agencies and ensure that no one else in your community is using that name. Publishing your fictitious name in a general circulation paper in the county where your business is located is one way to accomplish this.

If you are a corporation, naming your business is a formal process. When you begin the process of establishing your corporation and complete the required paperwork, the procedure for naming your business will be part of the documentation you will need to complete.

There are advantages and disadvantages to naming a business. Using your own name lends itself to better name recognition. If you are already established, this may be an advantage. Should you appear on television or get quoted in the newspaper, it is your name people will remember, not your business name. On the other hand, having a business name may give more credibility to your business in the public's eyes.

Before naming your business, you may want to secure the domain name for your Web site, especially if you want your business to be the same as your Web address. Check whether the domain name is available. Chapter 6 can provide guidance on this.

Tax Identification Number

In identifying your business for tax purposes or other situations where you are requested to use a tax identification number, you can use your Social Security number only if your business operates as a sole proprietorship. With the rise of identity theft, even sole proprietors (with no employees) should not use their Social Security numbers in business, as unscrupulous people may take advantage. In all business arrangements, it's best to apply for a federal Tax

Identification Number, also referred to as an Employer Identification Number (EIN). The application (Form SS-4, Application for Employer Identification Number) is available from the IRS Web site. When you apply, you will be provided an EIN easily and quickly (12).

Licenses and Zoning

Licensing for RDs varies from state to state. Consult the American Dietetic Association (ADA) Web site (http://www.eatright.org) to determine whether the state in which you are conducting business is a state that licenses RDs. If you are operating a business in a state that requires RDs to be licensed, it will be necessary for you to be licensed in that state even if you do not reside there.

If you are selling a product, such as a book or pamphlet that you have written, it will be necessary to obtain a seller's permit or license. This is necessary for reporting sales tax information with your state. Seller's permits and the laws governing them vary by state. You need to contact your state department of revenue to obtain information.

Before you set up an office in your home, make sure you have checked out all the zoning and code ordinances for your neighborhood with an attorney and acquire any permits or licenses needed to run a home-based business. It may be perfectly fine to operate a business out of your home, but if you are out of compliance with local ordinances and laws, you can be fined.

Insurance

As an employee, you might not have given much thought to the insurance your employer carried. As a business owner, you must consider several different types of insurance. There are many types of insurance policies. It may seem prudent to buy all, but the reality is you probably don't need to. Sit down with your business adviser and investigate what is essential for you to have as you start out. A brief overview of the common types of insurance policies used by most small businesses follows.

Professional Liability Insurance

Depending on the scope of your business, you will want to explore and decide on the appropriate type of professional liability insurance (ie, malpractice insurance) (13). Although you may not have a litigious mind, when you are in business there is a chance you will be sued. Because you are the "expert" in your nutrition business, if someone feels you have not lived up to what they expected, they can initiate a lawsuit (14). Professional liability insurance can protect you financially in a lawsuit. If you will be providing medical nutrition therapy to patients, you should obtain malpractice insurance. As an author, writer, consultant, or speaker, you will want to consider specialized insurance for that scope of work. Read through or have a lawyer read through your policy. It may or may not cover all your new activities as an entrepreneur.

General Liability and Property Insurance

You will want to obtain an insurance policy to cover the contents of your office in the event they are damaged in a fire or flood or are stolen. In addition, general liability insurance should be purchased to cover you if someone is injured in your office. Be sure to ask your insurance agent about any other policies they may deem necessary.

Health Insurance

If you've had the luxury of having someone else pay for your health insurance, be prepared when you need to purchase it on your own. Health insurance is expensive! There are several options available for the self-employed. Professional organizations, including the ADA, offer their members group policies as a member benefit. Another resource is the insurance available through the National Association for the Self-Employed (15). Search the Internet, ask family and friends, and explore other affiliations that offer group plans for health insurance you may be able to participate in to obtain premiums that are more competitive.

When you leave an employment situation with health insurance to start out on your own, you may be entitled to coverage through the Consolidated Omnibus Budget Reconciliation Act (COBRA). If you've been employed in an organization with 20 or more employees, your previous employer must extend your health insurance for 18 months. You are required to pay for this coverage. For eligibility requirements, consult the COBRA Web site (16).

Life Insurance and Disability Insurance

If you have dependents that rely on your income, it is a wise idea to investigate disability and life insurance policies. Disability insurance protects your earnings in the event that you cannot work by providing a percentage of your earnings on a monthly basis for a specified amount of time. Life insurance policies provide your beneficiaries with a payment in the event of your death.

If you have had policies with a previous employer, it may be possible to take over the payments to continue coverage with those policies. Insurance policies are also available through many professional organizations, including the American Dietetic Association.

Contracts

A contract is commonly defined as "an agreement between two or more parties for doing or not doing something specified. Contracts define your rights and obligations" (17). As an RD in business, you may be presented with a written contract. An example of this is when you become a provider for a managed-care organization, engage in spokesperson work for a public relations firm, or write a book. You may choose to present a written contract to a prospective client. For example, if you are asked to provide weight management classes for a health club, analyze restaurant menus, or perform nutrient analysis for a small food company, you want to have a clear understanding with the other party as to the work you are to perform and the compensation you will receive.

RDs question whether they should hire an attorney to write or review their contracts (3). If you are presented with a written contract, it is likely that an attorney for the organization prepared it. If you don't understand the contract, you should seek advice from legal counsel familiar with service contracts (3). If you have decided to draw up your own contract, a good guideline is the following: the more specific you are about the material terms of the agreement, the more enforceable it will be.

First Steps: A Summary

Here are the main points you should take away from this chapter:

- Advisers to your business may include attorneys, accountants, bankers, general business consultants, marketing consultants, public relations advisers, information technology consultants, and coaches. When inquiring about the services of these consultants, be sure that they are familiar with small business issues and their fees are in accordance with your budget. It is best to get referrals from colleagues in practice.
- You can structure your business as a sole proprietorship, a partnership, or a corporation. Each business structure has advantages and disadvantages. It may be a wise investment to discuss your business with an attorney, an accountant, or a business adviser to determine the most appropriate structure for your practice.
- You should write a business plan to determine your target market, organize your business structure and funding, and state the goals of your practice and how you hope to achieve those goals. A business plan is necessary to borrow money from a bank. There are many tools available to write a business plan.
- To conduct business, you need to explore the pros and cons of naming your business and the steps to obtain a business name, the licenses and permits you need to be in business, and the necessary insurance policies.
- You may be presented with a contract for certain consulting situations, or you may want to present a contract for your services. Depending on the specifics, hiring an attorney might be prudent.

References

1. US Department of the Treasury, Internal Revenue Service. *Independent Contractor or Employee . . .* Washington, DC: U.S. Department of the Treasury, Internal Revenue Service; 2008. Publication 1779.

2. Busey JC. Are all lawyers the same? *J Am Diet Assoc.* 2007;107:915–917.
3. Busey JC. When do you need a lawyer? *J Am Diet Assoc.* 2007;107:733–735.
4. US Small Business Administration. http://www.sba.gov. Accessed March 23, 2009.
5. Service Corps of Retired Executives (SCORE). http://www.score.org. Accessed March 23, 2009.
6. Lesonsky R. *Start Your Own Business.* Irvine, CA: Entrepreneur Media; 2007.
7. Marks G, ed. *Streetwise, Small Business Book of Lists.* Avon, MA: Adams Media; 2006.
8. US Small Business Administration. Forms of business ownership. http://www.sba.gov/smallbusinessplanner/start/chooseastructure/start forms of ownership.html. Accessed March 23, 2009.
9. Strauss SD. *The Small Business Bible: Everything You Need to Know to Succeed in Your Small Business.* Hoboken, NJ: John Wiley & Sons; 2008.
10. Williams B, Murray J. *The Complete Guide to Working for Yourself.* Ocala, FL: Atlantic Publishing Group; 2008.
11. Business.gov Web site. Business Name Registration (Doing Business As). http://www.business.gov/register/business-name/dba.html. Accessed December 5, 2009.
12. US Department of the Treasury, Internal Revenue Service. How to apply for an EIN. http://www.irs.gov/businesses/small/article/0,,id=97860,00.html. Accessed March 23, 2009.
13. Busey JC. Do food and nutrition professionals really need liability insurance? *J Am Diet Assoc.* 2007;107:1480.
14. Insurance Information Institute. Do I need professional liability insurance? http://www.iii.org/individuals/business/optional/professionalliability. Accessed March 25, 2009.
15. National Association for the Self-Employed. http://www.nase.org. Accessed March 23, 2009.
16. Consolidated Omnibus Budget Reconciliation Act (COBRA). http://www.cobrainsurance.com. Accessed March 23, 2009.
17. *Random House Unabridged Dictionary.* 2nd ed. New York, NY: Random House; 1993.

Chapter 3

Money Management: Setting Fees and Getting Paid

This chapter explores the essentials of money management. The skills required to work as a registered dietitian (RD) are not necessarily the same set of skills you need to run your own business. Traditional nutrition and dietetics programs do not require any business or management classes. To be successful in your own business, however, you must start thinking and acting like a businessperson. You may have fantastic ideas and be excellent at what you do, but before you even hang your shingle or sell your first product, you must have all your business systems in place. You need to be constantly aware of the bottom line. You must feel comfortable with being paid. Do not be afraid to ask for money!

Setting Fees

A common burning question from aspiring entrepreneurs is "How much should I charge?" Many factors must be considered when setting fees, but there are no hard-and-fast rules. Often the fee you set may seem a bit arbitrary. Two simple formulas for setting fees are presented in Boxes 3.1 and 3.2 (1–3).

Box 3.1 Axelrod's Formula for Setting Consulting Fees

How to charge to earn $100,000:

- $100,000 income divided by 200 days = $500 per day base rate
- $500 per day base rate + $500 per day for overhead = $1,000 per day
- $1,000 per day + 25% add-on for profit = $1,250 per day
- **Daily consulting rate = $1,250 per day**

Source: Reprinted with permission from Axelrod M. The consulting process: setting fees. The New Game Web site. http://www.thenewgame.com/axelrodlearning/consultingprocess.html. Accessed March 30, 2009.

Box 3.2 Bleich's "Three Times" Rule

To calculate the ballpark amount you will need to bill to meet operating expenses, triple your desired income to determine how much you need to bill annually. For example, to earn $50,000 a year, she estimates you will need to bill $150,000.

Source: Data are from references 2 and 3.

Factors to Consider

Desired Salary

Determine your desired annual income (it is important to be realistic) as a starting point. Do you want to earn about the same amount of money that you earned in your previous job and reap the benefits of being self-employed? Or, is your goal to earn more than you previously earned? Either way, there must be some tangible benefit to having your own business.

Expenses

Of course, to earn a salary, you must set fees that cover your expenses and provide a sufficient profit. Therefore, one of the first things you must do when setting fees is analyze what your fixed and variable expenses will likely be:

- **Fixed costs** are expenses you incur regardless of how much of a product you sell or the number of clients or patients you see. Examples of fixed costs include your rent, phone bill, insurance, and Internet service charges.

- **Variable costs**, on the other hand, are costs directly associated with the actual products sold or services provided. Your variable costs will increase as you sell more products or see additional clients, but these expenses will be offset by the income it produces. Depending on the type of business you run, you will want to calculate variable costs on a per person, per project, or per product basis.

The following are expenses you will incur:

- **Benefits:** It is very important to factor in the cost of replacing lost benefits when setting your fees. Benefits usually provided by employers include health, life, disability, and other forms of insurance, as well as 401K, profit-sharing, or pension plans. You will now have to pay for these benefits.
- **Taxes:** Whether your business is a corporation or a sole proprietorship, you will need to pay taxes, and these can be a substantial expense. For example, if you are self-employed, you must pay both the employer and employee's portions of the Federal Insurance Contributions Act (FICA) tax. Each of the FICA taxes is imposed at a single flat rate. Currently, the Social Security tax rate for employees is 6.2 percent and the Medicare tax rate is 1.45 percent, which accounts for 7.65 percent of your gross income. Because the employer is required to match this tax, a self-employed person is considered both employer and employee. The 6.2 percent becomes 12.4 percent, and the 1.45 percent becomes 2.9 percent. As a self-employed person, you now pay a whopping 15.3 percent of your income in FICA to the federal government.
- **Business and office expenses:** Business and office expenses are often referred to as overhead costs. When first starting out, you should be somewhat frugal but not so restrictive that you neglect to have necessary supplies and equipment to properly do the job. For a complete listing of the necessary office supplies and equipment you will need, turn to Chapter 4.

The Value of Your Time

In addition to the salary you'd like to earn and the expenses you will incur, you also need to consider your time when setting your fees. In a service industry, you are billing for your time. There are many things to consider. Determine your salable time—how much time can you really work, or more specifically, how many hours can you actually bill? Again, it is important to be realistic in your estimates. Build vacation time, sick days, holiday, and personal time into your formula. Figure out how many weeks of each you want.

Consider your non-billable time, which always seems to amount to more than you may think. This is the time spent on administrative work, such as returning and making phone calls, writing letters, checking e-mails, writing and placing advertisements, paying bills, sending bills, and other accounting. Think also about how much time you will be spending on marketing, networking, and continuing education, whether it is attending seminars, doing research in your office, or catching up by reading journal articles.

Special Considerations for Private Practice

RDs in private practice and those who accept contract work have unique concerns when setting fees. For more information on fee setting in private practice, refer to Chapter 8.

Special Considerations for Contract Work

When setting fees for contract work or classes, do not forget to factor in the following:

- **Travel time**: There may be time when you need to travel farther than the normal commuting distance. If you must travel to another city, take time off from another job, and/or spend the night, this should affect your rates substantially. Figure 3.1 provides an example of how to charge for travel time and other expenses incurred.
- **Preparation time**: Preparation time is a significant factor in the equation. If you need to analyze recipes, go shopping, prepare food, create a presentation or handouts, or do any research, your fees should reflect this.
- **Duplicating costs**: If you provide handouts or if you need to make copies for your own use in a project, don't forget to factor in duplicating costs. If you do not have your own copy machine, the cost of copies can quickly add up. When you do provide handouts, consider negotiating to have the client make the copies. To do this, you must be prepared in advance to get your handouts to the client. If you are the type who likes to make last-minute changes before you give a presentation, this may not work for you.
- **Length of the job**: The duration of the job is another important consideration when setting fees. How many hours is the client committing to? If you are signing a contract to provide services for a few months' time or more, you can probably afford to offer a slightly lower rate. A stable source of income, paired with a steady job reducing your marketing efforts, will allow for this.
- **Project fee versus hourly fee**: Consider whether a project fee or an hourly fee is more appropriate. Generally speaking, a longer project demands a slightly lower hourly rate.
- **Per-head rate**: A per-head rate is an option if giving a large presentation. This can be structured more than one way. You can charge a certain rate, for example $20 per person, for each attendee. The larger the turnout, the greater you will profit. Another option is to charge a flat rate for a

guaranteed minimum number of people attending, with an added rate for each additional person over that minimum; you get paid regardless of whether anyone attends. This latter option presents less risk (4).

- **Value of the service to the client:** If the services you are to provide are part of a larger project and they are necessary for the completion of the project, the practitioner is in a position to demand a high rate.
- **Priority work:** If one client wants work done immediately, you may have to put other projects on hold or cancel patients or other billable projects, and this will cost you. You may wish to pass that cost to the client who requests the priority work.
- **Company variables:** The size, financial status, and type of company may have an effect on what companies are willing to pay. However, it is important to realize that it is not your job to give your services away to struggling companies.

[Letterhead/logo here]

INVOICE

[Client name]

[Client address]

Date:

Supplies for interview: receipts attached	$________
Radio interview (includes travel to/from radio station)	
2 hours @ $_____/hour	$________
Television interview—Boston, [date]	
1 day @ $_____/day	$________
Hotel expenses: receipts attached	
Boston, [date]	$________
Travel expenses: receipts attached	
Airfare	$________
Taxi to and from airport	$________
Total	$________

Figure 3.1. Sample invoice. Reprinted with permission from Faye Berger Mitchell, RD.

Mistakes to Avoid

Clearly, setting fees is no easy task. In private practice counseling, you will have a set fee schedule. It should now be apparent, however, that a lot of thought must go into the process of setting fees for other contract work.

Never think that you must immediately state your fee to potential clients. Ask appropriate questions regarding the job—where, what, when, how many, how long, and so on—and tell them you will get back to them. Ask them how soon they need to know and get back to them in a timely manner, but don't let them push you into a fee you will regret.

Remember that once you win the job based on a given fee, you cannot go back with a "whoops, I miscalculated my fees." Therefore, it is always best to overestimate or cushion your fee a bit. Try to start with a high bid for your services and negotiate from that point. Often, you'll be pleasantly surprised that the client will agree to your fees. This strategy will allow for any unforeseeable glitches and will protect you from a potential costly mistake.

Most importantly, *do not undersell yourself!* You should ensure that you receive appropriate compensation for your services, consistent with what your clients are willing to pay. Make sure that the fees you charge are consistent with the value of your services.

Creating Effective Policies and Procedures

It is important that you institute your accounting and other administrative policies before you open your doors. Initially, if you are starting your business on a small scale, you may feel you can just "wing it." This is not recommended. You need to have policies in writing and systems in place. Let's begin with simple record keeping.

Where and how will you maintain a list of your clients' names, addresses, phone numbers, and other crucial information? Contracts, leases and other legal papers, employee paperwork (if applicable), and licenses all must be kept available as well. Those documents kept electronically must be backed up. All successful businesses have good bookkeeping and record-keeping systems in place. It is imperative to keep detailed records for the following reasons (5):

- **To monitor and track the performance of your business**: To understand which expenses are necessary and which can be cut, you must constantly monitor your business. Ultimately, this will tell you whether you are making money and assist you in making sound business decisions.
- **To determine your salary**: To know how much to pay yourself, you must know how much you have. It is as simple as that!

- **To track tax obligations:** If you maintain up-to-date and accurate financial records, it is much easier to gather accurate data for filing taxes and other returns or paying quarterly taxes. It will also decrease your accounting bills if you present these detailed records to your accountant when it comes time to prepare your tax returns.
- **To obtain a loan from the bank:** If you want to borrow money, banks request very detailed financial records.

Many software packages are available to make detailed record keeping quite simple for small businesses. However, regardless of the computer software program, you still need to enter the data. Information that needs to be entered includes the cash receipts (the money coming in) and the cash disbursements (the money going out).

Each transaction should be recorded and assigned to a category, such as office supplies, rent, and postage. If each transaction is accurately recorded, the cash balance on the software package will equal the cash balance in your company checking account. This is known as a balanced set of books. Obviously, this is desirable.

Make sure you save supporting paperwork for your income and expenses. These items may include bank deposit slips, copies of checks, credit card receipts, cancelled checks, bank account statements, invoices, and receipts for out-of-pocket expenses. This material is particularly important should you ever be audited.

To keep your finances straight, you will need to set up your system as if you have two separate businesses. One will manage your accounts receivable and allow you to send invoices out to clients and/or patients who owe you money. The other will record your income and expenses. That information will be used to file your income taxes and determine your profits.

Choosing Accounting Software

Software programs can perform all the necessary accounting and bookkeeping functions. There are many programs available on the market (6). Choosing the right system for your company is very important. You may want to speak with other business owners who have similar businesses. Also, ask the advice of your accountant.

To help you narrow your choice, consider which functions you want the system to perform. For example, you may want software that provides profit-and-loss statements, writes checks, and sends monthly bills. Again, your accountant can certainly advise you. You can also check the Internet for additional resources. Box 3.3 lists criteria you may want to consider before purchasing accounting software for your business (7,8).

Box 3.3 Factors to Consider When Choosing Accounting Software

Do you . . .

- Need something very basic or a program with versatility?
- Have inventory or will be selling a product?
- Want to track clients?
- Need payroll/have employees?
- Want to write checks?
- Want to do bookkeeping for taxes?
- Have international business needs?
- Need to send invoices, whether faxed or emailed?
- Want online banking access?
- Need customized reports?
- Accept credit cards?

Source: Data are from references 7 and 8.

Hiring an Accountant or Bookkeeper

If you are not very good at money management, you may prefer to hire someone to do your accounting and bookkeeping. This will allow you to spend your time on other aspects of running your business. For example, if you can bill $120 per hour for your time and pay a bookkeeper $50 per hour, you come out ahead. From a cost-benefit standpoint, you may be better off spending your time on providing services, developing your business, and marketing while leaving the administrative tasks to someone else.

The downside of hiring someone to manage your business finances, particularly when you are first starting out, is that it does cost money. Initially, most RDs going into business for themselves prefer to keep costs as low as possible. Also, when you are first getting started, it may be beneficial to have a better understanding of the financial aspect of the business. When you do the billing and accounting and perform other financial administrative tasks, you get a clear picture of what it actually costs to run your business and understand what is involved on the administrative end. As your business expands, you can then hire someone as an office administrator or even a part-time bookkeeper, depending on your needs. Weigh the options and decide which approach is best for you.

Getting Paid

How will you be paid for your products or services? Will you only accept cash and checks? Do you need to accept credit cards? And when will you get paid? These and other questions need to be answered.

Business Payment Policies

Your type of nutrition business will play a role in your payment policy. From the onset you need to establish your payment policy. Your customers or clients need to be informed of these policies.

Products and services can be paid for by check, cash, credit card, debit card, or online payment services. If you decide to accept payment via credit cards, debit cards, and online payment services, payment can be verified on the spot electronically. When a client or customer is paying by check, you may not want to release the product or schedule another appointment until the check has cleared.

When you seek to be paid for a service, much will depend on your policy, any contract that you have negotiated, and to whom you are providing services. If you are a speaker, writer, or in private practice, you will usually be paid after you have provided the service unless other arrangements have been made.

Collection of Overdue Payments

Establish a policy for collections when payment is not made as specified in your policy or contract. Send an invoice indicating the account is past due and requesting immediate payment by a certain date. If payment is not received, you may want to place a phone call inquiring why you were not paid. Most computer-generated invoices can be set up to automatically print a "past due" statement on the bottom of bills sent. When these approaches do not prompt action, consider sending a letter on your letterhead requesting payment within 10 business days. You can state, "If payment is not received within 10 business days of receipt of this letter, you will be contacted by our collection agency." In most cases, the letter will bring about payment. If not, depending on the size of the debt, it may be worthwhile to enlist the services of a collection agency. Some agencies retain a percentage of the total sum recovered; others charge a flat fee for each recovered account. To locate a collection agency, ask colleagues for recommendations or search the Internet.

Consider having a policy in place for handling returned checks. Determine what your bank charges you for returned checks, then work that charge into your fee structure. It is important to place this information on your new patient information sheet and/or post a sign in the waiting room. One great way to avoid returned checks and overdue accounts is to accept credit cards. This can also greatly reduce your accounts receivable.

Accepting Credit Cards

Before determining whether accepting credit cards is a viable option for you, it is necessary to do some research. The costs to the business owner are highly variable, so it is best to shop around. Often the credit card company will ask you to give an estimate of your expected monthly charges before quoting rates. A higher sales volume will generally provide you with lower monthly fees. Box 3.4 lists the options to evaluate before deciding which credit card processing company to use.

Box 3.4 Criteria to Consider When Choosing a Credit Card Processing Company

- Will you purchase or lease equipment?
- Is there Web site processing?
- Is there a monthly minimum charge?
- Is there a monthly statement fee?
- Is there an enrollment or application fee?
- Is there a set-up fee?
- What is the transaction fee? Is that fee fixed per transaction or is it calculated as a percentage of the transaction?
- Are there any additional fees for not swiping the credit card?
- How long is the contract?
- Are there cancellation fees?

Money Management: A Summary

Here are the main points you should take away from this chapter:

- When setting fees, factor in your desired salary, the cost to replace lost benefits, business and office expenses, and your salable time.
- Closely monitoring your finances is extremely important to assist you in determining the viability of your new company. Choosing the right accounting software will help.
- You must also have policies in place for billing, collecting past due accounts, and returned checks.

References

1. Axelrod M. The consulting process: setting fees. The New Game Web site. http://www.thenewgame.com/axelrodlearning/consultingprocess.html. Accessed March 30, 2009.
2. Biech E. *The Business of Consulting: The Basics and Beyond.* San Francisco, CA: Jossey-Bass/Pfeiffer; 1999:36.
3. Georgia B. The price is tight . . . isn't it? (industry trend or event). *Home Office Computing.* June 1999. http://findarticles.com/p/articles/mi_m1563/is_6_17/ai_63502624. Accessed August 16, 2009.

4. Lesonsky R. *Start Your Own Business*. Irvine, CA: Entrepreneur Media; 2007.
5. Marks G, ed. *Streetwise Small Business Book of Lists*. Avon, MA: Adams Media; 2006.
6. Strauss SD. *The Small Business Bible: Everything You Need to Know to Succeed in Your Small Business*. Hoboken, NJ: John Wiley & Sons; 2008.
7. Tyson E, Schell J. *Small Business for Dummies*. 3rd ed. Hoboken, NJ: Wiley Publishing; 2008.
8. Newman P. Which Accounting Software Is Best for You? Entrepreneur Web site. August 28, 2006. http://www.entrepreneur.com/money/moneymanagement/financialmanagementcolumnist pamnewman/article166216.html. Accessed April 19, 2009.

Chapter 4

Outfitting Your Office: What Do You Really Need?

Once you decide to go into business for yourself, you need to start thinking about the nitty-gritty of office set-up, such as what equipment, software, and supplies you need. This chapter covers the basics, and most of the information could apply to any registered dietitian (RD) going solo, whether in private practice or another type of entrepreneurial venture. Chapter 7 will discuss in more detail some issues related specifically to private practice.

Office Space

Before you determine what equipment and supplies you need, it is essential to determine where you will do business. For many types of nutrition consulting, your work duties can be performed almost anywhere and the issues regarding finding office space are minimal. In private practice, however, finding office space is a top priority and the decisions you make directly affect your clientele and your image. For this reason, a detailed discussion on finding space can be found in Chapter 7, along with other issues related to setting up a private practice. If you are not setting up a private practice, but you plan to work from home, pay close attention to the section on home offices in Chapter 7.

Office Essentials: Assessing Your Needs

Take some time to imagine going through a full day of work in your new office space. Visualize the entire process. What furniture will you need in your office? If meeting with clients, where will you greet them? What will the client do on entering your office? Will the client need to sit in a waiting room to complete some paperwork? What paperwork will there be? How will you furnish the waiting room? What do you want visitors to take away as their first impression? (Remember, first impressions are lasting impressions.) Continue this exercise as you jot down all the essentials that pop into your mind.

Once you have done this, you will have a greater feel for all the essentials required to set up your office. Make a master list of what you need. You can also ask yourself the following questions as a first step in preparing your list of essentials:

- Will you have employees working in the office? If so, it is important to have adequate workspace.
- Will clients be visiting often? Obviously, in private practice, the answer is "Yes." Consider the image you want to project and furnish accordingly. If you are setting up another type of consulting business, the more often you plan to see clients in your office, the greater the importance of projecting the right image with furnishings and decor.
- What can your budget accommodate? Clearly, your available cash flow will determine your purchases. Set your priorities in advance, and stick with your decisions.
- What equipment must you have? Decide what is essential to start with and what you can wait to purchase. For example, you must have chairs to sit on, but perhaps you can wait to purchase a copy machine and make copies at the local copy shop instead.

Furnishings

It is important to purchase furnishings and equipment wisely. These items can be extremely costly, but think of them as investments in the success of your business. There are numerous sources for purchasing office equipment and furnishings, including your local office supply stores or national chains. (Note: If you are subleasing, you may need to work with the furniture provided.)

Search the Internet for additional sources. If your budget is limited, you can check online auction sites for used furniture and equipment. Use caution before you purchase anything secondhand. Evaluate the cost of the item new and the condition of the used product.

When furnishing your office, think of your clientele. Make sure your furnishings are comfortable for them. If you plan to counsel obese clients, it is important to select sturdy furniture to accommodate them, make them feel at ease, and avoid any embarrassing moments. If furniture is low to the ground, some patients may have difficulty getting in and out. If you will be seeing families, you will need adequate seating. If you will be dealing with corporate clients, consider an upscale look. Pattern your office after other corporate offices. Maybe a conference room setup will work well.

It is important to consider the type of lighting. Do you like overhead fluorescent lighting or would you rather use lamps?

Equipment

To determine which equipment to buy immediately, you may want to analyze how much the purchase of that particular product will increase your productivity and profitability (1).

The Business Telephone

A telephone is a business essential. Having a designated telephone number for your business allows you to present yourself in a professional manner. Never use your home telephone line as your business line unless you are prepared to answer it with a professional greeting every time you pick up the telephone. Callers should always be greeted with your business name and/or the name of the person who is speaking (2).

Always answer your business telephone professionally. If you feel that it is important to have a real person answer the telephone and you cannot afford a receptionist or secretary, consider an answering service. Be aware that answering services can mishandle calls, which results in client complaints. Carefully screen services and get recommendations from other business owners before selecting one.

Voice mail provided by your local telephone company is a good option. Voice mail allows you to set up multiple mailboxes. If you plan to do different types of consulting, you can set up a separate mailbox for each and streamline your work. A standard answering machine is also a good solution.

There are many options for obtaining a telephone system. Although it is tempting to go with the least expensive option, especially when first starting out, consider the potential for growth and look to the future.

One simple solution is to purchase a cell phone that you carry with you. This is particularly useful if you do not spend a lot of time in the office or if you have multiple office locations. Some consultants prefer to have two cell phones, one for business and one for personal use. Further analysis of purchasing a cell phone is provided later in this chapter.

Instead of installing a telephone line in your office, you can have a second telephone line installed in your home and use either voice mail provided by your local telephone company or a standard answering machine. This allows you to be a bit more flexible with office space while you always maintain the same telephone number. For example, if you decide to sublet space on a part-time basis and eventually move into full-time space, you will not have to change telephone numbers as you move.

If you are renting office space in an office building and want to install a telephone line, you must install a business line. Even if you are working from your home, consider using a business telephone line. Often, a business line comes with a free yellow pages listing.

When setting up a home office, your choices for choosing a telephone may narrow slightly. You don't have the issues of multiple telephone lines for more than one location or moving your office. It is still important to have your telephone answered professionally, so consider an answering machine, voice mail, or an answering service. Decide on a residential or a business line, depending on your needs.

Computer

You must have a computer to do business. If you are not computer-savvy and do not plan to upgrade your skills, now is the time to forge a relationship with a good computer consultant or information technology (IT) specialist. A computer consultant or IT specialist is someone who plans, develops, operates, maintains, and evaluates computer hardware, software, and telecommunications. He or she can be an invaluable resource to your business. Paying a specialist the hourly rate can save you time and money in the end.

To locate a good consultant, ask other business owners for recommendations. Look for someone who is used to dealing with small businesses rather than large companies with huge networks. Get references and check them carefully. Also, ask the consultant the following questions (3):

- How do you bill?
- Are you available after hours? If so, do rates increase for after-hours calls?
- Can you help me determine which hardware and software I need?
- Can you help determine which new gadgets will help with my productivity and are worth the investment?
- Finally, can you set up all the computer systems I need?

If your family shares a computer, consider investing in one that is strictly for your business use. You want to have access to the computer at all times so that you can work when someone else in the house is using the computer.

Technology can save hours of time if you choose the right tools. It can also become costly if you make mistakes when purchasing. Some equipment is necessary for running a successful business; some is optional. Purchase the essentials immediately and then nonessential items as your budget allows.

If you find that you do need to purchase a computer for your business, the next section will review some basic considerations. Enlist the help of your new IT consultant rather than relying on the salespeople at the computer store to guide you through this process.

Computer Hardware

Your first decision is whether to purchase a laptop computer or a desktop computer. If you will be traveling to different locations, be giving presentations, or want round-the-clock access to your files, you will need a laptop. If you see patients in a location other than your main office, a laptop will allow you to enter your new patient information as well as process fees and collections immediately after each visit. You can also work on other projects if you have a gap in your schedule. A laptop provides you with the freedom to do your work when and where you wish.

Your next decision will be whether to choose a Mac or a PC. Macs are known for their simplicity and ease of use, and they tend to be less susceptible to worms and viruses than PCs. Basic PCs, on the other hand, can be more affordable. PCs provide a greater variety of software programs. Some software is not compatible with the Mac operating system, and users must purchase additional software to make certain programs compatible.

When purchasing hardware, it is usually best to avoid the least expensive equipment. However, a top-of-the-line computer is rarely necessary. Purchase a computer with a warranty from a reputable and reliable store. If being without your computer will put you out of business, you should purchase a service contract as an "insurance policy." This will allow for continued productivity in the event that your computer malfunctions and needs repair.

Data Backups

One of the most essential yet often forgotten tasks you must include in your daily routine is to back up your computer files. Don't wait until you have a computer disaster to learn this important lesson. Your two main choices for backup are to use a remote server or put the saved data on media. Remote servers are encrypted online backup systems. Backup media include CDs, DVDs, and external hard drives. Both options are inexpensive, so consider using both methods.

CDs and DVDs are a great choice for individual files that you may never need again but should keep just in case, such as past client records. An external hard drive is recommended for files you want to access but do not necessarily need stored on your computer. Backing up certain data on an external hard drive will save space on your computer. Thumb drives (also known as flash drives) are great for traveling and transferring files but not for storage. Finally, for important files, encrypted online backups are essential. Many companies provide this service. Keep in mind that any physical device such as an external hard drive is subject to failure.

Mobile Communication Devices

Mobile communication devices include cellular phones, smart phones, and personal digital assistants (PDAs). In addition to these, new devices are regularly emerging in the marketplace.

The functions of mobile communication devices vary and overlap. When purchasing a mobile communication device, consider how it can best serve you in your practice and how you might foresee using it.

Purchasing a mobile phone number specific for your practice can keep you in touch with your patients even when you are not in the office. When the cell phone rings, you will know it is a professional call. You can decide whether you wish to put on your "professional hat" at that moment and answer the call. Returning phone calls in a timely fashion can help build your practice, especially when it's a prospective patient or client.

Be aware that when using a cellular phone exclusively as your practice's phone number, you may be unable to obtain a business listing in the phone book. However, you can arrange call forwarding from your business landline to the designated cellular phone.

Mobile communication devices can help keep you organized. They can substitute for a laptop on the road, keep your schedule and appointments, allow you to check e-mail, and maintain your contact list. You can add software such as nutrient-drug interaction and nutrition analysis databases to these devices. You can also add other practice-related applications, such as those that in combination with paid services allow you to accept credit cards.

Carefully analyze which features you need, as the prices of mobile devices vary greatly depending on their features. You may find that you are paying for duplicate features, which is unnecessary. For example, if you are carrying a laptop to your office and have Internet access, you may not need that feature in your handheld device. See Box 4.1 to determine whether a handheld device is right for you.

Box 4.1 Is a Handheld Device Right for You?

If you are considering purchasing a handheld device to add to your arsenal of technological gadgets, here are some key questions to ask yourself:

- Do you enjoy using computers and electronic devices?
- Are you away from your office for a significant portion of your workday?
- Do you need or wish to stay connected to your work life when you're not actually working?
- Do you travel frequently and want a smaller alternative to your main computer?

RDs typically use their mobile devices for Internet access, e-mail, calendar, and contacts (and, of course, phone calls). If your existing phone and computer are enough, you will not need one of these devices. If you are ready to choose a mobile device, however, consider size, weight, features, and cost. When considering cost, don't forget to factor in the fee for monthly plans in addition to the cost of the device. Box 4.2 provides a list of features to consider when shopping. Determine those you need before you head off to the store.

Box 4.2 Features Available in PDAs

- Calendar
- Contacts
- E-mail
- Phone
- Mobile/cellular access to data
- Input devices (keyboard, touch-screen, and scroll wheel)
- Camera
- Bluetooth
- GPS
- MP3 player
- Voice recorder
- Video player
- Ability to use and edit common file types (such as Microsoft Word)
- Ability to synchronize with other systems and computers
- Compatibility with applications you use, such as patient/client assessment tools

You must have a system for keeping an up-to-date contact list and calendar, so if you decide not to go with a handheld device, you should know what you will use instead. If you still have questions, consider asking your colleagues and friends about what devices they use and why. You might discover functions you never knew you needed.

Fax Machine

Medical practices are used to faxing laboratory reports and other medical information before patient visits. Health Insurance Portability and Accountability Act (HIPAA) privacy regulations affect your ability to fax information (see Chapter 7). Still, the ability to send and receive faxes is important for any office. As with the other equipment, fax machines vary in price. A basic machine may be all that you need. Another option to consider is sending and receiving faxes through your computer, therefore eliminating the need for an additional piece of equipment.

Copy Machine

Copy machines can be quite costly yet may be necessary for conducting business on a daily basis. Do you photocopy ideas and notes for clients at the close of a counseling session? Do you frequently photocopy information in preparation for a client meeting or during a counseling session to support educational concepts? Weigh the benefits and convenience of having the machine available versus the time and expense of going to the copy shop. A copy machine might be a piece of equipment that can be purchased later, as your income increases. Another option is to purchase an "all-in-one" machine for your computer. These machines print documents from the computer, scan documents and books, and function as copy machines. This alternative can save you money because you will be purchasing one machine rather than four.

Postage Machine

Some entrepreneurs think they must purchase a postage machine. Others do not mind the occasional run to the post office; it can provide a needed break. Some businesspeople report that they rarely mail anything because they use e-mail and other Web communication services.

If you will be mailing primarily letter-sized envelopes and don't have a postage machine, you will need to purchase large quantities of stamps and have them available at all times. Another option is to purchase stamps online from the US Postal Service.

If you sell a product through the mail, a postage machine may be a good investment. To determine the value of a postage machine for your business, you could start without one and analyze your turnaround time in sending products out and how much time you are actually spending at the post office.

Post Office Box

Some consultants who work out of their homes opt to rent a post office box for receiving mail. This helps keep business mail separate and may appear to be more professional as it can list the PO box number as a suite number.

Shared Equipment

If you share an office suite with one or several others, often you can share the costs associated with fax machines, copiers, postage equipment, and furnishings in the waiting area. If you do this, however, make certain to designate who is responsible for handling equipment failures, maintenance, and other related situations.

Business Supplies and Forms

You cannot run a business without certain supplies and forms. Some basic supplies are necessary regardless of your setting or the type of consulting.

Business Cards and Logos

Creating business cards can be fun, frustrating, and exciting at the same time. Your business card can be your first introduction to potential clients. A properly designed card becomes a powerful marketing tool and presents you in a professional manner (4).

You may choose to start with simple cards that feature your name, phone number, and e-mail address. Many computer programs allow you to design and print your own business cards. This is an easy, inexpensive way to go when first starting your business. Many office supply stores print very basic, affordable business cards. Surf the Web for further resources. Many sites not only offer reasonable prices but also offer helpful tips.

As your business grows and as your budget permits, consider adding a logo to your business cards and other materials. A well-designed logo creates a lasting impression and definitely contributes to name recognition. You may want to hire a graphic artist to design your logo. What image do you want to portray? Are you more traditional or contemporary? Do certain colors appeal to you? Do you want two-color printing? If so, note that it will cost you more but may differentiate you from the crowd.

Once you design your logo, keep in mind that you will be using it on all your forms and marketing materials, including invoices, brochures, letterhead, labels, and any other forms you develop (3). Your logo can also be incorporated into your Web site and presentations.

Keep in mind that just as your business will grow and change over time, the same principles can apply to your logo; the image you create today may not be the one you'll use in future, and that's not unusual in the business world.

Refer to Box 4.3 (5) for advice on designing business cards. Use the business card checklist in Box 4.4 (6,7) for tips on creating your cards. For examples of business card templates, see Figure 4.1. Although the cards are generic, they can give you ideas for layout and design. To give your card pizzazz, add your logo and/or some graphics. When it comes to designing business cards, there are no rules. It comes down to personal choice and affordability.

Box 4.3 Designing Your Business Cards

- **Tip 1: Make sure your cards are legible.** Don't use all CAPs, *italics,* or underlining. Use a standard font that is easy to read. Make sure the type is big enough and the color is easy for people to read.
- **Tip 2: Don't use glossy or metallic paper.** Often when you hand someone your card, they want to make a note on the back of it. Have your cards printed on a paper stock that someone can actually write on.
- **Tip 3: Use the back of the card.** Take advantage of the extra real estate on the other side to add valuable information about your business. Include a map to your location, key points about your services, or an appointment reminder.
- **Tip 4: Get the advice of a professional designer.** If you can't afford to have a professional graphic designer design your entire card, at least get a consultation. Sketch where you want your logo on the card and other information, such as your name, address, phone number, Web site, and e-mail address. Take this information along with the computer file containing your logo to a graphic designer for advice. Even a short consultation will improve your card.

Source: Adapted with permission from: HomeBusinessWiz.com. 5 Tips for Designing Effective Business Cards. http://www.homebusinesswiz.com/2006/11/5_tips_for_designing_effective.html. Accessed June 11, 2009.

Box 4.4 Business Card Options

A good business card requires certain elements. Consider the following items:

- Your Name
- Title
- Credentials
- Name of your business
- Address
- Telephone number(s)
- Fax number
- E-mail address
- Web site address
- Tagline
- Logo
- Graphic image(s)
- List of services
- Your photo
- Space for noting the next appointment

Some of these items are optional, and it is not possible to fit them all on one small card. Determine which ones are appropriate and most important for your business card.

Source: Data are from references 6 and 7.

Nutrition Services

Jane Doe, MS, RD
Registered Dietitian, Author, Speaker

555 Fictitious Street
Suite 1200
Chicago, Illinois 55555
(555) 555-5555
Fax (555) 555-5555
nutritionservices@fictitious.com

Jane Doe, MS, RD
Registered Dietitian, Author, Speaker

Nutrition Services

(555) 555-5555
Fax (555) 555-5555
nutritionservices@fictitious.com
555 Fictitious Street
Suite 1200
Chicago, Illinois 55555

Jane Doe, MS, RD
Registered Dietitian, Author, Speaker

Nutrition Services

Your Sports Nutrition Specialist

555 Fictitious Street
Suite 1200
Chicago, IL 55555
(555) 555-5555
Fax (555) 555-5555
nutritionservices@fictitious.com

Figure 4.1 Sample business cards. Cards designed using the business card template at DesignYourOwnCard.com.

Determine which choices make sense for you in your situation and have fun creating a unique card.

Letterhead

Your letterhead should be designed as a package with your business card. Envelopes are also usually purchased at the same time. If you have not yet developed a logo, at least use the same font style and type size on business cards, letterhead, and envelopes. Some entrepreneurs have decided they do not need printed letterhead. They use computer-generated letterhead on an as-needed basis. You can create your letterhead on your computer with unique fonts. It need not be fancy, but it is important to convey a professional image.

Forms

Even if most of your paperwork is kept on your computer, forms are often necessary to gather the information needed to enter into the computer. It is recommended that you keep hard copies of most stored information on file. Forms you will need include the following:

- A **client or patient information sheet,** or contact sheet. This allows you to collect necessary information such as name, address, and phone number on new clients or patients. Refer to Chapter 7 for an example.
- A **fax cover sheet**. See Figure 4.2 for an example of a simple yet effective cover sheet that can be composed on your computer.
- **Invoices,** particularly if you are selling a product.
- **Checks**. If you are writing your checks with an accounting software package, you will need compatible checks.

Standard office software packages provide many business form templates. Simply add your personal and/or business information to the templates to customize them and print them as needed from your computer, as discussed later in this chapter. Another option is to purchase standard business forms such as checking and banking supplies, invoices, and statements through your local print shop or office supply store, or from various Web retailers. As with all the business items mentioned, prices vary.

Office Supplies

Remember to stock up on other miscellaneous supplies, such as pens, pencils, tape, paper clips, phone message pads, and stapler and staples. Make sure you have all the necessary printer and fax cartridges and paper you need. Always have extra on hand.

Computer Software

You can purchase a variety of software to use in your business. Investigate and determine what you will need and actually use. Nothing may be more

RD's Name and RD's Logo

Digest This Information . . .

Date: ______________________

To: ______________________

Fax Number: ______________________

From: ______________________

Number of Pages: ______________________

Comments/Message: ______________________

____

____

____

____

____

Note: This transmission may contain CONFIDENTIAL information and is intended for the addressee only. Unauthorized use of this information may be a violation of criminal statutes. If this information was received by someone other than the addressee, the recipient shall immediately notify the sender at the telephone number or address below and will be informed as to its proper disposal. Under no circumstances should this information be shared, retained, copied other than the addressee.

Corporate Office · 128 Dietitian's Lane • New York, NY 55555 • (212) 555-5555

Figure 4.2 Fax cover sheet. Reprinted with permission from Litt A, Mitchell F. Be Your Own Boss Starter Kit. 2007.

frustrating than spending money on software that you never use. Consider consulting with colleagues to determine which software they have found the most useful.

When you purchase a computer, it usually comes with an office software package, but you may have to purchase it separately. Typically, this includes a word processing program and other programs, such as a spreadsheet application and a presentation program.

Office Management Software

You can use your computer's software to enhance your business and streamline your work in numerous ways (see Box 4.5). Software packages can handle all your administrative tasks. For example, it is possible to keep records of all new clients and track how each was referred to you by using a spreadsheet. If you want to determine who your top referral sources are, you can easily access that information.

Box 4.5 Putting Office Management Software to Work

Jan Patenaude, RD and certified LEAP therapist, counsels her clients in her nationwide practice by telephone and the Internet. She has made her "office" mostly paperless by adapting standard word processing, spreadsheet, presentation, and e-mail and calendar software on her laptop. She also uses her laptop to send and receive electronic faxes. By keeping everything virtual, she's able to work while traveling. As long as Jan has her laptop, she's "in her office."

Jan uses her software to:

- Maintain a folder on each client, including his or her medical history, test results, client information and progress notes.
- Schedule appointments and maintain a task list.
- E-mail and paperless fax to clients, referral sources, or physicians.
- Track clients and referral sources.
- Market her services using the Internet via e-mail, letters, articles, Web postings, message boards, and Listservs.

Creating Forms

You can create forms using your word processing program. Creating templates as your original, you can make as many copies as you need. There are many different documents you can build and have available as needed. Be creative in how you can use your computer software. An investment of time in developing documents will pay off in the long term.

Create templates that can be used as contracts. Customize them for various types of consulting positions. For example, use the same contract template for a speaking engagement, a corporate wellness workshop, or an assignment to create menus for group homes.

If creating these forms does not appeal to you or you simply do not have the time, there are other options. You can purchase the forms as hard copies and scan them into your computer (provided you have a scanner). This allows you to print them out as needed. You can also purchase forms on disk or as a download. Chapter 14 lists resources where you can find these products. You can also hire a tech-savvy RD to help you.

Developing Educational Handouts

You can also use word processing software to produce specific and unique educational materials. For example, you could develop handouts for diets you address frequently or marketing materials for talks that you give. It is very easy to individualize handouts for each patient or speaking engagement. For example, if you have a handout on treating hyperlipidemia and your patient has lactose intolerance, you can customize the hyperlipidemia handout by deleting all sources of lactose and adding substitutes for lactose-containing food. Save this file, and if this patient situation should arise again, you are ready. Perhaps you have been contracted to provide two separate presentations, "Healthy Snacking for Kids" and "Healthy Eating on the Go." You can use much of the same information with a few tweaks for each event. If you have a flair for design, use clip art and different fonts to jazz up your educational materials to maintain the reader's interest (8).

Creating Spreadsheets

Spreadsheet software can be used in a variety of ways. You can track your productivity by developing monthly graphs to determine the growth of your business. You can also create charts to determine your reimbursement rates from different insurance companies, if you accept insurance. You can track media contacts and pitches so you can follow up in a timely manner.

Using Presentation Software

Presentation software can be used to maintain the audience's attention when addressing a group or counseling a patient. For example, you could develop an educational series that can be shown to patients during their visits, or create a presentation geared directly toward potential clients, patients, or referral sources and e-mailed as an attachment or put on your Web site.

Voice Recognition Software

Imagine writing a business proposal or follow-up letter to a referring physician without your fingers ever touching the keypad on your computer. How is that possible? Voice or speech recognition programs allow this convenience.

Some computers provide this as a standard feature, or you can purchase the software separately as well as a combination headset with microphone. The beauty of using a voice recognition program is that most likely you can speak faster than you can type. The program will allow you crank out your letters and other typing functions with speed and save time. This software can be used virtually with all aspects of your computer.

Accounting Software

A good accounting software package is an asset to your business and will save you valuable time. You can keep track of all your financial data and client billing with the right program. For most small businesses, there are many good programs to handle accounting and billing. Chapter 3 reviews the basics of choosing accounting software. When in doubt, you can always consult with your accountant or business adviser.

Virtual Assistants

Starting out in your new business will entail many expenses. You may not be able to afford the expenditure of employing someone to assist in your administrative tasks. On the other hand, if you spend too much of your time attending to administrative duties, you lose precious networking, marketing, and development time. A virtual assistant may be the perfect compromise.

A virtual assistant can sound futuristic, but RDs in business commonly use them. This is a self-employed person who works from his or her home while remotely managing your business or practice and performing the same services of an administrative assistant. A virtual assistant may work part time for you, but to others it may seem like you have full-time help. Virtual assistants typically manage a number of clients at the same time. Contracting the services of a virtual assistant may allow you to have the help you need and keep it affordable.

Virtual assistants typically provide support via e-mail, the Internet, phone calls, or fax. Working relationships with a virtual assistant can be long term until your needs change. A virtual assistant can manage most of your administrative functions without being physically present in your office. For example, imagine that your patient who is scheduled in two hours cancels. Your virtual assistant can contact your patients and move their appointments up or squeeze in a new patient. However, a virtual assistant cannot open the door for a client, water the plants, file charts, or perform other tasks that require a physical presence.

Fees for a virtual assistant can be a retainer for a minimum of hours per month and then by the hour over the minimum. The costs can be similar to having someone physically present in your office, but the services of a virtual assistant may be used more efficiently.

Outfitting Your Office: A Summary

Presenting a professional image is of the utmost importance. There are so many decisions you must make when setting up your office. Carefully assess the options, determine your requirements, and figure out which expenses can wait until you are more solvent. Remember, though, you have to spend money to make money!

The following are some key points from this chapter to consider:

- Before you see clients or patients, you must secure office space. Determine how much space you need, where you want to be located, and what type of space will work.
- Determine whether a rented, shared, or home office will meet your needs, or if you would do better in an alternative location.
- Once space is secured, you must determine what furnishings, equipment, and supplies you need and budget accordingly.
- A well-designed logo for your business card, stationery, and other printed materials creates a lasting impression and contributes to name recognition. Hiring a graphic designer can be a wise investment.
- You can use software in different ways to maximize your productivity.

References

1. Mintzer R. *The Everything to Start Your Own Business Book.* Avon, MA: Adams Media; 2002.
2. Babener J, Stewart D. Setting Up a Home Office. ESTEEM: the Self-Esteem Review Web site. 1993:2. http://www.mlmlegal.com/homeoffice.html. Accessed December 23, 2003.
3. American Dietetic Association Nutrition Entrepreneurs Dietetic Practice Group. Where to hang your shingle: home or rented office? In: *Nutrition Entrepreneurs Toolkit 2009.* Chicago, IL: American Dietetic Association; 2010.
4. Gaebler.com. Designing Effective Business Cards. http://www.gaebler.com/Business-Cards.htm. Accessed June 11, 2009.
5. HomeBusinessWiz.com. 5 Tips for Designing Effective Business Cards. http://www.homebusinesswiz.com/2006/11/5_tips_for_designing_effective.html. Accessed June 11, 2009.
6. About.com: Desktop Publishing. Business card lesson plans: resources, checklists, variations. http//desktoppub.about.com/od/lessonplans/l/aa_bizcardextra.htm. Accessed August 21, 2009.
7. Ferree E. Information to include on your business card. Small Business Brief Web site. Available at: http://www.smallbusinessbrief.com/articles/marketing/000893.html. Accessed August 21, 2009.
8. Clairmont C. A hard look at software solutions to ease your workload. *Today's Dietitian.* 2001;3:24–27.

Acknowledgment: Dina Aronson, MS, RD, President of Welltech Solutions, contributed to the section on mobile communication devices.

Chapter 5

Tools and Tips for Marketing

You may be on the cutting edge of diabetes management, or author a bestseller, or have the highest success rate with helping lactating mothers, but if no one knows about you, your business or product fails. Success in business is all about marketing. Marketing separates you from your competition and lets your clients know you are out there. Good marketing translates into a successful business.

To market effectively, you must build a plan around the "4 Ps" of marketing: product, place, price, and promotion (1). These topics can be systematically addressed by creating a marketing plan. The marketing plan is different from the business plan addressed in Chapter 2. A business plan is the blueprint that guides you as you get your business up and running. Your marketing plan is a strategic plan to get your name and business out to customers to make money! It isn't theoretical; it's a practical plan of action (1–4).

Many small businesses may develop a business plan but stumble through the marketing process. Reasons offered for ignoring marketing plans include insufficient cash, lack of knowledge, and low priority. However, marketing is everything. To successfully market your services, your marketing plan will define the following:

- Your target market
- The service or product you are selling
- Tools you will use to ensure that your product reaches the market

It is as basic as that. Don't get too bogged down with the fine points. Whether you are marketing your private practice or a new nutrition product, you need to develop a plan that will be revised, refined, and reformulated as your business develops.

Your Target Market

Who needs or will use your services or products? Marketing your services or products requires you to be specific and objective. To identify your target market, you will need to learn characteristics of the population you wish to reach as well as your competition, and how your services or products are priced in the marketplace. You must also find out about trends in the marketplace and answer how (or if) your target market is presently having their needs met.

Your research will help you learn about the population you wish to reach. What is their socioeconomic profile? Where are they now turning for the service or products you hope to offer them? How much are they paying? This research will help you to conclude where your business is most needed or will most likely succeed.

Conducting an analysis of the marketplace will help you to identify what services or products are being provided and what is missing. If you are pursuing a business in which some other registered dietitians (RDs) are already providing the same or similar services or products, assess what needs are not being met. You may uncover an area of your business not yet tapped. This allows you to position your business advantageously. The positioning of your business will project the image and ranking relative to your competition. The question you may ask is, "Where do I want to be in relation to my competition?" (5).

Thorough marketing research should reveal information about your competition. Your competitors can include other food and nutrition professionals and other professionals or persons. Your goal in assessing the competition is to determine how your services will meet a client's needs in a way that the competition does not.

Analyze the competition by assessing their strengths and weakness (see Figure 5.1) (5). Compare them to your own. To set yourself apart from the competition, ask yourself what is special, unusual, or different about your experiences or services. How well are your competitors performing? Is there an area of the marketplace not yet being addressed?

Tools for obtaining information about your competition can range from a formal mailed survey or an online survey tool that targets your identified audience. It can also be as simple as picking up the telephone or sending an e-mail. Depending on your business, information gathering may entail learning what the commercial programs and local hospitals offer, purchasing books or products of your competition, exploring Web sites of your competition, and even contacting other food and nutrition professionals who are your competitors.

Many RDs view their competition as the enemy. This is a shortsighted analysis. In fact, other food and nutrition professionals can be your greatest referral source if you market yourself properly.

1. Competitor's name: ______________________________

2. Services or products offered: ______________________________

3. Location of service or method of distribution for products (physical or virtual): ______________________________

4. Years in business: ______________________________

5. Image: ______________________________

    a. Method of marketing: ______________________________

    b. Quality of service or product: ______________________________

6. Performance of the services or products: ______________________________

7. Price for services or products: ______________________________

8. Methods of payment accepted: ______________________________

Strengths of competitor (the strengths become your strengths):

____

____

____

Weaknesses (looking at the weaknesses of the competition can help you find ways of being unique and benefiting the consumer):

____

____

____

____

Figure 5.1 Evaluating the competition. Adapted with permission from Pinson L, Jinnett J. *Steps to Small Business Start-Up. Everything You Need to Know to Turn Your Idea into a Successful Business.* Chicago, IL: Kaplan Publishing; 2006: 221. Copyright © 2006 Kaplan Publishing.

Be a courteous colleague. Do not "step on toes." Too many of the same nutrition businesses in one location may not reflect well on the profession. Colleagues working together to ensure certain niches are covered in a geographic area will present a more unified professional image.

A careful analysis of your own strengths and weaknesses will allow you to refer to other RDs when you cannot fulfill a need. This not only allows you to assist your client or customer, but it may also result in reciprocal referrals from other RDs.

To find out which services or products are most needed, you need to track consumer trends. Read annual reports from trade organizations, professional publications, and government publications. Immediate information on trends is available simply by reading newspapers and magazines. They can provide insights into issues such as what readers think is hot, which foods they are purchasing, and present diet fads. Although you don't need to be a part of every diet trend, you do need to be aware of them to speak convincingly to your clients. It is not necessary to be the first, just the best. Box 5.1 provides additional resources for determining trends and ideas.

Box 5.1 Resources for Tracking Food and Nutrition Trends

Amercian Dietetic Association (ADA) Daily News (http://www.eatright.org/dailynews)
The Daily News List is a daily newsletter informing ADA members of news affecting food, nutrition, and health. To get the Daily News in your mailbox each day, go to the ADA Web site.

Association for Consumer Trends (http://www.consumerexpert.org)
ACT is a nonprofit organization that connects professionals to trends, resources, and insights to create innovation. It provides networking and trend tracking via conferences, teleconferences, trend-related Web sites, and e-newsletters and blogs.

Food Marketing Institute (http://www.fmi.org)
This Web site provides resources for consumer behavior and attitudes on a wide range of issues that are important to understanding the grocery shopper. Topics include spending patterns, satisfaction ratings, importance of products and services, types of stores shopped, nutrition, and food safety concerns.

Marketresearch.com (http://www.marketresearch.com)
This Web site compiles and sells market research reports by industry, market research publisher, and geographic area.

Springwise.com (http://springwise.com)
An inspirational Web site for the entrepreneur with a free weekly e-newsletter that scans the world for new business ideas and concepts.

Trend Central (http://www.trendcentral.com)
This Web site offers free sign-up for daily e-mails that cover a wide spectrum of trends in a variety of categories, including lifestyle.

Trendwatching.com (http://wwww.trendwatching.com)
This Web site focuses on consumer insights and behavioral trends and the hands-on marketing and business opportunities they present. Provides a free monthly newsletter.

Formal marketing research can be daunting and quite costly, especially for the new RD just getting started. Be creative to find the information you need without spending your entire marketing budget. You don't need to rely on professionally developed questionnaires or sophisticated market surveys. To keep expenses down and methods manageable, you can use some creative resources that are readily available to you. Web searches can be a good place to start.

Focus Groups

Traditional focus groups are conducted with a group of neutral individuals who are not going to benefit directly from your service. When manufacturers are introducing a new product, they always conduct focus groups to get feedback. You can think the same way. Focus groups are an inexpensive way to perform market research.

Suppose you have an idea to offer a nutrition lecture series for new parents. To determine whether this is a good idea, consider asking a pediatrician's staff to serve as your focus group, or better yet, request the names of five to ten new parents who may be interested. Ask if you can learn their opinions of your idea. Because members of focus groups expect to receive something in return for their time, offer to provide the first class to them as a thank-you.

Perhaps you want to develop educational materials for the athletes you counsel. After you do an Internet search to determine the resources already in print on this topic, take your idea directly to the athletes. Call your local "roadrunners" group. Offer to give a lecture, and in return ask the participants evaluate your ideas.

Volunteer to give a free lecture to a group of senior citizens residing in a retirement community. In return, gather feedback on an idea to provide "cooking for one" classes. Those attending your seminar have just served as your focus group. The only cost to you is the time you spend preparing and presenting a lecture.

Advisory Boards

An advisory board can help you develop a successful business while also serving in a mentoring capacity (1). The purpose of an advisory board is to provide you with objective guidance and contrasting points of views in your business development. Ask another health care provider, your mentor, and a client to serve as your advisory board, or colleagues, professional or business friends, or family members you know who may have more experience or will provide a totally different perspective. Arrange an informal brainstorming session at a convenient time and location. This can be in person, or on a conference call or online chat. Offer to buy them breakfast or send a token gift in return for serving as your advisory board for your newly formed business. Find out what they think is lacking in established businesses, get their input on your office location, find out what they think is reasonable for you to charge for your services, and any other questions or concerns. Your advisory board will be flattered to be part of your business venture (6).

What You Are Selling

Marketing a tangible product is somewhat different from marketing an intangible professional service. The information that follows applies to both services and products, although you will find that some strategies may not apply to or be appropriate for your business.

Successful marketing requires a "hook," something that makes you or your business unique (1). Think about what will attract people. It's not about the features of what you are selling, but what the benefits are. People will remember benefits (2). When physicians decide to refer a patient to a private practice RD, they are interested in two things: how the RD will help the patient and how the RD will save the physician time. Although your resume may be impressive, the resume is not what helps the patient—it's the benefit they will reap from being referred to you.

Your Mission Statement

Your hook can be your unique approach, a product that's timely with a trend, or something that will make people remember your business. To define your marketing hook, start by developing a mission statement about your business. In your mission statement, include who you are, how you can help your customer, and a brief summary of your philosophy. What's important is the "help." Ask yourself the question (1), "Am I providing a solution for my client whether it's for a need, a desire, or a problem?" Once complete, who you are will become clearer to your target population. This will also highlight how you are different from your competition. Be honest and upfront about your philosophy. Don't hide behind your philosophy, regardless of how unconventional it might be. Just be sure that your statement reflects *you*. That is what will separate you from the pack. A good mission statement will also help to keep you focused when marketing. For assistance in creating a mission statement, refer to Figure 5.2.

Niche Marketing

Developing a niche and marketing to that niche can be beneficial. Your niche could be a specific aspect of nutrition, such as diabetes, food allergies, or vegetarians. Or it could be a certain age group, such as elderly persons or children. Or it might be based on special skills you possess, such as your fluency in Spanish, your geographic location, or your willingness to go to the client. A niche can even be providing superior-quality products or services that surpass the competition's. However, it's not the niche that will determine the success of your business, but how you run the business (1).

People form impressions of others within the first 20 to 30 seconds. It is critical that you prepare your personal "promotion" and mission statement. Plan what you will say. Your preparation will help you gain better results in all your marketing activities.

Using 20 words or less, describe who you are and what you do (be creative and interesting):

____

____

____

Using 20 words or less, describe how your services will benefit the consumer:

____

____

____

Figure 5.2 Who or what are you marketing? Formulating a mission statement.

Marketing to a niche can help target your marketing efforts. Your market may be overweight persons; however, a focus on a particular segment of that population will help you with marketing that is more specific. The tools you might use to market to overweight middle-aged executives, for example, will be quite different from the tools used to market to overweight teenagers. For actual examples of niche marketing, refer to Box 5.2.

For many reasons, it might be necessary to be open to all aspects of business when you first start. As your business grows, you might find that the population you wanted to work with was not what you expected. Be open to everything, but remember you don't have to "do" everything. What you love will emerge, and it will most likely be what you are good at.

Price Factors in Marketing

Pricing your services needs to be a part of your marketing plan. From a marketing standpoint, it never makes sense to market yourself based on price. Marketing on price can devalue the quality of what you provide. You do not want potential clients to choose to see you simply because you are the least

Box 5.2 True Examples of Niche Marketing

Constance Brown-Riggs, MSEd, RD, CDE, CDN

"I've established myself as an expert on the subject of nutrition, diabetes, and cultural issues that impact the health care of people of color. I operate CBR Nutrition Enterprises, a multipronged company that provides medical nutrition therapy (MNT) to patients, among other consultation services. My primary niche market is people with diabetes. African Americans with diabetes make up the sub-niche. There are very few books or educational tools that address health concerns unique to African Americans who have or are at risk for diabetes—thus my microniche developed. My microniche has given me the greatest boost in marketing and building my business. I self-published *Eating Soulfully and Healthfully with Diabetes* (2006) and parlayed that into numerous speaking engagements across the nation to both lay and professional audiences. The subniche and microniche have provided a solid platform, enabling me to secure an agent and publisher for a second book targeting African Americans with diabetes."

Denice Ferko-Adams, MPH, RD

"My company provides team-based health campaigns led by RDs to corporate clients nationally. For 20 years, I have specialized in worksite wellness campaigns. My niche developed by accident: a fitness center director asked me to run a team-based weight loss competition. We expected 50 people to join. When enrollment hit 499, I had to renegotiate my contract and provide 3-days-a-week sessions. Two weeks into the program, I was asked to develop a healthy cafeteria campaign. At the end of the program, the outcomes were impressive. My telephone rang for the next two years. I found my niche! Today, I offer more refined health campaigns with an Internet component, and I have perfected cooking demonstrations to reach 100 people at a seating. Why reach only 10 to 20 people when you can impact hundreds? The worksite holds tremendous potential for RDs!"

Anu Kaur, MS, RD

"I have had personal and professional experiences with terminal illness, in particular cancer and HIV populations. It has taught me how people seek out complementary care without informing their health professionals because they feel judged. As a result, I became passionate about being more versed in complementary therapies and understanding the evidence-based science around Eastern modalities, such as yoga and *pranayam* (breathing).

I enjoy explaining complementary therapies in terms that can be appreciated by all, especially those more familiar with Western-based medicine. After I started my own nutrition company I worked with a coach to identify my niche by acknowledging what I enjoyed the most and what came naturally to me. It was one of the best things I ever did for myself and highly recommend it. Through the powerful questions my coach posed, I identified my passion and niche of preventive medicine and integrative MNT.

I focus on stress-management of yoga and lifestyle changes with wellness coaching. My clientele includes anyone who likes this integrative approach of mind-body-spirit. I have observed that many South Asian Indians seek out my services in particular. I have been able to grow my business and market myself via my Web site, nutrition and yoga workshops, speaking engagements, and writing. Over the years as I have come to fully embrace my niche by seeking out mentors and colleagues in integrative medicine and continue my lifelong learning in this area."

expensive. Although price may be a factor when someone is deciding whether to purchase your service or product, it makes better business sense to market based on other factors, such as success rate, quality, philosophy, or expertise.

Tools and Methods for Reaching Your Target Market

Potential clients will know of your business through your marketing efforts. The goal of marketing is simple: get your name out there and keep it out there in a cost-effective way. There are many marketing tools available. When selecting marketing tools and strategies, you will need to consider your market. The tools you use may be different if you are marketing to a health club, a physicians' practice, a corporation, or a consumer group in the community. Focus on what seems appropriate to the market. Ultimately, you want to know who your customer may be so you can begin to think like your customer and identify the most effective way to market to them.

There are four general categories for promoting your services: networking, advertising, publicity, and word of mouth. Finding the right mix of promotional activities to get your name out and keep it out in an affordable way is your goal (1,2,5).

Networking: It's Not What You Know . . . It's Who You Know

Networking is defined as "the deliberate process of exchanging information, resources, support, and access in such way as to create mutually beneficial relationships for personal and professional success" (7, p.17). New entrepreneurs are sometimes uncomfortable with the concept of networking. Some view it as "using" others. True networking is building relationships that work two ways. It is about giving *and* receiving.

Networking is not simply going to an event, handing out your business card, and collecting other people's business cards. Networking requires you to have a plan to connect with others, share information, and receive something in return to further your professional or personal goals (7).

Finding Your Networks

Any situation where you can meet people, share your vision, gather information from the group, and hopefully offer them something in return is a network. You can start by creating a list of your existing networks. This list should include your personal and professional acquaintances. Your personal networks could include your relatives, your children's school, as well as your place of worship, softball team, and community association.

Your professional networks include your colleagues at work (if you are still employed), dietetics organizations, other health professionals such as doctors and therapists, organizations such as college alumni groups, and civic organizations.

In addition to the American Dietetic Association (ADA), you will want to join and become an active member in other professional organizations where you can meet a targeted audience. Explore membership in business networking groups outside the world of dietetics in the vicinity of your business, such as the chamber of commerce. Simply becoming a member of an organization is not networking. Being an active and participative member means you give and receive. Dietetic practice groups, health organizations such as the American Diabetes Association, and professional organizations such as the National Speakers Bureau will provide opportunities to share and learn from others with similar interests and goals.

Online social networks can be other forums for networking with colleagues, friends, and family (8,9). See Chapter 6 for more information on social network Web sites. Be aware that these are social Web sites, and you need to consider the image you portray as you mix your personal and professional lives. If you post a risqué photo of yourself or a controversial political point of view, it may affect a potential customer's willingness to do business with you.

Remember to network with competitors. One of the best existing networks is other RDs. RDs new to self-employment fear that RDs with established businesses would perceive them as competition or a threat. However, other RDs can be an excellent referral source. Get to know about their businesses so that when you get a referral you cannot handle, you can reciprocate. Referring to others is an important aspect of doing business.

Networking Strategies

Learning how to network is an art. Attend professional meetings, social gatherings, and even family events with a networking frame of mind. Don't wait for people to seek you out. You must make the effort to get to know your networks. Think about who your networks are and put yourself in a position to be active within those networks. If you are focusing your practice on diabetes management, become active in the local American Diabetes Association chapter. If you are specializing in geriatrics, look at networking opportunities offered through the AARP.

Take advantage of your membership in organizations and the networking opportunities available. Professional organizations, including the ADA, offer formal networking events. Toastmasters International Clubs (http://www.toastmasters.org) as well as business and civic groups also provide formal networking classes.

Every time you attend a meeting, social gathering, or even a family dinner, you can network. Set a networking goal for yourself for each event you attend. Networking goals can include meeting a new person, providing a referral or resource, and following up with a new contact within five days of the networking event.

Make your address book or contact list meaningful by keeping names memorable. When you meet someone, use the back of their business card to jot down something about your meeting to help you remember them. It could be a shared birth date, their recent promotion, or their love of baseball. Rely on this when you reconnect. People will be impressed that you've taken an interest in them. They are more likely to share.

Do not attend a function with a negative attitude. If you get caught in a conversation that is not productive, excuse yourself. Avoid toxic people. They will not be helpful to building your network.

Invite conversation by practicing a welcoming introduction. When first introducing yourself, have an "elevator speech" prepared—that is, a creative, memorable speech about yourself that is no longer than the time spent in an elevator ride.

Think of ways to encourage people to tell you about them. This is relationship building. It may take many introductions and exposures before people remember who you are. Come up with 10 items you can share with someone. Use key words to make it easier for people to remember you. Refer to Box 5.3 for guidance (10).

Box 5.3 Develop a Powerful Self-Introduction

Your first impression should be a lasting impression. You want to tell someone what you do, not who you are. The keys to a lasting self-introduction:

- **Clear:** People know what you do.
- **Concise:** Keep it short, sweet, and simple. Say it in 7 to 10 seconds.
- **Distinctive:** Catchy, while professional.
- **Relatable:** Use layperson terms and examples so that the listener can relate.
- **Engaging:** Connect with whom you are speaking. Your words, tone, eye contact, and body language play a role.

Which self-introduction sounds better? "Hi, I'm Mary Smith. I'm a registered dietitian. I specialize in diabetes," or "Good afternoon, I'm Mary Smith. I help people with diabetes understand how they can eat all foods to improve their blood sugars. I'm a registered dietitian."

Source: Adapted from Fisher D, Vilas S. *Power Networking: 59 Secrets for Personal & Professional Success*. Marietta, GA: Bard Press; 2000:77–80. Adapted with permission from the authors. Copyright © Donna Fisher and Sandy Vilas.

Networking is about exposure and having fun. Plan to network at least once a week in a variety of settings. Networking can include lunch with a colleague or a power walk with a friend. Always follow up a formal or informal networking function with a note, e-mail, or phone call thanking the person for his or her efforts in helping increase your network. For more networking tips, refer to Box 5.4 (11).

Box 5.4 Practice Makes Perfect

- **Make names memorable.** When you meet new people, don't rush introductions. Repeat their names and associate them with something that will make them easy to recall. Repeat your name a few times, too.
- **Invite conversation.** When asked what you do, tell of a talent or skill. Share a time you saved the day, solved a problem, or served the client.
- **Business cards are not handbills.** The number of cards you hand out doesn't measure successful networking. Instead, pour your energy into each conversation and exchange cards when necessary.
- **Network with competitors.** Get to know and trust your competition so you can refer business that's not in your area of expertise. Everyone wins.
- **Have fun.** It is fine to network in informal settings! If you look like you enjoy what you do, people will be more inclined to refer to you. Sell your passion.
- **Say thanks.** Look for appropriate yet creative ways to express appreciation to people who've helped you. Always offer to pay the tab if you've networked over a meal. A fruit basket, a bouquet of flowers, a massage. At a minimum, always send a thank you note.
- **Finish with the future in mind.** End conversations with people imagining they will be in your circle for years. Make dates to explore how you can help each other.

Source: Reprinted from Waymon L, Baber A. No-nonsense marketing. *Your Company*. 1993; (Summer): 37, with permission from the authors. Copyright © 1993 Anne Baber and Lynne Waymon, the authors of *Make Your Contacts Count: Networking Know-How for Business and Career Success* (New York, NY: AMACOM; 2007). For more information: see the Web site http://www.contactscount.com or call 301/589-8633.

Anyone you meet is a potential resource for you. Learning how and when to massage those connections is important. Practice a subtle but direct approach. Asking someone, "What can you do for me?" is a turnoff. Craft your questions carefully. For example, ask, "Who else should I speak with?" There will be times when it is inappropriate to network, and there will be situations where you might not be interested in networking!

Networking is an ongoing activity. For as long as you are in business, you will need to keep your networks alive. Always be "on." You never know who that person in line at the grocery store may be.

Advertising

Good advertising means getting the word out often. For advertising to be effective, the message must be repeated several times. There are plenty of low-cost advertising tools. Regardless of which you use, employ two basic advertising concepts: your advertising must be catchy and your audience must encounter it repeatedly (1,2,9). In *The Small Business Bible* (2), Steven Strauss explains that you may see the same advertisement repeatedly and never notice it until the day you need what it advertises. Great ads solve problems—does yours?

When you are starting out, choose the most appropriate media and upgrade as you can afford it. Advertising allows you to control your message. Take the time to plan a well-designed ad. If you can't afford to have it professionally designed, have it evaluated by friends and colleagues. Take their input seriously, and revise your advertising until the message is presented in a clear, concise, and catchy way.

Newspapers

Newspapers can be good advertising tools, although ads in some newspapers can be very costly. If you live in a large metropolitan area, advertise in a small community-based newspaper. It will be more affordable and reach a more targeted audience.

Think carefully about ad placement. If your paper has a health edition or food edition, placing an ad in that section will reach an already interested audience. If you are focusing on sports nutrition, have your ad placed on the sports page. Some newspapers offer "bulletin boards" that advertise classes, community events, or lectures. This is free advertising. If you can, be sure to take advantage of this opportunity.

When planning your newspaper ad, remember to budget for several releases. Good advertising needs to appear several times. A one-time newspaper ad will likely not generate the attention you want. Consider smaller ads appearing more often rather than a larger ad less frequently. When buying bulk advertising—that is, running the same advertisement multiple times—you will be offered a discount. Also, do not forget to design your ad so that it is punchy and informative.

Yellow Pages

Advertising in the yellow pages is targeted to a captive audience. The person searching the yellow pages has already determined they need to "buy" that service or product. It is generally inexpensive to place an ad. If you have a business telephone number, you might be entitled to a free listing, which is simply your name, address, and phone number in a specific category. Consider placing a display ad in several different categories. For example, weight loss, nutrition consultants, and dietitians may all be appropriate ad placement categories. Placement and size of the ad is important. Consumers will call the first ad they see, and they believe a larger ad means a more reputable business (2). Free design services are offered by many yellow pages; however, "free" may mean your ad will look like other ads in the book.

The yellow pages do not have stated criteria for who can advertise, so you might find yourself competing with large diet centers or unlicensed professionals. Think carefully about what type of client you want to attract and advertise with that in mind.

The online yellow pages are an updated option to the print version. A listing is free for a business phone number, but there are fees for a display ad.

Nonprint Media: Television and Radio

Airtime, regardless of the market, is expensive. A paid commercial is probably beyond the budget for most RDs just starting out. Cable and satellite TV are less expensive than network TV but may not be a wise use of your marketing money (12). If you are trying to advertise an event as opposed to your own business, networks and radio stations may offer the opportunity for a public service announcement. Exposure and name recognition are important, so do not pass up this opportunity if it exists.

Web Sites

A Web site is an essential tool in doing business. No matter the size of your business, the stage of your business, or where you conduct your business, a Web site can provide equal footing with the established big players (2). If you start your business using a spare bedroom in your home, on the Internet no one will know. A Web site provides you with the opportunity to communicate better with your potential or existing clients, sell a product or service, or establish credibility in the marketplace, among other things.

Developing, maintaining, and promoting a Web site does not have to be costly, but it can be time-consuming. Think through your purpose and your target audience before committing time and resources to developing one. A Web site can be a useful marketing tool. Anywhere you market your business, like an advertisement or business cards, you can include and direct customers to your Web address. Your Web site becomes a golden opportunity for customers to learn more about you and your business. For more information on Web sites, refer to Chapter 6.

Direct Mail

Direct mail includes any promotional piece that connects directly with the consumer. There are many options available to you, each with its unique selling power. Direct mail includes e-mails, postcards, brochures, announcements, and newsletters. Even a follow-up letter to a referring physician is a form of direct mail.

Targeted mailing lists can be purchased from several different organizations. If you are advertising to other RDs to promote a class or product, you can purchase mailing lists from the ADA that are targeted for geographic regions or by specialty area. Other professional organizations sell lists, too. Your local medical society may be a good source if you are mailing to physicians or other health professionals.

To access an existing mailing list, think about the target group you identified and what other services they may use. If you are offering a class for new parents, think about the products all new parents will be purchasing and contact that source to see if a list is available. You can also generate your own mailing list for free from your e-mail address book and other personal contact lists.

E-mail

E-mail is an effective way to market. The most basic use of e-mail as a marketing tool is sending every e-mail with your "signature," which provides complete contact information about your business. This is free advertising each time you send an e-mail. Take advantage of this. Another way to use e-mail as a marketing tool is to use an e-mail marketing Web site. These Web sites assist in developing professional, polished-looking e-mails for a nominal fee and can provide other services as well (2). Chapter 6 provides additional information on the uses of e-mail.

Brochures

A printed brochure allows you to go into detail about your business and can be especially helpful when marketing a service (9). Brochures can be relatively inexpensive to create. To keep costs down, brochures can be created on a computer. Important elements to highlight would include your philosophy and what makes your business unique. It's also nice to "give" something away on the brochure, such as a sample recipe or a healthy eating tip.

When designing the brochure, always keep the audience in mind. For example, a brochure to send other professionals may have a different look from a brochure you will distribute at a health club. Your brochure should look professional and help you to establish credibility. For further guidance, refer to Box 5.5.

Flyers

Flyers can be an inexpensive and creative way to advertise. Like brochures, they allow you to discuss your service in a more personal way. A well-designed flyer can promote a professional image. Distribute them with thought. Rather than leaving your flyers on car windshields, strategically place them on community bulletin boards, in a physician's office waiting area, or as a giveaway at a local road race. Just be sure to ask permission before distributing them. To make them meaningful, include fast-food facts, holiday tips, or even a recipe of the month. Be sure the flyer includes the important information about you and your practice.

Announcements

Announcements are most successful when you are established and have something new to announce. For example, a new partner, new location, or new program might be appropriate reasons to send an announcement. There are likely better ways to spend your marketing budget than sending announcements

Box 5.5 Guidelines for Developing a Brochure

- Identify your audience. This determines the tone of your brochure.
- Consider the purpose of the brochure. It could be to:
  - Distribute at lectures
  - Mail to prospective clients
  - Send to referral sources, such as physicians, therapists, or schools.
- Keep samples of brochures that you like. It is easier to identify features you like and don't like and adapt them to accommodate your unique approach than to create a brochure from scratch. If a professional will be assisting you, bring the brochures with you.
- Make a "dummy" brochure by folding paper and laying out items.
- Brochures are generally 8.5 × 11.5 or 8.5 × 14 inches. They need to be folded to fit into a business envelope for mailing.
- Brochures are generally divided into three panels, using the front and back of the paper.
  - One panel is used for the headlines. This is where you prominently display information about yourself: name, credentials, address, telephone number, e-mail address, Web site URL. You would also put your logo here, if you have one. This is what your audience will read first. It should move the reader to call you.
  - One panel is where you describe your services or products. Emphasize how you will help a prospective client, how someone will benefit from your services or products, and how your services or products are unique.
  - One panel is where you might give away advice, add a recipe, include testimonials (make sure to get permission), and insert your picture (optional).
- Make sure the language you use is appropriate to the audience you seek. This is not the place to be clinical or show off your vocabulary. Use the active voice when writing and avoid clichés. Choose simple words that will excite people and motivate them to call you.
- The typeface you select must be reader friendly. Use of a variety of fonts, and bold and italics type to allow information to stand out. Be careful not to make it too busy as that is a turnoff.
- The quality of the paper you use is determined by your budget. Use the best you can afford, but your money will be better spent on the creative portion and developing snappy copy.
- Let your personal style show through, even if a professional is designing it for you.

to let people know you have opened a new practice. Because your name won't be recognized, the persons you wish to reach may never read the announcement before it's tossed in the trash. Announcements can be sent via the mail or as an e-mail. For a generic announcement, see Figure 5.3.

Jane Doe, M.S., R.D.

Is pleased to announce the relocation of her practice

Nutrition Consulting Services
121 Main Street
Anywhere, USA

(333) 222–2222
(333) 222–2223 fax
anynet.com

Figure 5.3 Generic announcement.

Follow-Up Letters, Thank-You Notes, Cards, and Gifts

An overlooked piece of direct mail is the follow-up letter you mail to a physician or a thank-you note you send to a referral source. With so much reliance on e-mail, receiving a letter or note the old-fashioned way can provide a personal touch to make you stand out, which customers may really appreciate. Follow-up letters are direct mail pieces with very targeted and receptive audiences. You might also include an article on a relevant nutrition topic. The name of the game in advertising is to keep your name out there. Always include business cards and a brochure or other promotional material, if possible.

Sending holiday cards to your referral sources and client base is direct mail advertising. It is another way of keeping your name out there. Purchase or design cards that reflect you and your practice. Add a personal note. Also consider sending holiday gifts to referral sources. A fruit basket, a nice cookbook, or a subscription to a health newsletter or magazine are all appreciated gifts. National Nutrition Month and Registered Dietitian Day provide opportunities for marketing your services by sending a gift, article, or card.

Newsletters

Although a newsletter is a great way to advertise, it should not be the first tool used to promote your business. Creating a newsletter is time-consuming, and publishing can be expensive unless it is distributed as an e-newsletter; that is, electronic newsletters sent via e-mail. It can be added to your "bag of tricks" when you are looking to grow and diversify your business, but consider your target population and what they will read (13). For example, if marketing to seniors, consider that they will more likely read paper newsletters sent via snail mail than e-newsletters.

Directories

Many organizations publish the names of all members in their directories, and some directories include paid advertisements. Look for opportunities to be listed or advertise in multiple directories. For example, your dietetic practice group or the local chapter of the American Heart Association or of Women in Business may have directories that will reach different populations. Medical societies often publish directories for physicians and other health professionals. If your medical community publishes a directory but does not include RDs, suggest they add the section. It will make their directory more complete.

Search the Internet for directory Web sites that include nutrition businesses or services. Create a profile or listing for your business on these directories. When prospective clients search your name on the Internet, they can be guided to your listing. On some of these sites, visitors can post reviews of your business. Check what others are reading and writing about your services.

Remember to think of all your networks: your child's school, garden club, and place of worship. Do they publish a directory? Does it reach your target audience? If so, advertise in it.

Directories can be a very inexpensive form of advertising. Sometimes a reprint of your business card can take the place of a formal ad.

Publicity

Publicity is basically free advertising. It includes anything that gets your name to the target population. It can be a quote you've given to a newspaper, an article you've written, or publicity flyers distributed for a talk you are giving. Your target market will view good publicity as more credible than paid advertising. Readers often think that you must be credible if an article features you or relies on you as an expert, or if you've been asked to speak to a group. Publicity tends to have greater longevity than paid advertising. Readers will likely remember it better than advertising. The key is learning how to become noteworthy enough to attract good publicity.

As you seek publicity, remember that you cannot fully control what is said about you. For example, when you are interviewed, the interviewer can use your comments in any way they might fit into a story. Although reporters are not out to make you look bad, they do determine what they write about the interview. You can request to review the article for accuracy prior to publication, but this doesn't give you control of the message.

Press Releases and Press Kits

The first step in attracting publicity is to develop a press release. Send a press release to anyone who might have any interest in what you are doing. Perhaps you have a new software program to analyze recipes, a new piece of equipment to measure percentage of body fat, or you are starting a cooking program for senior citizens. These could all seem newsworthy to the right media source. According to Jeff Crilley of the Newsroom PR, a press release can lead to free publicity (14).

You should create a press kit if you plan on promoting yourself or an event to the media or to organizations interested in hiring you to speak. For more information on press releases and press kits, see Chapter 12.

Writing for Publicity

Having a byline and getting published is great publicity. Although many RDs are paid for writing, others write to gain name recognition or as a stepping-stone to larger projects. If you are writing for free, negotiate for free advertising space in return for writing an article.

Writing takes time, talent, and drive. You do not need to start with a large daily newspaper to be published. Think about what your target market reads. Perhaps you are working with a pediatric population. Writing for a locally produced parenting magazine or newspaper or even contributing an article for the local Parent Teacher Association (PTA) newsletter would provide you with exposure to your target population. If your interest is in sports nutrition, find a local fitness center with a monthly newsletter and volunteer to write an article. Perhaps you are interested in conducting supermarket tours. If so, check if your local supermarket chain might be interested in having you write a column for their newsletter. Chapter 12 has more information on writing opportunities.

Publicizing Yourself with Reprinted Articles Written by Others

If you do not have the time or interest to write an article, find a relevant article written by someone else and distribute copies to raise awareness of a topic related to your business. Let readers know that you are a local expert on that topic. Before you distribute any published material, be sure to request permission to have it reprinted. Costs for reprint permissions vary extensively. Some articles may be free of charge; others can be quite expensive to use.

Getting Quoted as an Expert

To become the local expert, you will need to develop relationships with the local media. Learning how to work with the media is an art that is not mastered overnight. Offer yourself as an expert by sending them a press release about a program you are presenting in the community and providing a press kit including information about your practice, or simply calling them to respond to a story they ran. The media will appreciate your availability as a credible source rather than as an RD who is trying to get her name in print (15).

Reporters appreciate hearing about story ideas. However, not all ideas are considered. For serious consideration, a story idea should be unique, topical, or present a new angle on a previously covered topic. If one reporter is not interested in the topic, ask if he or she is aware of someone who might be interested. Be persistent, but do not be a pest (15).

Generally, reporters always need the information yesterday. If a reporter calls you, be sure to respond in a timely way. Often, the reporter will use the first person that returns their call. If you know the time and topic of the interview, be prepared. If you are not prepared with an answer when a reporter calls, ask if you can return the call in 15 minutes. In that time, collect your thoughts. Have a few important "sound bites" of information. Limit your answers to the questions asked. The more you talk to reporters, the more comfortable you will become asking them to repeat what you've said to minimize the risks of being misquoted. Follow up promptly with supporting information requested. If you don't know the topic, the best thing you can do is to provide them with the name of someone who does.

Realize that this process can be frustrating. You might provide 45 minutes of your time and in return receive a two-second sound bite or a one-sentence quote. Sometimes you might receive no mention at all. Follow up by contacting the writer after the article has appeared. Give them feedback. Thank the reporter for including your information or for consulting with you, even if you were not mentioned.

Notice when RDs are quoted in the press, then contact them and ask how they became a resource to the media. If an RD has a relationship with the media, advise him of your expertise. Professionals should recognize their limitations and, if they are aware of your expertise, may refer the media to you. Refer to Chapter 12 for additional help on working with the media.

Speaking Engagements and Presentations

Name recognition and keeping your name visible are the cornerstones of marketing. One easy way to do this is by making yourself available for speaking engagements. To find opportunities, join speakers' bureaus, such as the National Speakers Bureau (http://www.speaker.org) or the speakers' bureaus of your professional organizations. You will learn how to become a better speaker and, with some marketing, can be called upon as a speaker.

Nutrition is a topic of interest to almost everyone, including your colleagues. It's important to learn how to speak publicly to different audiences. Research your audience before giving the talk. Do not focus on selling your services or products to the audience. If you do a good job, the audience members may request a business card. Also, be sure to have handouts available when you speak. And, of course, always include contact information.

As you look for speaking and presentation opportunities, concentrate on your target market. If you want to target physicians in practice, you may offer to provide a lunchtime presentation on a relevant topic at their office. If pediatrics is your focus, present at a PTA meeting. Your goal is for the referring sources to see you as the expert. For examples of timely presentation topics by the month, see Box 5.6. For additional information on public speaking techniques and strategies, see Chapter 12.

Box 5.6 Hot Topics for Presentations

January: How to keep those New Year's resolutions

February: The latest thoughts on heart health

March: National Nutrition Month . . . know your registered dietitians

April: Getting ready for summer . . . comparison of latest diet trends

May: Fast-food choices

June: Eating well when eating out

July: Picnic safety

August: Back-to-school lunch

September: Satisfying snack foods

October: Yikes . . . it's Halloween

November: Thanksgiving is only one meal

December: Navigating your way through the holiday season

Health Fairs

Many organizations conduct health fairs, and these events can be opportunities to market your services, network, assess interest in topics, showcase new products, or get feedback on educational materials you sell or use. If the health fair reaches your target audience, it is a good way to get your name out and earn credibility. Although a health fair that doesn't reach your target population is unlikely to bring you business, it may be a good opportunity to practice speaking with an audience that you probably will not address again. Be wary of health fairs that charge a fee. Consider whether it is prudent to spend your marketing dollars on such fees.

Community Involvement

Investigate the possibilities of donating a free consultation to a targeted auction or community event. Schools, places of worship, and charitable organizations may hold auctions to raise funds. Auction catalogues and publicity for the event will serve as your free advertising. You can give back to your community and receive free publicity for your service.

Word of Mouth

A satisfied customer is your best marketing tool. You can't control this free advertising, but it is the best advertising. Being competent, caring for your client base, and a little luck with satisfied clients are what will ultimately promote your services.

Tools and Tips for Marketing: A Summary

"It takes money to make money." You need to determine not whether you can afford marketing, but how much you can spend on marketing to get the biggest bang for your buck. Be realistic. Very few RDs will be able to foot the bill for a large marketing campaign. That does not mean you should forego marketing. It simply means you need to do your research and invest your money where you will reap the biggest returns. Marketing dollars must be spent wisely. The effectiveness of marketing needs to be constantly monitored. As discussed in this chapter, there are less expensive ways to market—seek out these opportunities. Be creative. Advertising allows you to control the message but is more costly. Publicity and word of mouth, although free, do not allow you to control the message, only to influence it.

Marketing is a dynamic process. You do not create a marketing plan, try it out, and go into business. From the inception of your business until you retire, you need to be marketing, and reevaluating and revising your marketing methods as needed. Marketing should be fun and allow you and your business to shine.

Evaluate your marketing knowledge and get professional help where you feel inadequate. Tap into free services offered through organizations including the ADA and the Small Business Administration, your local chamber of commerce, and public libraries.

Draw up a plan, think creatively, and go for it. Keep the following vital points in mind:

- The "4 Ps" of marketing are product, place, price, and promotion. These all come together in the essential marketing plan.
- Analyzing your target market will help you to learn about the people who will buy your services or products. It should also reveal information about your competition. Knowing your competition is important in defining your own business and marketing your services.
- Successful marketing requires a "hook." Think about all the things that are unique about you and your business. Networking is essential to your success. Find out where your networks exist and learn how and when to network effectively.

- Advertising needs to be repeated to be meaningful. One-shot ads are generally not worth the investment.
- There are many different media—including newspapers, yellow pages, radio and television, Web sites, direct mail, e-mail, brochures, announcements, flyers, follow-up letters, holiday cards, newsletters, and directories—that are available to you for advertising. Evaluate the cost, image, and effectiveness of each for your particular practice.
- Publicity is free advertising. You have little control over what is said about you, but it tends to give credibility to your services. To position yourself for publicity, create a press release or press kit, write an article, or offer your expertise to the media. Free publicity also comes from giving talks, volunteering at health fairs, and being involved in your community.
- A satisfied client is the best form of advertising.

References

1. Tyson E, Schell J. *Small Business for Dummies*. Hoboken, NJ: John Wiley and Sons Publishing; 2008.
2. Strauss S. *The Small Business Bible: Everything You Need to Know to Succeed in Your Small Business*. 2nd ed. Hoboken, NJ: John Wiley and Sons; 2008.
3. Westwood J. *How to Write a Marketing Plan*. 3rd ed. Philadelphia, PA: Thomson-Shore; 2007.
4. Rogoff E. *Bankable Business Plans*. 2nd ed. New York, NY: Rowhouse Publishing; 2007.
5. Pinson J, Jinnett J. *Steps to Small Business Start-Up. Everything You Need to Know to Turn Your Idea into a Successful Business*. 6th ed. Chicago, IL: Kaplan Publishing; 2006.
6. Comaford C. Don't Go it Alone: Create an Advisory Board. Business Week Web site. February 1. 2007. http://www.businessweek.com/smallbiz/content/feb2007/sb20070201_669782.htm. Accessed May 3, 2009.
7. Baber A, Waymon L. *Make Your Contacts Count: Networking Know-How for Business and Career Success*. 2nd ed. New York, NY: AMACOM; 2007.
8. Brown D. Networking moves online. *J Am Diet Assoc*. 2009;109:210–211.
9. Lesonsky R. *Start Your Own Business*. Irvine, CA: Entrepreneur Media; 2007.
10. Fisher D, Vilas S. *Power Networking: 59 Secrets for Personal & Professional Success*. Marietta, GA: Bard Press; 2000.
11. Baber A, Waymon L. No-nonsense networking: a guide to cultivating new business contacts. *Your Company*. 1993;(Summer):34–38.
12. Levinson J. *Guerrilla Marketing: Easy and Inexpensive Strategies for Making Big Profits from Your Small Business*. New York, NY: Houghton Mifflin; 2007.
13. Mathieu J. Tips for publishing a top-notch newsletter *J Am Diet Assoc*. 2007; 107: 384–385.
14. Crilley J. *Free Publicity*. Dallas, TX: Brown Books; 2003.
15. American Dietetic Association. Working with the Media: A Handbook for Members of the American Dietetic Association; 2009. http://www.eatright.org/cps/rde/xchg/ada/hs.xsl/media_20576_ENU_HTML.htm. Accessed April 27, 2009.

Chapter 6

Using Technology to Enhance Your Business

Technology is changing so fast it can be difficult to keep up. To compete in today's market, however, you must change with the times. Although you do not need to run out and purchase the latest and greatest gadget the minute it appears on the market, you do need to be aware of new technology and assess its usefulness to you. For example, in today's market, you cannot effectively do business without using the Internet. If used properly, the features of the Internet can be quite an asset to your business. This chapter will explore ways to use technology to enhance your business.

E-Mail Marketing

E-mail has greatly increased productivity. In most cases, e-mail has replaced the telephone call and US mail. Registered dietitians (RDs) use e-mail to communicate with business associates regarding business issues and to schedule meetings. They also communicate by e-mail with other health care professionals regarding a particular patient (provided they comply with the Health Insurance Portability and Accountability Act regulations) and use e-mail to send proposals to potential clients.

E-mail can also be used as a marketing tool. For example, you can collect e-mail addresses from your patients or clients and e-mail them the "recipe of the month" or the "nutrition tip of the month." Make sure you have permission from the recipients, however. You do not want to be the source of unwanted e-mail.

There is a downside to e-mail. Checking e-mail can be time-consuming, and you may become sidetracked by certain e-mails. Some RDs find it helpful to set up a separate e-mail addresses for business and personal use so they can focus on one at a time. Others schedule specific times of the day to focus solely on e-mail to increase productivity and decrease distraction.

Listservs and Electronic Mailing Lists

Electronic mailing lists and Listservs are wonderful free tools for RDs. A Listserv is a forum for discussion via e-mail. You can subscribe to Listservs that pertain to your area of interest. Be mindful that when you send an e-mail message to a Listserv, everyone who is subscribed receives the e-mail (1). RDs use Listservs to obtain clinical and business advice from colleagues across the country, announce consulting positions, and locate referrals for their patients who are moving.

The American Dietetic Association (ADA) has a general Listserv open to all members. Most of ADA's dietetic practice groups (DPGs) also have Listservs, which are more specialized by area of practice. Even within the DPGs, Listservs exist among subgroups. For example, the Nutrition Entrepreneurs DPG has a general Listserv for its members as well as specific Listservs for RDs who specialize in private practice, writing, speaking, Internet and business technology, corporate health, and coaching. Participating in the DPG Listservs requires DPG membership.

If you choose to subscribe to multiple Listservs, the volume of mail can become overwhelming. Consider the option of receiving the information in the digest version. This will provide you with a daily summary rather than multiple e-mails coming in throughout the day. Another option is to set up a separate e-mail address for Listserv subscriptions. Then you can check that address periodically.

Netiquette

"Netiquette" refers to "Internet etiquette." General netiquette guidelines have been around for years. The need for guidelines arose as e-mail became the primary communication tool used in business. Many professionals, however, forget to abide by basic netiquette guidelines (Box 6.1) (2).

It is also important to be aware of any specific netiquette guidelines set for subscribers by an individual Listserv. For example, ADA has specific general guidelines for all ADA Listservs, and the DPGs take it a step further by providing specific guidelines for their purposes. Each DPG outlines their netiquette guidelines on their Web site. Box 6.2 provides an example of Nutrition Entrepreneurs' netiquette guidelines (3).

Box 6.1 Netiquette Guidelines

- **Be clear.** Always include a subject line.
- **Use appropriate language.** If you are emotional, do not send the message. Save it and review it later.
- **Be brief.** People are more likely to read a short message.
- **Be selective.** Information on the Internet is very public.
- **Get permission from the originator to forward e-mail messages.**
- **Obey copyright laws.** Do not use others' images or content without permission.
- **Do not send spam.** Remember, it is electronic junk mail.
- **Cite others when you use their work.**

Source: Adapted with permission from *The Ten Commandments of E-mail "Netiquette."* Study Guides and Strategies Web site. http://www.studygs.net/netiquette.htm. Accessed March 9, 2010.

Box 6.2 Nutrition Entrepreneurs Practice Group's Netiquette Guidelines

The following are points of conduct and protocol that will improve the experience of all participants in the lists. Adherence to these suggested practices is strongly encouraged.

1. Unless responding to a message in which the author has specifically asked for private replies, a participant should send any reply to the list so the response is shared. Addressing a copy to the sender is usually not required, but is acceptable.
2. A participant should include a descriptive subject line in each posting. If using the digest mode and wishing to respond to a post, the participant should be sure to use a subject header that matches the original post. A participant should sign every message with the name, organization, phone number, and e-mail address of the sender. Promotional tag lines should be kept to a minimum.
3. Where it is appropriate to reply only to the original sender, as with "me too" or "I agree" messages, the participant should refrain from replying to the entire list unless the message will be of interest to the majority of contributors to the ongoing discussion.
4. The language of a written message can be ambiguous and subject to different interpretations. Each participant should carefully consider the phrasing and choice of language in his or her message to ensure that the intended message is conveyed. Although the list is private and confidential, all participants should also consider the effect of their message if publicly distributed or read by a third party.
5. A participant should refrain from sending jokes/chain letters/junk mail, religious messages, or spam, as well as e-mail attachments that might contain viruses or virus warnings. In addition, each participant has an obligation to other participants to take appropriate steps to avoid the spread of viruses through the list, including the installation of virus protection on all computers by which the list is accessed.

Source: Reprinted with permission: Nutrition Entrepreneurs DPG. Online Discussions Netiquette and Terms of Use. Available at: http://www.nedpg.org/members/listservs/NetiquetteFINAL.pdf. Accessed: April 19, 2010.

Research on the World Wide Web

Staying current is essential in the field of nutrition. Your patients or clients will want your opinion of the latest diet or today's news about food safety. To stay current, you can read online editions of major newspapers, such as the *New York Times*, *Wall Street Journal*, or *Washington Post*. You can also subscribe to the *Daily News* e-mail published by ADA's Knowledge Center. It provides a daily summary of nutrition and health articles from major media outlets. Another great ADA feature is *ADA New in Review*. Each month, *ADA New in Review* compiles articles from scientific and professional periodicals of interest to food and nutrition professionals, as well as reviews of dietetics-related books and Web sites. This new members-only benefit is available online (http://www.eatright.org/adanewinreview).

You can access educational materials online, but be aware of legal rules regarding the distribution of such documents to patients or clients. Materials published by the US government are generally part of the public domain and usually can be distributed without asking permission. Other material on the Internet is copyrighted. Many Web sites allow you to reprint copyrighted documents for free if you are using them for educational purposes (4). However, you should always verify that reprints are permitted before you distribute materials. You may need a signed release from the copyright holder. Some copyright holders will charge a fee for use. Another option is to direct your patients or clients to some of the sites you deem appropriate and accurate.

Marketing on the Web

One way you can use the Web as a marketing tool is to subscribe to online referral listings. ADA's Nationwide Nutrition Network provides a referral listing at no charge to ADA members. Be sure to check other associations, such as the American Diabetes Association or the National Speakers Association, for opportunities to list your practice or services.

It is common to list your company e-mail address with your business telephone number for contact information on the referral listings. Once you do, be prepared for inquiries via e-mail about your services. If you do not have a Web site, you may find it beneficial to save some marketing materials, such as your biography and information about your business, as electronic documents. You can then send them to potential patients or clients as you receive e-mail requests.

Setting Up a Web Site for Your Business

The Internet has changed the way we do business. Having a presence on the Web by developing a Web site will lend credibility to your business or practice. When potential new clients contact you, they often assume that you have a site and ask for your URL (Web address) to obtain more information about you and your services. Having a Web site is your opportunity to control the message about your practice or company. The information potential clients receive is what you decide is important.

If you have the time, interest, and inclination, you can develop your own Web site. Alternatively, you can hire a Web site designer to develop it for you. If you decide to hire a designer, look at other sites he or she has created. See if they appeal to you. Explore different Web sites of colleagues and of those outside the food and nutrition industry. Get a sense of those Web sites you like. What is it you liked about them? Consider the layout, ease of navigating the Web site, the color scheme, and graphics. Make a list of components and features you may want to include on your site.

Even if you hire a designer, you must be involved in each step. Once your site is designed, you will need to host it yourself or hire someone to host and maintain it. If you decide to create your own Web site, you should set aside some money from your business to hire someone down the road to redesign what you have created. Not everyone needs an expensive Web site, but most businesses at some point need to bring in professionals to expand a Web site or give it a design that reaches the desired target market. These goals can be achieved without a huge financial investment.

Planning Your Site

Before you approach a Web company to set up your Web site, you must have a plan in place. First determine the purpose of your Web site. Box 6.3 provides 10 basic purposes of a Web site (5). Identify one as your primary purpose. This will influence many decisions such as design, content, site organization, and navigation. Next, identify any secondary purposes for your site. As you think about these issues, you will want to remember who your target market is (see Chapter 5).

Box 6.3 Ten Basic Purposes of a Web Site

1. Improve and increase the image and visibility of your business
2. Attract new customers in your local area
3. Attract new customers from outside the local area
4. Better serve current customers
5. Complement your advertising
6. Start a new venture online
7. Sell a product or service
8. Use as an online brochure for business
9. Provide educational content and resources
10. Share your passion and expertise

Source: Data are from reference 5.

Choosing a Domain

The domain is your Web site name and URL address. Some RDs prefer to use a catchy name related to nutrition or the product they sell, while others prefer to use their own names. To determine whether a domain is available, check with a domain provider, such as Network Solutions (http://www.networksolutions.com) or Register (http://www.register.com). You may want to purchase the same domain name with ".com," ".net," and ".org" to protect yourself from a competitor directing traffic to its site. Also, consider common misspellings and purchase them.

Keep in mind how people will find you. If someone is searching for your services, what will he or she type into the search engine? This may help you come up with your domain name. Having a domain name that matches what people enter into their search engine can place your page higher in search results. For example, if someone searches "Atlanta diabetes information" and your Web site URL is atlantadiabetesinfo.com, it will have a greater chance of coming near the top of the results list. The best domains are easy to remember and spell and are associated with the services and/or products you provide.

Once you determine that your desired domain is available, you can purchase it. Purchase from a reputable domain provider such as Network Solutions or Register. Be aware that some domain services make it difficult and time-consuming to choose alternatives for hosting and may require a multi-year commitment.

Choosing a Hosting Company

A Web host puts your Web site on the Internet. When choosing your hosting company, remember that the cheapest is not the best. Hosting is a minimal expense, so it is worth paying extra for better service. When making your choice, make sure the company provides the following services:

- Around-the-clock support
- Daily backups of your site
- Web site traffic reports

If you plan to sell products from your site, it is not recommended that you use the shopping cart offered by the hosting company. It can be extremely costly should you decide to change hosting companies in the future. Look for a reputable company that offers a full e-commerce system that is transferable from host to host, provides support, and has been in business for several years. This last factor is important because many companies come and go. Be sure to choose a company that is keeping up with changes in technology and the marketplace and will be around for the long term.

Choosing a Web Developer or Designer

When you hire professionals to help build your Web site, you can use freelancers or a Web site development company. A Web site company typically will be full service and can help you with branding, marketing, search engine optimization, design, e-commerce, updating, content management system, a blog, or anything else you will need. If you want to create some of the Web site yourself, hiring freelancers to do a specialized part of the project may be your best option. Keep in mind with this option that you will need to put together specific details on what you need the freelancers to do, oversee them, and test out the result.

To find a Web site developer, get recommendations from colleagues and search the Internet for sites you like the look and feel of. If a site appeals to you, contact the site and ask which company it used and solicit feedback. Look at the portfolio of the design company, and ask other candidates to show their portfolios. Also, browse Web sites they have designed and evaluate the following (6):

- Are the sites easy to navigate?
- Do all the links work?
- Is the content updated?
- Do the designs have a fresh, cutting-edge look?
- Do all the forms work?
- Do newsletter sign-ups work?
- Do the "contact" sections work?
- Do the sites work in more than one browser?

Think twice before using a friend of a friend who does design on the side or an uncle's teenage neighbor who is known as a computer whiz. If you are going to hire someone, choose a professional. Get a minimum of three bids before you make your decision.

Building a Do-It-Yourself Site

If you prefer to create your own Web site, there are programs and Web sites available to assist novices. These programs allow you to develop Web pages visually without having to know the technical aspects of Web building and design. Designing your own site is fine for a basic site, particularly when you are first starting out and budget is a concern. To locate a Web design program, enter "Web authoring software" into your search engine. Look for recent reviews of each program before you make a decision. As your practice or business grows and you want to add more complicated components to your site such as video clips or forms to download, it will be worthwhile to invest in a professionally designed site.

Essential Web Site Features

Regardless of who is designing your Web site, certain features are essential. These include a home page, graphics, and navigation. The home page will provide a purposeful first impression, guide visitors around your Web site (7), and tell first-time visitors about what you do or sell. You don't want visitors to dwell on this page; rather, you want to pull them inside to browse the site. Graphics emphasize or bring out a point on the page; they should not be used to simply make a page "pretty." Ease of navigation is very important to users. If they cannot find what they need quickly, they will become frustrated and leave the site. Navigation helps guide visitors through a site.

All sites should include an "about" page, a contact page, and a privacy policy. The about page provides a description of who owns and is behind the site. The contact page is self-explanatory—it provides a way for visitors to contact you. You can provide an e-mail address or phone number, but consider providing both. This is also a great place to provide your office location and directions to your office. Contact information should be very easy for visitors to find when navigating your site. A privacy policy is provided for ethical reasons. The purpose of a privacy policy is to build trust online and inform visitors to your site that you will protect and respect their privacy. Your customers or clients will feel more secure if they know that any information they submit to you will only be used in ways they have authorized. There are numerous online tools available to assist with creating a privacy policy. Simply type "privacy policy for Web sites" into your search engine to take advantage of the free resources.

Another common page is the FAQs (frequently asked questions) page. Include those questions that take a significant amount of time to answer on the phone. You can use FAQs to plant questions that draw users into identifying the need for your product or service. For example, posting "With so many nutrition books out there, is a registered dietitian really worth the money?" will allow you to tout the benefits of seeing an RD and explain why visitors to your site should schedule an appointment.

Traffic Reports

When you are setting up your Web site, it is important to have access to some form of traffic report. This report can tell you how well your Web site is doing. Some hosting companies charge extra for this service, so carefully investigate whether you will be using their reports. You can monitor how many views each page receives and make changes to your site accordingly. Monitoring traffic reports and taking action based on these reports requires some skill. It may be wise to hire a professional to steer you in the right direction.

Updating and Adding Content

Businesses with Web sites should develop a plan for updating content on a regular basis. This will keep your visitors coming back, keep your site from becoming stale, and increase your ranking in search engines. Daily updating is probably unrealistic, especially if you are doing everything by yourself, but consider weekly or monthly updates. New content might include recipes, FAQs, links, or new product reviews.

Your Web site is an extension of your business. It takes time and energy to develop and maintain a professional site. However, if you nourish it properly, it will thrive and grow.

Multimedia Tools to Enhance Your Business

Once you are using the Internet to streamline your work and you have developed your Web site for marketing, you may want to take technology to the next level. Many multimedia tools, including video clips, podcasts, Webinars, teleconferences, and telecounseling can be added to your technology toolbox to increase your business or enhance your products and services.

Video Clips

One of the simplest ways to enhance a Web site is to add video clips. For example, many RDs post video of themselves giving television interviews, teaching classes, or conducting cooking demonstrations. What a great way to showcase your talent and expertise.

Podcasts

A podcast is an audio file available on the Internet that you can listen to on computers and handheld devices. Vodcasts include video in addition to audio. (Some people include videos under the term "podcast.") Some podcasts are offered for free while others require payment to download. For example, some medical journals offer free podcasts of their articles, sometimes with added content (8).

There are many ways for RDs to enhance their businesses by offering podcasts. Consider providing free podcasts on various nutrition topics via your Web site. This could be an excellent way of regularly updating your site and encouraging repeat visitors. For example, you could post a weekly or monthly podcast that provides sports nutrition tips and recipes. Alternatively, you could charge a nominal fee for downloading podcasts, particularly if you have an interesting area of expertise and produce podcasts that people are willing to buy. Some RDs turn the classes they teach into podcasts for purchase. Box 6.4 provides examples of ways in which RDs are incorporating podcasts into their businesses.

Making a podcast is fairly easy. There are numerous "how to" articles available on the Internet to walk you through all the steps. You can even find podcasts on how to make a podcast! You need specific equipment to make a

Box 6.4 Using Podcasts to Enhance Nutrition Businesses

Marjorie Geiser, MBA, RD, NSCA-CPT

Marjorie has been presenting the Professional of the Month series as a podcast since 2005. Initially, they were free to anyone who wished to listen, but now she uses them as a value-added service for paid members who sign up for her coaching membership program. She also records most of her teleconferences and offers them as podcasts to compliment her home-study courses, which are available for purchase for continuing professional education (CPE) credits.

Janice Newell Bissex, MS, RD, and Liz Weiss, MS, RD

Janice and Liz have co-hosted a weekly podcast, *Cooking with the Moms*, since 2008. Each week they dish about fast and healthy recipe ideas and helpful mealtime tips that help families eat a more nutritious diet. The free podcasts are available on their Web site (MealMakeoverMoms.com) or can be downloaded from iTunes. In addition to their Web site and blog, Meal Makeover Moms' Kitchen, they see the podcast as another way to broaden their social media network. Revenue from the podcast is generated through corporate sponsorship.

Molly Kellogg, RD

Molly uses free podcasts to support her mission of advancing the counseling skills of nutrition professionals. Live roundtable conference calls a few times a year are recorded and posted on her site. Molly also offers recorded conference calls as a value-added benefit to her Counseling Intensive workshop. Calls held a month after each workshop allow participants to share successes and encourage taking further steps. Most of these monthly conference calls are recorded so members can listen again or catch up if they couldn't make that week. Some of her podcasts provide revenue in the form of teleclasses on various counseling topics held live and then offered as recordings.

podcast, but it is fairly inexpensive and not complicated. If you decide to offer podcasts, make sure they are done in a professional manner.

Webinars, Teleconferences, and Telecounseling

Many traditional face-to-face activities have now become technological. It is possible to receive continuing education, conduct business meetings, and even counsel clients from the comfort of your own home if you have the right equipment.

The term "Webinar" is short for Web-based seminar. It is a presentation, lecture, workshop, or seminar that is transmitted over the Web. Webinars are interactive. Generally, participants call in or listen through audio on the computer, and a guided slide presentation or videos are provided for participants to watch while an expert talks. Participants can type questions or ask them over the phone. Many RDs receive continuing education through Webinars. Webinars can also be used to provide nutrition education programs to the public. Perhaps you have developed a great presentation for executives on "healthy eating on the run." Consider filming your presentation, turning it into a Webinar, and marketing it to area law firms.

Teleconferences are telephone meetings among two or more people. Traditionally, teleconferences were audio only, but with added equipment, it is now possible to include video images. Teleconferences tend to be used more to hold meetings or disseminate information.

Some private practitioners are providing telecounseling. They use a Webcam (a camera attached to their computers that allows clients to see them) to counsel patients—virtually. There are many types of Webcams available for purchase, and some computers have them built in. "Telehealth" is evolving and becoming more common. Should you decide to go this route, carefully investigate the following (9,10):

- Confirm state licensing and/or credentialing laws for providing nutrition counseling and medical nutrition therapy across state lines. State laws vary.
- Verify that your professional liability insurance will cover electronic counseling.
- Check with third-party payers to make sure they cover and pay for telecounseling.

Social Media

Social media are Web-based applications that allow interactive conversations to take place among many people. When you use blogs, microblogs (such as Twitter), and online communities (such as Facebook, LinkedIn, YouTube, and Blip), you are participating in social media and building a social network that can help your business grow. With social media, you can reach many people quickly and easily, which raises your profile, amplifies who you are, and helps build your reputation. Furthermore, you have the potential to be more influential and escalate the value of your opinions, thoughts, and ideas. This is great currency for any entrepreneur. Best of all, you don't need a big budget. The main "cost" associated with participating in social media is your time.

Blogs

Blogs (short for Web log) are Web pages in which the content consists of individual written entries (posts) that may contain text, photos, video, and audio. Blogs display the most recent content first and older entries follow down the page, much like a diary. Blog authors write posts in a conversational style to encourage dialogue. Readers interact with the blog author and each other by leaving questions or comments. A blog is a great forum for engaging in conversations on trends and topics that matter to you and are also in line with your business. Blog authors have a chance to let their style and personality shine through their topic choices, writing ability, and dialogue with readers.

Blogs are easy to set up and maintain. If you would like to start a blog, be sure to come up with a theme that supports your business goals and professional interests. Successful blogs tend to be centered on a specific theme and deal with current issues people want to talk about. Some RDs love to cook, so they use their blogs as a way to share photos, test recipes, and get feedback from others. Others may only blog about their practice specialty, like polycystic ovarian syndrome, diabetes, or celiac disease.

You can expect to spend 30 to 60 minutes on most blog posts and maybe even more time when you are first getting started. There's no standard length for posts, but people don't like to read long pieces online—they prefer to skim. Aim to keep most blog posts between 300 and 500 words, use bolded headings and bullet points, and include visual media, such as photos or videos. These tactics will improve the readability of your blog posts. If you have a hard time sticking to the word count, work on your writing skills. Try to edit your pieces or split them into several posts.

Authoring a blog is a great way to position yourself as a knowledgeable expert. If you want more paid communications work, blogging may help you get it. Your blog posts and video clips are essentially writing samples and demonstration reels you can use to pitch a story idea. Blogging also helps increase your Web site's search ranking, which allows your target customers to find you more easily without the cost of paid advertising.

Blogging has its disadvantages as well. You have to learn how to use the software and publish posts on a regular basis. Keeping a blog up to date can be a serious time commitment. You have to write often (at least a couple posts a week), respond to reader comments, filter out spam, and build an audience of readers. Usually, audience-building involves reading and commenting on other blogs or linking to them in one of your own posts.

It is possible to obtain a free or inexpensive blog. Vendors that provide free or inexpensive blogging applications include Wordpress (http://www.wordpress.com), Blogger (http://www.blogger.com), and TypePad (http://www.typepad.com).

Most blog communities allow you to sync your blog via real simple syndication (RSS) or start your own blog within the community. The power of blog communities is the power of numbers. Everyone involved benefits from traffic to their content.

People often ask, "How can I make money with my blog?" If you're looking to earn money directly from the blog, you may be able to participate in an advertising program, such as Google's AdSense (https://www.google.com/adsense/login/en_US). Essentially, you allow ads to display on your Web page and get paid each time someone clicks on the ad. There are a few downsides. You can't control the type of ads that display on your page (for example, ads for supplements or diet products could be shown). To make a significant profit, you need to generate many clicks, and when someone does click on the ad, traffic is sent away from your Web site. Chances are, if your blog is popular, the monetary benefits you reap are not substantial enough to outweigh the downsides. Carefully weigh the costs and benefits of allowing advertisements.

If you have contacts with companies, you may be able to sell them ad space on your blog or Web site. This way you can align your business with products you believe in. For example, if the theme of your blog is eating healthfully on the run, you could consider contacting a restaurant chain or food manufacturer to advertise their healthy products on your blog. Make sure the blogging program you use allows paid advertisements. You can also get paid for your writing skills. Some Web sites will pay a small fee per post. Volunteer to write posts to practice and springboard those blog posts as writing samples. This may turn into an opportunity to blog with a company willing to pay for your writing.

Twitter

Twitter (http://www.twitter.com) is a social media Web site that asks you one question: "What are you doing?" You have 140 characters to answer that question and share it with people who follow you. Twitter is considered a microblog because of the space limitation it imposes. When you create an account with Twitter, you set up a profile and look for people to "follow." You can find people to follow based on topic area under categories they provide, such as "health" or "food and drink," or perform a search using your own keyword. Alternatively, you can enter your e-mail address, and Twitter will find your contacts that also have accounts. You can invite friends not on Twitter by entering their e-mail addresses. When you follow people, their "tweets" show up on your home page. You view the chatter and let the fun begin!

Twitter is an easy way to stay on top of what people in your network are blogging about, reading in the news, or doing for their jobs that may be of interest to you. You can skim your Twitter stream to get quick tidbits of information, discover news, and share it with your followers (called a "retweet"). You can ask questions of people in your network, such as, "Anyone have healthy, kid-friendly snack ideas?" You can share links to your recent blog posts, videos, or special promotions to get the word out quickly. Twitter even has a theme called "follow Fridays" where users suggest other people to follow every Friday. It's like giving a virtual recommendation.

Twitter is currently developing new features to manage your contacts. You can create lists that allow you to group people you follow into categories (for example, "RDs"). You can also use Twitter's trending tools that allow you to follow the conversations going on in your region just by clicking a button.

Many companies have created applications to help you manage your Twitter presence. Tweetdeck (http://www.tweetdeck.com) allows you to review conversations from multiple Twitter accounts and other social networks all on one screen. You can post one update from Tweetdeck to display on several of your social media pages, which saves you time and keeps you in the conversation. You can also text Twitter an update from your mobile phone.

Twitter can be a very powerful marketing and networking tool. You can use it as a free way to market yourself, establish yourself as an expert, and connect with your business contacts. A Twitter account is much easier to set up than a blog and less time-consuming to manage. If you're not yet doing anything with social media, Twitter may be a great place to start. Without question, there is a learning curve to using the features, understanding the lingo, and maximizing the networking benefits of Twitter. You'll need to try it out for yourself and find ways to make it work for you.

Facebook

Facebook (http://www.facebook.com) is a robust social networking Web site that allows people to create a profile, find "friends," upload photos and videos, connect their blogs to their Facebook page, join groups and causes, raise money, and host events—to name a few features. It's easy for people to stay connected using Facebook.

One of the useful Facebook features for business owners is the "pages" feature for branded entities. Businesses, individual products, nonprofits, public figures, music groups, sports teams, TV shows, and Web sites are all examples of branded entities. If you have a presence on Facebook, you can create a public page for your business and invite your contacts to become "fans." Anyone with a Facebook account can join your page, which allows all of your fans to communicate with you and each other. This enables you to establish your own online community around your business. You can provide special offers and incentives to your fans, ask them for feedback, or share news and information.

If you want to set up a Facebook page, all you need to do is create an account on its Web site. You will need to provide your name, valid e-mail address, and birthday (for age-appropriate content and advertising controls).

Facebook has customizable privacy permissions that allow you to select what profile information is public and what is for friends only. Some entrepreneurs are not comfortable with "mixing business and pleasure" and don't know whether they should "friend" clients, business colleagues, and family. This is a personal decision, and, ultimately, the most important thing is that you are authentic on social media. Proceed with caution. Based on your area of practice, you may need to be careful about what your clients and professional contacts see. If you want to keep professional connections away from your profile, you can decline their "friend" invitation and send them a request to join your fan page instead.

The right column on Facebook pages contain paid advertisements. (That's how the company earns revenue.) You can place an ad to promote your business to your target audience, but it will cost you. The pricing of Facebook ads is based on an auction system where ads compete for impressions. You submit an ad, choose keywords, submit a bid (a maximum price you are willing to pay per click), and provide your credit card. When you run your ad, you are charged only for the number of clicks or impressions that you receive. You can set a daily budget so you don't spend more than you want to. Once you reach your limit, Facebook will remove your ad.

The advantage of advertising on Facebook is you can target their 350 million users by many demographic and psychographic filters. If your audience is on Facebook and you have some advertising money, consider the value of using Facebook's powerful targeting tools to stretch your dollar. As a first step, expand your network on Facebook through people you already know and consider paid placement when you have funds available for advertising. If you decide to move forward with an ad, consider offering a discount to people who mention the ad so you can measure your return on investment.

YouTube

YouTube (http://www.youtube.com) is one of the oldest social media sites. Essentially, it is a place to store and share videos. Although people can comment on videos, YouTube does not have the power of Facebook as a social networking Web site. However, it integrates well with other Web sites. You may decide to record video blogs, which you can do using a simple video camera. You can post the videos to YouTube, embed them in your blog, and upload them to Facebook. If you are interested in speaking, spokesperson, or media opportunities, you can start by recording your own videos. Think of it as practice and a way to build up examples of your work.

YouTube allows you to record a video to sell yourself. Highlight your unique qualities, background, and anything else that makes you stand out. YouTube limits video file size, so most videos need to be less than 10 minutes in length. This is rarely a problem, because most people prefer to watch short videos (one to three minutes). Copyright laws require that you must own the video to post it on the Web. For alternatives to YouTube, check out the Web sites Vimeo (http://vimeo.com) and Blip (http://blip.tv).

Social Media Strategies

Be strategic as you explore how you can use social media in your business. Your business plan is a great place to start. Look at your business goals and ask yourself, "How can social media help?" If you're considering a blog, be sure to ask yourself "Why do I need to blog?" For example, if you are starting to build your counseling business, maybe you want to blog to establish yourself as an expert. Maybe you decided to self-publish a book and want to start a blog to help promote your book. This will help justify the time investment you'll put into building your presence in social media. Think about the people you need to connect with—whether they are people you know or those you need to learn from. Explore the leading social media Web sites and services. Once you decide you want to participate, you'll need to create accounts at the various Web sites. Keep in mind, you can't just set up a profile and abandon your social media presence. Your intention should be to stay involved for the long haul. Success may not come overnight—but the only way you will really know if it works for you is to try it out.

After you have a social media presence, you need to integrate it. Maximize your reach and minimize your time investment by making sure your Facebook fans know how they can follow you on Twitter. Think of your Web site as "home base," and make sure there is a place on your Web site that links to your entire social media presence. The trend now is to use graphic icons and buttons for the social networking sites. To find free icons, search "social media graphics" or ask your Web designer.

As social media take hold, the tools to manage them will likely grow in simplicity and ease of use. Here are a few ways to integrate your social media presence:

- Your blog may have a free widget that pulls your Twitter feed and Facebook status updates.
- Facebook has an application that will automatically update Twitter when you update Facebook.
- LinkedIn (http://www.linkedin.com) can update your status from Twitter.
- Services such as Ping.fm (http://ping.fm) allow you to claim your social media profiles and update all of them at once from one place.

If you find yourself searching for quick ideas of how social media may fit into your private practice, Box 6.5 should help get those entrepreneurial juices flowing. Box 6.6 provides an example of how one RD uses social media to enhance and market her business.

Box 6.5 Ten Ways to Use Social Media to Promote Your Business

1. Read current blogs in your specialty area to stay on top of news and professional information.
2. If you have an e-newsletter, include your recent blog posts or recipes for your clients.
3. Find blogs you like to read and offer to provide a one-time guest post. This gives you the feeling of blogging with minimum time investment.
4. Start a blog on your nutrition specialty area. Post your thoughts, tips, and timely news related to your area.
5. Create a LinkedIn account and find contacts that may help you achieve a business goal.
6. Tape short videos of yourself giving nutrition tips and upload them to social networking sites that support video, such as YouTube, Blip.tv, and Facebook.
7. "Tweet" story ideas to members of the media to get a story spot or quotation.
8. Find local health experts important to your area of expertise to follow on Twitter and read their blogs. Start communicating with them to develop a referral network.
9. Tell your clients to check your blog or Twitter account for added-value services you provide.
10. If you'd like to write a book, start by blogging some of your ideas to get feedback from readers. This can help you make decisions that will improve your proposal or manuscript.

Box 6.6 Putting Social Media to Work

Evelyn Tribole, MS, RD, is in private practice in Newport Beach, California, and has written seven books, including the bestsellers *Healthy Homestyle Cooking* and *Intuitive Eating* (co-author). She has increased her business for her Intuitive Eating Pro Teleseminar series by creating a group called Intuitive Eating Professionals on LinkedIn. Evelyn thought that LinkedIn was the best choice among the various social media options because it focuses specifically on professionals. The purpose of the Intuitive Eating Professionals group is to unite health professionals who help people create a healthy relationship with food, mind, and body through intuitive eating practices. Ultimately, it is a place to share resources, network, and collaborate. For Evelyn, this group has been a wonderful experience, rich with discussions from distinguished scientists and practitioners from different fields. Evelyn also uses Twitter. She regularly sends "tweets" related to her specialty areas—eating disorders, intuitive eating, and celiac disease. This in turn has resulted in media interviews (including on CNN radio—from one tweet!) and an increase in members for her LinkedIn group.

Evelyn provides the following tips for those who want to jump into the social media game:

- Offer useful information so you can be of service to your contacts.
- Be consistent in how often you use social media to develop relationships for future business.
- Be a trusted resource.
- Create objectives clearly defining what you want to accomplish with various social media to be effective.

Social media is not just a passing trend. While the thought of entering into uncharted territory may be overwhelming, using social media as a marketing and communications tool is necessary for your business to thrive and prosper. If you are a little hesitant to jump in, take advantage of the many free resources available on the Web. If you use a Web designer, make sure he or she is on top of social media. Take small steps when first getting started to gain confidence, and before you know it you will be a social media pro.

A Day in the Life of a Tech-Savvy RD

Dina Aronson, MS, RD, is a nutrition consultant, author, editor, and speaker who works from her home office in Montclair, New Jersey. She depends on technology for her consulting work. Table 6.1 summarizes Dina's current projects and how she uses technology to get the job done. Dina notes that while technology is related to her work, she uses it mainly as a tool to enhance her productivity. Her expertise as an RD is her most valuable skill. For example, for her meal plan consulting work, she uses nutrient analysis software and her knowledge of nutrition and foods. Combining both areas of expertise, she is able to create meals that meet predetermined requirements and best suit the needs of the customer.

Table 6.1. Technology Applications in an RD's Business

Project	*Technology Used*
Consulting for a Web-based company on the production of meal plans	• Nutrition analysis software • Internet • E-mail
Managing Web sites for wellness clients and updating her own Web sites	• Graphic design software • FTP client (to transfer files) • Internet • E-mail
Writing a diet book and various articles	• Word processing software • Online bibliographic databases (such as PubMed, Google Scholar)
Social marketing for her business	• Blogging software • Social media sites (such as Twitter, Facebook, and LinkedIn)
Ongoing work: checking e-mail, organizing activities, scheduling meetings, prioritizing tasks, paperwork, and billing	• Personal digital assistant • E-mail • Financial management software • Online document processing software

Using Technology to Enhance Your Business: A Summary

Depending on your interest level, the opportunities you have had, and maybe even your age, you may or may not be using technology to your best advantage. If the task of putting technology to work for you is daunting, find someone who can assist you with that task. Find mentors with expertise in technology and offer to assist them with some aspect of their practice. The Nutrition Entrepreneurs DPG has a technology subunit dedicated to helping RDs advance their technological knowledge and skills.

Once you begin to use all your new "toys," you'll be accomplished in no time. With each technological addition, you won't be able to imagine how you ever did without it. Keep in mind the following key points:

- RDs can use e-mail to communicate with other health professionals, provide patient counseling, and send out "new patient information." They can also stay connected by participating in electronic mailing lists.
- The World Wide Web can be used for monitoring nutrition news, accessing educational materials, and marketing your practice.
- Having a presence on the Web by developing a Web site will lend credibility to your business or practice. Although it is possible to design a Web site yourself, consider hiring a professional for a more polished presence on the Web.
- Social media are Web-based applications that allow interactive conversations to take place between many people. Social media, if used

properly, can help you reach many people quickly and easily, raise your profile, and help build your reputation. Social media participation can be time-consuming but ultimately it is a great marketing tool.

References

1. Aronson D. Make the most out of e-mail. *DBC Dimensions*. Fall 2003:6.
2. The ten commandments of e-mail "netiquette." Study Guides and Strategies Web site. http://www.studygs.net/netiquette.htm. Accessed March 9, 2010.
3. Online Discussions Netiquette and Terms of Use. Available at: http://www.nedpg.org/members/listservs/NetiquetteFINAL.pdf. Accessed: April 19, 2010.
4. Clairmont C. A hard look at software solutions to ease your workload. *Today's Dietitian.* 2001;3:24–27.
5. Belicove ME. The purpose-driven Web site. *Entrepreneur Magazine*. June 2009. http://www.entrepreneur.com/magazine/entrepreneur/2009/june/201650.html. Accessed June 27, 2009.
6. Crowder DA. Pouring the foundation. In: *Building Web Sites for Dummies*. Hoboken, NJ: Wiley Publishing; 2007.
7. Nielsen J. Site design. In: *Designing Web. Usability: The Practice of Simplicity*. Indianapolis, IN: New Riders Publishing; 2000.
8. Mathieu J. Blogs, podcasts, and wikis: the new names in information dissemination. *J Am Diet Assoc*. 2007;107:553–555.
9. Busey C, Michael P. Telehealth—opportunities and pitfalls. *J Am Diet Assoc.* 2008;108:1296–1301.
10. American Dietetic Association. Telehealth. http://www.eatright.org/Members/content.aspx?id=7341. Accessed January 31, 2010.

Acknowledgments: Content for the "Setting Up a Web Site for Your Business" section was provided by Teresa Pangan, RD, PhD, owner of Webnoxious (http://www.webnoxious.com) and co-owner of Feed Your Career (http://www.feedyourcareer.com). Content on social media was provided by Rebecca Scritchfield, MA, RD, ACSM (http://www.elitenutritiondc.com).

Section 2

Everything You Need to Know About Private Practice

Chapter 7

Private Practice Particulars: Office Set-up and HIPAA

Now that you have decided to go into private practice, you must determine where to see patients and acquire furnishings, computer equipment, and office supplies. This chapter focuses on specific issues pertaining to setting up a private practice, such as the layout of office space for nutrition counseling, the supplies and materials that a registered dietitian (RD) in private practice needs, and concerns about compliance with the Health Insurance Portability and Accountability Act (HIPAA).

Finding Office Space

One of the most important decisions you will make as you set up your practice is where to find office space. Before you begin your search, ask yourself the following questions (1):

- How much space do you need?
- Can you share space?
- Do you want to be accessible by public transportation?
- How much storage space do you need?
- Is it necessary for you to be in a traditional setting, such as an office building?
- Is subletting an option?
- Can you work from home?

It is prudent to keep business costs as low as possible when you are first starting out, but don't make decisions based solely on economics. Keep the future in mind as you make your decisions. If you anticipate growth, make sure the space can accommodate you in the next few years (1,2).

As you think about office space options, consider doing a market analysis. For example, if you are leaving a clinical position in a hospital to start a private practice and plan to receive referrals from the physicians you worked with in that hospital, your office should be in close proximity to that setting. (Special note: If this is your plan, make sure you have not signed a noncompete agreement with your current employer before you select a location.)

Once you have determined the general location for your office, you then need to begin to consider other variables. Refer to Box 7.1 for a list of issues to consider before deciding on office space.

Box 7.1 Issues to Investigate Before Deciding on Office Space

- **Bathroom access:** Will there be a bathroom in your suite or in the hall? Do clients need a key to access the bathroom?
- **Signage:** Can you place your name in the directory, on a nameplate at the entrance to the office, and/or at the entrance to your individual office? Who pays for signage?
- **Security:** What type of security does the office provide? Is there a security person in front of the building or a code for access, or must visitors be announced? Appropriate security is particularly important if you will be counseling or consulting after regular business hours.
- **Snow removal and grounds keeping:** Who is responsible for the grounds around the office?
- **Cleaning:** Does the rent include a cleaning service?
- **Utilities:** Does the rent include utilities? Do they shut off after regular business hours? Is there a way you can pay to use them after business hours?
- **Kitchen area:** Do you want a small kitchen area in your office? If you will be there for long periods of time, you may want to have a place where you can make coffee or tea, refrigerate items, or place a microwave.
- **Parking:** Is parking available for you and your clients? Is there a parking fee? If so, will this deter patients?
- **Other fees:** Will the landlord make you responsible to pay a share of the building taxes and/or insurance?
- **Handicap accessibility:** Is the building in compliance with the Americans with Disabilities Act?
- **Elevator access:** Many people who are not classified as "disabled" still have difficulty climbing stairs.
- **Furniture:** Is the furniture you see in the office now available for your use? (This is more applicable if you are subleasing.)

Renting

Renting is the most traditional way to obtain office space. Check with commercial realtors and newspaper advertisements or ask around to learn of available space. Renting office space can be costly. You will be asked to sign a lease, usually for at least a year, and a security deposit is usually required. If you sign a lease for longer than one year, you could prevent rent increases for the duration of the lease. If changes to the space are needed, such as painting or reconfiguration, you can negotiate with the landlord. In some cases, such changes may be your responsibility. Remember, everything in the lease is negotiable, so if you want changes, it's worth asking for them (3).

Co-leasing

Still considered renting, co-leasing is basically sharing the office space. Two or more professionals join forces, allowing them to share rent and many other expenses. You can still expect to sign a lease, but you each have an equal voice in making decisions.

It is important that you define all the parameters in writing before you enter into this type of agreement. The office must accommodate the needs of both professionals, and you must divide the available time evenly. Your schedules must mesh. Should you need to switch days, you may not have that option. Even if you and your partner are extremely compatible, you still may want to invest in separate phone lines.

Co-leasing can be a great arrangement for two private practitioners. Consider pairing up with another RD whose skills and expertise complement yours. For example, perhaps you have a specialty in weight management and eating disorders. Consider sharing with someone who is a certified diabetes educator and specializes in cardiovascular disease. You then have an automatic referral system.

Subleasing

Subleasing is an option that works well for many professionals. Again, you are still renting space but with a slightly different type of arrangement. It is often possible to find another professional with an office available certain days of the week or for specific times in a day. You may even find a vacant room within an office available to sublet by the month.

Subleasing space in a physician's office can be an ideal situation for private practitioners. Most physicians do not use their offices one day per week and would welcome some extra revenue. There may be extra unused space within the office that is available, or the physician may offer you the use of his or her office. Although there may be no room for personalization, it is a great option when you are first starting out.

Another option is to sublet extra office space or a room available within a professional office suite or health club. When subleasing, keep in mind that you may not be dealing directly with the owner of the space, so there are limitations.

The arrangement for determining rent for a sublease can vary widely. Some professionals have paid "rent" by giving the physician a percentage of total billings. The percentage the physician receives can range from 20 percent to 50 percent. This arrangement is not recommended, because it may be viewed as fee splitting. Fee splitting, otherwise known as kickbacks, is not advised. Recent regulations have tightened up on physicians benefiting financially from referrals to other health care providers. In certain situations, fee splitting has been deemed illegal.

Other sublet options include paying a set fee for the space by the hour, day, week, or month. Another possibility for RDs in private practice is for the physician's practice to pay the RD a consulting fee for seeing patients. Physicians consider this a value-added service to their practice. In return, the physician's practice benefits from the ability to offer patients more comprehensive medical care within the office; it also saves the physician valuable time by taking care of patients' nutrition questions.

Whether you sublet or are paid a consulting fee, consider the following variables when negotiating:

- Who will do the scheduling?
- Will the office receptionist greet the patients and provide them forms to complete?
- Who will do the billing?
- Can you use the fax, copy machine, and phone lines?
- Will business cards be provided?
- Who pays for educational materials?
- Who will take care of cleaning the space if subleasing?
- Are office supplies (such as paper goods, pens, and sticky notes) included?
- Is furniture included, or do you supply your own?
- Who decides on decor?

All of these goods and services cost money and therefore should be factored into the equation.

Other options to explore include the offices of psychotherapists, social workers, and other mental health professionals. Their offices are often available during their down times, and many of these professionals are used to subletting their space. Because you may be sharing space, this puts a natural limit on your available hours. It will require you to set regular office hours, thus limiting your flexibility.

When subleasing, you still may be required to sign a lease, or at least have an agreement in writing. Some sublet situations will require a one-year lease. If possible, consider negotiating a month-to-month lease, with the stipulation of a two-month notice period if either party wants to change the lease terms. This will allow you to assess whether the arrangement is working for both parties.

In a sublet arrangement, make sure you are able to have all your supplies conveniently available. Having to wheel a scale or a cart containing all your papers in and out of the room each time you are in the office can quickly become tiresome. Consider installing your own telephone line if you have any concerns about sharing a telephone.

Investigate whom you are subletting from. Be careful about associating with someone who may not have the best reputation. You do not want your practice to be affected by another's poor reputation.

Traveling Office

Some RDs in private practice can avoid the hassle of finding office space by making home visits. They simply gather their necessary supplies in a box and make house calls. This allows them to really see what their patients are eating, check pantries, and perform feeding evaluations. The downside is that they have to be extra vigilant in making sure they have everything they need and that they are in a safe environment. It is also important to charge accordingly—travel time should be considered when establishing fees.

Executive Office Suite

An executive office suite is an office arrangement that typically includes a receptionist, access to a conference room, and a specified day or days during the week that you have an assigned office space. Generally, you pay à la carte for each service you desire. There are many companies that manage executive office space for lease with a variety of different services and amenities; therefore, it is necessary to shop around and visit different offices to determine which is the best fit for your business.

Home Office

The home office is likely the most affordable option and the one that presents the smallest financial risk. However, some professionals find it difficult to stay on track when working at home.

If you choose to use a home office, make sure your office space is private if you will be seeing patients or clients there. If this is the case, ideally you should have a separate office in your home. Some professionals have been successful in creating home office space by partitioning off a section of a common room.

Consider how comfortable you feel having strangers come to your home. Do you have a separate entrance? Will patients, clients, or customers enter through your front door? What about a waiting area—will it be your living room? Can you keep your house neat and quiet enough to receive clients in a professional manner? Some clients feel more comfortable coming to your home, whereas others feel the opposite.

A third option is to have both! Some private practitioners sublet office space on a part-time basis for seeing patients and perform their administrative duties and non-patient-related projects from their home office.

If you will not be receiving clients in your office, you may prefer to use a separate office in your home. Box 7.2 (4) lists the advantages and disadvantages of working from your home. Carefully review this before you make your decision.

Box 7.2 The Pros and Cons of Setting Up a Home Office

Pros

- No commute
- Greater work flexibility
- Lower start-up costs
- Clients or patients relax more quickly
- You can "squeeze in" home chores

Cons

- The possibility of professional isolation or loneliness
- Can be hard to stay disciplined
- Difficult to have meetings
- Clients or patients are less comfortable in a home setting
- Hard to set boundaries

Source: Adapted with permission from Nutrition Entrepreneurs, a dietetic practice group of the American Dietetic Association. Where to hang your shingle: home or rented office? In: *Nutrition Entrepreneurs Toolkit 2009*. Chicago, IL: American Dietetic Association; 2010. http://www.nedpg.org.

It is also important to set limits for yourself when working from home. You can do so in the following ways (3):

- Try to set a work schedule and stick with it. Make sure you leave time for your personal life.
- Arrange for child care when necessary. It is very difficult to meet your clients' needs while working around kids' schedules.
- Take breaks throughout the day. Time away from your desk will ultimately increase your productivity. Get out of the office (house) at least once a day.

You may find it helpful to dress professionally when working from home. How you dress may affect how you feel about your work. While working in your pajamas may sound appealing, it may be beneficial to get dressed as if you are going to an outside location to provide a clear delineation between work and home.

Having a home office may have some tax advantages. You are able to deduct your home office from your taxes if any of the following are true:

- Your home office is the *principal place* from which you conduct your business.
- Your home office is used for meeting with patients, clients, or customers in the normal course of doing business.
- You have a separate building on your property, which you use as a home office.

Even if your home office does not meet these criteria, you may be able to claim a tax deduction for it. However, there may be limitations to the amount you can deduct. See your accountant or business adviser for further assistance with this matter.

Other Possibilities

There are many places to find office space. Think of allied health professionals and the fitness industry, and don't forget to think outside the box for other possibilities. Box 7.3 provides some suggestions for your search.

Box 7.3 Possibilities for Office Space

- Physician's office
- Psychotherapist's office
- Dental office
- Occupational therapist's office
- Physical therapist's office
- Day spas
- Executive office suites
- Massage therapist's office
- Chiropractor's office

Visualizing Your Office

As you set up your office, take some time to visualize going through your routine. In addition, you should think about your patients from the moment they step in the door until you have ended the session and it is time for them to leave. Do you want to present a "medical" or a "counseling" image? When counseling, it is recommended that you not place a desk between yourself and the patient. The preferred counseling arrangement is to sit next to or across from the client, without a barrier. This fosters communication.

Sharing your space with another health professional can raise special concerns for your private practice. For example, if you share an office with an occupational therapist, will the office accommodate the other person's equipment and still leave enough space for you? If a doctor offers an exam room for counseling, does the configuration of the medical equipment in the room lend itself to counseling patients? You must be able to visualize how that space will work in a counseling situation.

Nutrition Counseling Supplies

A well-stocked nutrition counseling office is different from that of any other health practitioner. The tools required to effectively counsel patients and teach them about nutrition are unique.

Nutrient Analysis Software

Some RDs remember having to perform nutrient calculations by hand. Analyzing a recipe or a three-day food diary was tedious and time-consuming work. Enter nutrient analysis software. Today's programs have streamlined the work of RDs, allowing them to spend more time with their patients or market their programs and practices.

Nutrient analysis software is a valuable addition to any food and nutrition practice. Many packages are available for a reasonable price. Explore options listed in Chapter 14 or ask colleagues for their feedback on the various nutrient analysis programs. If you want to try multiple programs, download trial versions or attend the American Dietetic Association's (ADA's) Food and Nutrition Conference and Expo, where many companies exhibit their products.

Nutrient analysis software can aid in clinical assessment. It can help you determine the adequacy of a patient's diet and highlight specific deficiencies. In private practice, this software can be a powerful teaching tool. Providing analysis to your patient helps them visualize their nutrition goals. The printouts provide tangible evidence and feedback, which help them stay focused. Before you purchase nutrition software, evaluate what you need it to do (see Box 7.4) (5,6). Make a list of essential features and rank them in importance. Depending on your practice setting and your patient population, your needs may vary.

Providing nutrient analyses to your patients is a value-added service. It takes additional time to analyze a patient's diet. Determine whether you want to provide that service to your patients as an additional benefit. As an alternative, you may want to charge for the service separately as a way to generate

Box 7.4 Questions to Evaluate Nutrition Software

- How reliable is the nutrient database?
- Can you manipulate data in various ways—e.g., subtract an ingredient from a recipe?
- Can you track numerous patients simultaneously?
- Can you add food items to the database?
- How often is the database updated?
- How easy is it to find a food from the database?
- Can you plan meals at various calorie levels with various nutrient distributions?
- What type of printouts can you get?
- Can you customize printouts?
- Are updates free?
- Will more than one person use the software? Is that authorized?
- Do you need access to the software at more than one location?
- Is technical support provided?

Source: Data are from references 5 and 6.

further revenue. It can be a great marketing tool. Some RDs offer nutrient analysis as a stand-alone service.

If you have a specific need in your practice that a general nutrient analysis software package does not meet, consider purchasing niche software. For example, if you see many patients with diabetes, you may want to purchase a specialized program that is geared toward that patient population. There are programs that assist you in teaching your patient about diabetes nutrition. One specialized program explains diabetic meal planning principles and enables the patient to plan sample meals. It also allows you to enter the patient's needs and help them make correct food choices (7).

Nutrient Analysis Web sites

In addition to nutrient analysis software, there are nutrient analysis Web sites, including some that charge fees for services. Some sites are geared toward professionals, while other, simpler sites appeal to the general public. These nutrient analysis Web sites come and go. You may want to poll colleagues and patients to see which ones are most commonly used.

Nutrition Charting Programs

Programs specifically developed for medical nutrition therapy are available to practitioners in private practice. By maintaining patient and physician information on your computer, your practice can be primarily paperless. The amount of time involved with record keeping can be substantially reduced.

You will no longer have to file charts at the end of the day. Any paper received, such as referrals from physicians, laboratory test results, or patient food records, can be scanned into a file and saved in the patient's name. You may find it beneficial to keep hard copies of the most important information.

These programs allow data to be entered for each patient, such as medical information, weight history, nutrient analysis, physical activity, and laboratory test results. Programs can accommodate the Nutrition Care Process and include billing functions, as well. Learning how to utilize all of the functions can be time consuming but will pay off in the end. Box 7.5 provides an example of how one RD made the shift to an electronic practice.

Box 7.5 One Registered Dietitian's Electronic Practice

Dara Bergen, MPH, RD, CDN, is the proprietor of the private practice Forest Hills Wellness, in New York. Dara and her staff specialize in weight management, diabetes, cardiovascular disease, bariatric surgery, pre- and postnatal care, and gastrointestinal disorders.

Electronic records were incorporated into Forest Hills Wellness from its first day. Originally the office space did not have room for file cabinets, so Dara decided that electronic health records (EHRs) would be a great space saver. Dara also liked the idea of less clutter in the office and the ease of charting from home.

An advertisement in the *Journal of the American Dietetic Association* for an electronic charting system designed specifically for RDs caught Dara's eye. After reviewing the features of this nutrition-specific charting and practice management software and comparing its pricing to other products, Dara decided it was what she was looking for. The program is used at Forest Hills Wellness to chart sessions, send letters to referring physicians, track laboratory test results, and electronically send bills to insurance companies. Employees can also scan a copy of a client's insurance card and signed HIPAA form, so the practice is almost paperless.

Dara's advice to colleagues considering switching to an EHR is to not fear the transition. From her experience, Dara believes you don't need to be very tech-savvy to use an EHR. If you are comfortable with basic computer programs, then you should be able to navigate the software. Going electronic in her practice had another benefit. Dara states, "Charting and billing time reduced significantly, and we were able to see double the clients and significantly increased the bottom line within one year."

Educational Materials

Patient education materials are crucial to imparting nutrition information to your patients. When patients walk out of the office with well-structured, clear, and pertinent educational material in hand, they feel as though they have received their money's worth.

Many RDs create their own nutrition handouts and tailor them to their patient population. When you are first starting your practice, however, time is an issue. You need to devote your time to marketing and developing your business. Why reinvent the wheel? There are many excellent materials available, so purchase what you need. For example, ADA publishes numerous client education items for purchase.

Many companies and enterprising RDs sell educational materials designed specifically for nutrition counseling. Food- and health-related companies, as well as other types of councils and agencies, such as the Dairy Council and the Food Marketing Institute, often provide free materials to RDs. For example, many of the large manufacturers of calcium supplements provide educational pamphlets about calcium. Review materials before you give them to patients and make sure the message agrees with your philosophy. The material might be free, but if it promotes an idea or a product that you do not fully endorse, then the cost is too high. Chapter 14 lists selected resources for obtaining educational materials.

Food Models

Food models are a helpful visual aid for teaching patients about portion size. If you worked in a facility that provided food models, you may not realize how expensive they are. If your counseling style depends on models, your office will not be complete without them. As the models are expensive, research pricing carefully and plan to work them into your budget.

Other Supplies

In addition to the supplies described previously, you may need others. What you need depends on the type of practice you have and the patients you counsel. Some items that you may find useful in private practice include measuring cups and spoons (to demonstrate portion sizes), food labels or actual food packages, a flip chart for diagramming concepts to patients, and of course, a well-stocked library with plenty of reference books. On the other end of the spectrum, you may also want to have coffee, tea, and water available for your patients. There are many variables to consider.

Medical Equipment and Nutrition Assessment Tools

Scales

A medical scale is a wise investment. A beam-balance scale is the most accurate. When choosing a scale, think about your patient population. For example, if you counsel obese patients, consider purchasing a scale that accommodates greater weights. A counter for the beam-balance scale can increase the scale's weighing capacity to 450 pounds. There are also some accurate portable scales on the market, but they do not accommodate individuals who are morbidly obese. Practitioners who share an office or who make home visits, however, find portable scales their only option.

Body Fat Analyzers

Body fat analyzers can be very helpful to RDs in private practice. They allow patients and practitioners to measure progress in ways other than a regular scale. Patients ask RDs to analyze their body fat, and the analysis can be expected as part of the nutrition assessment. Sports dietitians find them to be a useful tool, as do eating disorder and weight management professionals.

You need to first decide whether it makes sense to provide body fat analysis to your patients. If so, decide whether to provide it at no charge or use it as a value-added service. Some RDs charge an additional fee for the service as a way of recouping the expense of the equipment.

If you want to incorporate technology rather than use calipers to measure body fat, there are many handheld products on the market. Also, consider scales that can measure body fat. It is important to assess their reliability and accuracy before you purchase one. Evaluate their accuracy with different patient populations—for example, individuals with anorexia who have very low body fat. Ask other professionals what they recommend and do your own research. Select a technology that works best for your practice and your patients.

Metabolic Testing

Another gadget that can enhance your practice is a calorimeter. This tool measures resting metabolic rate using indirect calorimetry. It is a useful tool for RDs working with athletes, people who diet chronically, or patients with eating disorders. Metabolic testing can add value to your practice in assessing a patient and as another source of income. As with body fat analyzers, you should research the options, ask for recommendations, and select the brand that fits your practice and patient population. Before you invest in this equipment, carefully analyze whether you need this data or if good clinical judgment can suffice.

Diabetes Management Tools

If you counsel patients with diabetes, a blood glucose monitor and insulin pump will be useful. Contact companies that manufacture these tools and request a demonstration model to use in your office.

Patient Forms

You will need a variety of patient forms in your private practice. Using office management software, you can develop, customize, and revise your forms, even purchased standardized ones. You can e-mail the forms as an attachment, post them on your Web site, and fax or send them by mail to your patients. This can streamline your work.

Registration Forms

The first form you will need from your patient is a patient registration form (see Figure 7.1). Some RDs post this form on their Web site and request that the patient download, complete, and bring it to the first visit. This can save time as the patient does not have to complete the form in the waiting room during the appointment time. Consider providing the following information on your patient registration form:

- Contact information
- Insurance information
- Doctor and other health professional contact information
- Referring entity information
- Problem or reason for visit

You may also want to provide a payment policy form for patients to sign. This will let them know your policies, whether you will bill insurance as a courtesy to your patients, and what will happen if insurance won't cover the cost.

A release of information form should be given to and signed by any patient who requires coordination of care with other health care providers. This form gives you permission to communicate with authorized health care providers regarding your patient's treatment. It is also possible to gather this information on the HIPAA form (see next section), but some RDs prefer to use a separate form that can be readily accessed. Also, patients do not always think to list health care providers on HIPAA forms. Instead, they tend to list family members with whom they will allow you to communicate.

HIPAA Forms

Under the HIPAA privacy rule, each covered entity must provide a notice of its privacy practices to all patients and make a good-faith effort to obtain written acknowledgement from patients of their receipt of the notice (8). The government has outlined specific policies and procedures to which covered entities must adhere, such as posting the privacy notice and computer access procedures, to comply with HIPAA (see Box 7.6) (9). Most hospitals or large clinic facilities have a privacy notice that covers all practitioner services provided at that location. However, RDs in private practice will need to create a personalized privacy notice and patient acknowledgement form to meet the HIPAA requirement. A sample HIPAA privacy notice and patient written acknowledgement confirming receipt of privacy notice (Figure 7.2) are accessible from the members-only section of the ADA Web site (10).

Nutrition Assessment Forms

Nutrition assessment forms are essential. Some practitioners have more than one assessment form. They may use different forms for different types

Patient Registration Form

Name: ______________________________

Home address: ______________________________

____

Date of birth: ______________________________

Social Security number: ______________________________

Telephone number: Home ( ) ____________ Work ( ) ____________

Cell ( ) ____________ E-mail address ____________

Occupation: ______________________________

Employer: ______________________________

Name of person responsible for bill: ______________________________

Address: ______________________________

____

Telephone number: Home ( ) ____________ Work ( ) ____________

Cell ( ) ____________ E-mail address ____________

Referred by: ______________________________

Reason for referral: ______________________________

____

Current doctor: ____________ Phone number: ( ) ____________

Doctor's address: ______________________________

____

Figure 7.1 Patient registration form. Reprinted with permission from Litt A, Mitchell F. Be Your Own Boss Starter Kit. 2007.

Box 7.6 HIPAA Guidelines for Small Providers

1. Does your office conduct *all* the following transactions on paper, by phone, or by fax (from a dedicated fax machine, as opposed to faxing from a computer)?
   - Submitting claims or managed care encounter information
   - Checking claim status inquiry and response
   - Checking eligibility and receiving a response
   - Checking referral certifications and authorizations
   - Enrolling and disenrolling in a health plan
   - Receiving health care payments and remittance advice
   - Providing coordination of benefits

   If your office does not conduct any of the above standard transactions electronically and if you do not have someone else conduct them electronically on your behalf—such as a clearinghouse or billing service—**you are not a covered entity and HIPAA does not apply to you.**

2. Do you bill Medicare and are you a small provider with fewer than 10 full-time-equivalent employees? Effective October 16, 2003, Medicare may not pay claims submitted on paper, with certain exceptions. One of the major exceptions is for claims submitted by "a small provider of services or supplier." The term "small provider of services or supplier" means:
   - A provider of services with fewer than 25 full-time-equivalent employees, and
   - A physician, practitioner, facility, or supplier (other than provider of services) with fewer than 10 full-time-equivalent employees.

   If you do not meet the small provider exception, effective October 16, 2003, you will be required to submit your Medicare claims electronically. Once you begin submitting claims electronically to Medicare, your answer to question 1 above would be "no," and you would become a covered entity under HIPAA.

Note: Small providers must comply with HIPAA regulations if they perform any of the following tasks electronically: submit claims, check claim status, check eligibility, check referral certifications and authorizations, enroll in a health care plan, receive health care payments and remittance advice, or provide coordination of benefits.

Source: Reprinted from Centers for Medicare & Medicaid Services. HIPAA Information Series: 2. Are You a Covered Entity? http://www.cms.hhs.gov/EducationMaterials/Downloads/Areyouacoveredentity-2.pdf. Accessed March 18, 2010.

of patients. Some may shorten their assessment for managed care patients if their time with the patient is limited. Consider a three-day diet intake form, a food-frequency checklist, a food journal sheet (see Figure 7.3), a food history questionnaire and assessment form, an RD summary form (Figure 7.4), a telephone intake sheet (Figure 7.5), and a progress note form (Figure 7.6).

Patient Written Acknowledgment Confirming Receipt of Privacy Notice

[Print on clinic letterhead, if applicable]

I have received [insert clinic's name] HIPAA Privacy Notice.

________________________________ (patient/client signature)

________________________________ (date)

Figure 7.2 Form for patient confirmation of receipt of privacy notice (typically printed as full-page form). Reprinted with permission from American Dietetic Association. http://www.eatright.org/Members/content.aspx?id=7514. Accessed March 15, 2010.

Date/ Time/ Where	Degree of Hunger	Before (Thoughts, Feelings, Activities)	Food Eaten	Degree of Hunger	After (Thoughts, Feelings, Activities)

Figure 7.3 Excerpt from a food journal worksheet. Reprinted with permission from Litt A, Mitchell F. Be Your Own Boss Starter Kit. 2007.

Registered Dietitian's Summary Sheet

Patient's name: ______________________ Date: ______________________

Patient's comments: ____

____

Diagnosis: ______________________

Height: __________ Weight: __________

IBW: __________ Usual Wt: __________

Estimated calorie needs based on BEE:

____

Manifestations

- ☐ Purging
- ☐ Laxative use
- ☐ Diuretic use
- ☐ Fasting
- ☐ Very low calorie intake
- ☐ Excessive exercise
- ☐ Bingeing
- ☐ Excessive calorie intake

Pertinent medical history:

____

____

____

____

____

Nutritional status

Food Groups	Inadequate	Adequate
Milk	☐	☐
Meat	☐	☐
Fruit/Veg	☐	☐
Grain	☐	☐

Estimated daily caloric intake: ______________

% of daily calorie needs consumed: __________

No. of excess/deficient calories per day: ________

Specific excess/deficiency: ______________

Plan

Education on: ______________________

Refer to: ______________________

Follow up: ______________________

Meal plan: ______________________

Letter sent to: ________ Date: ________

Patient's insurance: ______________________________

Dietitian's signature: ______________________________

Reimbursement: Yes ☐ No ☐

Figure 7.4 Registered dietitian's summary sheet. Reprinted with permission from Litt A, Mitchell F. Be Your Own Boss Starter Kit. 2007.

Telephone Intake Sheet

Patient's name: ______________________________

Parent's name: ______________________________

Telephone numbers:

Home: ____________ Work: ____________ Mobile: ____________

Reason for referral: ______________________________

Referred by: ______________________________

Scheduled date: ____________ **Time allowed:** ____________

REQUESTED:

Lab work: ______ Growth chart: ______ Food diary: ______ Picture: ______

Policy reviewed: ____________ **Philosophy reviewed:** ____________

Figure 7.5 Sample telephone intake sheet (usually printed as full-page form). Adapted with permission from Litt A, Mitchell F. Be Your Own Boss Starter Kit. 2007.

Page: ________

Patient name: ______________________________

Progress Notes

DATE	NOTES

Figure 7.6 Sample progress notes (usually printed as full-page form). Adapted with permission from Litt A, Mitchell F. Be Your Own Boss Starter Kit. 2007.

Superbill

A superbill is the foundation for insurance reimbursement. This form is a necessity. RDs who do not file insurance claims for their patients present them with a completed superbill. The patient is encouraged to file the superbill with the insurance carrier for reimbursement. If you have the time, you can create a superbill on your computer. Collect samples from other health care providers as you visit them and pattern yours after these samples. It is easier, however, to purchase superbills for a nominal fee. Chapter 8 provides more information about superbills and the issues concerning reimbursement and the private practitioner.

Patient Charts

There is more than one way to keep pertinent patient information. Each practitioner has a preferred way to do so. Some use a manila folder with the patient's name on the front tab; others keep notes in their laptop. In your patient charts, you should keep copies of patient registration, insurance information, progress notes, payment information, and food journals. Charts should be securely kept in a locked file drawer. If you share an office space, make sure that no one else has access to your charts.

Waiting Room Reading

Once you have all your patient counseling supplies, the last step is to stock your waiting room with reading material. Consider some health-related publications, but make sure the messages they give are consistent with your philosophy. For example, if a particular publication touts the latest low-carbohydrate diets and you do not believe in them, this may not be what you want your patients to read while they wait to see you. A daily newspaper and standard periodicals, such as *Time, Newsweek*, and women's and men's magazines, are usually safe choices.

Is Your Office Ready?

Before you open your office to patients, use the checklist in Figure 7.7 to make sure you have covered every detail.

Setting up your office should be fun and exciting. This step really seals the deal. You are in business for yourself!

- ❑ Procure space
- ❑ Sign lease
- ❑ Arrange for painting, carpeting, construction work, or other changes to space
- ❑ Order nameplates for door and directory
- ❑ Purchase furniture; set delivery date
- ❑ Arrange for cleaning service (if necessary)
- ❑ Obtain parking space (if necessary)
- ❑ Obtain keys
- ❑ Notify security
- ❑ Order telephone line(s)
- ❑ Order fax line
- ❑ Arrange for Internet access
- ❑ Decide on answering system
- ❑ Purchase cell phone
- ❑ Design logo
- ❑ Order stationery, business cards, announcements
- ❑ Purchase insurance:
    - ❑ Malpractice
    - ❑ Theft and fire
    - ❑ Liability
    - ❑ Disability
- ❑ Purchase office equipment:
    - ❑ Computer
    - ❑ Copy machine
    - ❑ Fax machine
    - ❑ Personal digital assistant (PDA)
    - ❑ Scale
    - ❑ Food models
- ❑ Set up billing/bookkeeping system
- ❑ Purchase or create educational materials
- ❑ Purchase or create office start-up forms:
    - ❑ HIPAA Privacy Notice
    - ❑ Patient Written Acknowledgment Confirming Receipt of Privacy Notice
    - ❑ Nutrition assessment forms, food-frequency questionnaires, food diaries, and other nutrition forms
- ❑ Purchase office supplies:
    - ❑ Stapler
    - ❑ Paper
    - ❑ Pens and pencils
    - ❑ Cartridges
- ❑ Establish office policies—such as hours, fees, payments, schedule
- ❑ MARKET!
- ❑ NETWORK!

Figure 7.7 Checklist for setting up an office. Adapted with permission from Litt A, Mitchell, F. Be Your Own Boss Starter Kit. 2007.

HIPAA: The Bottom Line

In addition to setting up your office as a physical space, you need to set up your practice to meet its legal obligations to patients. Among the most important concerns in this regard is HIPAA. As noted previously in this chapter, HIPAA refers to the Health Insurance Portability and Accountability Act. This 1996 act establishes standards for electronic transactions and "Standards for Privacy of Individually Identifiable Health Information" (8). Trying to decipher the regulations and figuring out how they apply to your practice can be quite confusing. In this section, we cover the most important facts, outline what you should do in your practice, and provide you with resources for more information.

Covered Entities

HIPAA regulations apply to "covered entities," which are defined as health plans, health clearinghouses, and health care providers who transmit health information electronically (11). Exceptions exist for providers with fewer than 100 full-time-equivalent employees and those who do not transmit claims electronically (12). Therefore, solo practitioners who conduct all business activities and health care transactions by paper, telephone, or fax (from a dedicated fax machine, as opposed to faxes sent via computer) are not considered covered entities and are exempt from the regulations. Refer to Box 7.7 for more information (13). If you are still not sure whether you are a covered entity or if you just want to cover all the bases, you can go to the HIPAA section of the Centers for Medicare & Medicaid Services (CMS) Web site (14).

HIPAA imposes certain obligations on covered entities with respect to their use, disclosure, and maintenance of personal health information (PHI) (12). PHI is any information that connects medical information to a patient's name. Opinions may vary as to what constitutes PHI. When a patient signs his name on a sign-in sheet, is that PHI, or does it become PHI if the sheet lists "reason for visit"?

It is best to review HIPAA information on CMS's Web site (12), check ADA's resources, or consult with an attorney who specializes in HIPAA if you have specific questions. Answers can vary because you are dealing with interpretation of the law. The points covered in Box 7.7 may also help (13).

Implementing HIPAA Policies and Procedures

These are the regulations. So how do they translate to what you need to do in your practice to comply with these laws? The following are some policies and procedures you should implement in your office setting (12,14,15).

- All patients must be notified in writing of your privacy practices at their first appointment.

Box 7.7 HIPAA Obligations for Covered Entities

Covered entities must:

- Designate a privacy officer who is responsible for development and implementation of the covered entity's policies and procedures;
- Designate a contact person or office who is responsible for receiving complaints and providing further information about the covered entity's privacy practices;
- Train all the members of its workforce on the covered entity's privacy policies and procedures, as necessary and appropriate for the members of the workforce to carry out their job functions;
- Implement appropriate administrative, technical, and physical safeguards to protect the privacy of Personal Health Information (PHI);
- Enter into business associate contracts with persons that provide certain services to the covered entity, the provision of which involves the use or disclosure of PHI;
- Provide a process for individuals to make complaints concerning the covered entity's privacy policies and procedures;
- Develop and apply appropriate sanctions against members of its workforce who fail to comply with the covered entity's privacy policies and procedures;
- Implement policies and procedures that are designed to comply with the requirements of the Privacy Regulation (e.g., develop and implement processes for complying with a number of new patient rights);
- Develop a *Notice of Privacy Practices* that explains how the covered entity will use and disclose an individual's PHI, the individual's rights with respect to his or her PHI, and the covered entity's legal obligations with respect to PHI;
- Develop an authorization form for certain non-routine uses and disclosures of PHI; and
- Determine which members of the workforce need access to what types of PHI in order to perform their job functions.

Source: Reprinted with permission from American Dietetic Association. Additional covered entity obligations under HIPAA. Prepared by Mintz, Levin, Cohn, Ferris, Glovsky, and Popeo, P.C. April 2002. http://www.eatright.org/Members/content.aspx?id=7504 Accessed March 15, 2010.

- Each patient must sign a written acknowledgment stating that he or she received the privacy notice.
- The HIPAA privacy notice should be posted in your office (for example, laminated or in a display rack) and on your Web site (if applicable).
- Business associates with whom your practice shares patient information—such as computer consultants, attorneys, accountants, your billing company, or anyone who has access to your patient's PHI—must sign a privacy contract or business associates' agreement with your practice.

- If your computer contains any patient information, you must protect that information, such as use a password to access data.
- Fax and e-mail communications should have a confidentiality disclaimer (see Box 7.8).
- If computer screens display patient information, they cannot be visible to anyone other than you and your employees.
- Your file cabinets should be locked when not in use.
- You must request permission to leave messages on home or office answering machines regarding patient information.
- You should ask whether mailings should be sent to an address other than the home address.

Box 7.8 Sample E-Mail Disclaimer

This e-mail message and any attached files are confidential and are intended solely for the use of the addressee named above. This communication may contain material protected by any and all privileges associated with the provision of health services. If you are not the intended recipient or person responsible for delivering this confidential communication to the intended recipient, or if you have received this communication in error, then any review, use, dissemination, forwarding, printing, copying, or other distribution of this e-mail message and any attached files is strictly prohibited. If you have received this confidential communication in error, please notify the sender immediately by reply e-mail message and permanently delete the original message. If you have any questions concerning this message, please contact [insert registered dietitian's name]. Thank you.

Note that these are just some of the ramifications of HIPAA. The laws have been put into place to protect patient confidentiality. If you are a covered entity, make sure your office is HIPAA-compliant before you open your doors.

Private Practice Particulars: A Summary

The office of the private practitioner has a unique set of requirements. It is important that you consider your patient population and their needs when planning your space.

Some final notes:

- Before you decide on your location, consider a market analysis—where will your patients come from?
- Consider subleasing, sharing space, or a traveling or a home office to keep costs low when first starting out.

- As you set up your office, visualize the kind of relationship you will have with patients and the type of experience you want them to have from the start to finish of the counseling session.
- Many specialized forms, supplies, and equipment are needed to furnish your office. The materials you need depend on the type of practice you establish.
- Take the time to review HIPAA regulations and have all necessary forms if you are a covered entity.

References

1. Mintzer R. *The Everything to Start Your Own Business Book.* Avon, MA: Adams Media; 2002.
2. Lesonsky C. *Start Your Own Business.* Irvine, CA: Entrepreneur Media; 2007.
3. Friedman C, Yorio K. *The Girl's Guide to Starting Your Own Business.* New York, NY: HarperCollins Publishing; 2003.
4. American Dietetic Association Nutrition Entrepreneurs Dietetic Practice Group. Where to hang your shingle: home or rented office? In: *Nutrition Entrepreneurs Toolkit 2009.* Chicago, IL: American Dietetic Association; 2010.
5. Fiske H. 2002 Nutrition software review. *Today's Dietitian.* May 2002. http://www.todaysdietitian.com/newarchives/td_0502.shtml. Accessed July 11, 2009.
6. Prestwood E. 101 questions to ask before you buy nutrition software. *Today's Dietitian.* 2000;2(2). Reprinted at http://www.dietsoftware.com/101.shtml. Accessed July 11, 2009.
7. Clairmont C. A hard look at software solutions to ease your workload. *Today's Dietitian.* 2001;3:24–27.
8. US Department of Health and Human Services. Summary of the HIPAA Privacy Rule. http://www.hhs.gov/ocr/privacysummary.pdf. Accessed May 12, 2010.
9. Centers for Medicare & Medicaid Services. HIPAA Information Series: 2. Are You a Covered Entity? http://www.cms.hhs.gov/EducationMaterials/Downloads/Areyouacoveredentity-2.pdf. Accessed March 18, 2010.
10. American Dietetic Association. Patient Written Acknowledgement Confirming Receipt of Privacy Notice. http://www.eatright.org/Members/content.aspx?id=7514. Accessed March 15, 2010.
11. Michael P, Pritchett E. The impact of HIPAA electronic transmissions and health information privacy standards. *J Am Diet Assoc.* 2001;101:524–528.
12. Health and Human Services. Understanding HIPAA Privacy: For Covered Entities. http://www.hhs.gov/ocr/privacy/hipaa/understanding/coveredentities. Accessed August 25, 2005.
13. American Dietetic Association. Additional covered entity obligations under HIPAA. Prepared by Mintz, Levin, Cohn, Ferris, Glovsky, and Popeo, P.C. April 2002. http://www.eatright.org/Members/content.aspx?id=7504. Accessed March 15, 2010.
14. Centers for Medicare & Medicaid Services. HIPAA: Are You a Covered Entity? http://www.cms.hhs.gov/HIPAAGenInfo/06_AreYouaCoveredEntity.asp. Accessed March 29, 2010.
15. Bodman S. Privacy, please: new rules may protect patients, alter hospital, office practices. *Washington Post.* April 8, 2003;HE:01.

Chapter 8

Private Practice Business Decisions

Now let's talk about making money in your practice. You want to be paid for the services you rendered. Right? Remember, when you get to the checkout line in the supermarket, you must pay. It's the same in your office with your patients. At the end of each counseling session, the time comes for you to be paid.

Office Payment Policies

Before you begin to see patients, you need to establish your payment policies (see Box 8.1). Will you accept reimbursement from private insurance carriers, or will your practice be entirely fee for service? Do you plan to become a third-party provider? These options are discussed in detail later in this chapter.

Once you set your office payment policies, you must clearly inform your patients of them. Present your policies in writing at the time of their first appointment. Each new patient should sign a form stating he or she has read and understands the policies and is responsible for payment. Inform the patient that payment is collected at the time of the visit. Patients then know what to expect. See Box 8.2 for a sample statement.

Even if you implement a fee-for-service policy, there may be situations when you have to send bills. If you do need to bill for your services, do so in a timely manner. Bill within a month of the date of service.

Box 8.1 Options for Structuring Your Payment Policies

- **Receive fee for service.** Some registered dietitians (RDs) find it beneficial to set their practices up as "fee for service." The policy is simple. Payment is due at the time of the appointment. You are paid by patients and provide them with a completed superbill (the form that contains the diagnostic and procedure codes). Patients then submit the completed superbill to their insurance carrier for reimbursement.
- **Accept third-party reimbursement.** Many RDs accept third-party payment (insurance). They see the patient and then submit the claim to the patient's insurance carrier to receive payment or reimbursement. Most carriers require that the RD becomes a provider to receive direct reimbursement. Options include private insurance companies, Medicare, and Medicaid.
- **Join networks.** Some RDs find it beneficial to join networks. Referred to as "access programs," the patient—not the employer group or insurance company—pays the RD for the service. When RDs join the network, they usually agree to provide services at a discounted rate.

Box 8.2 Sample Payment Policy Statement

Payment for services is due at the time services are rendered, unless other arrangements have been made in advance. I accept Master Card, Visa, American Express, cash, and checks. I will be happy to help you with an insurance claim form for reimbursement if I am not a provider of your insurance. Assignment is accepted only from those insurance companies for which I am a provider. However, if your insurance company denies coverage, you are financially responsible for the payment.

Source: Reprinted with permission from Ann M. Silver.

Third-party payers specify a deadline for claims submission. Many private insurance companies require claims within 90 to 120 days from the date of service. Medicare accepts claims up to 12 months. After 12 months, Medicare will reduce payment for delayed submission.

To minimize billing, which costs you time and postage, establish the routine of collecting payment at each visit. There will be exceptions. It is often difficult to obtain payment after visits from teenagers and young adults whose parents are paying the bills.

How Will You Be Paid?

In determining your office policies, you need to decide *how* your patients will pay you. Will you only accept checks and cash for fees for service and co-pays? Or do you also want to accept credit and debit cards?

When you accept cash, there are no additional costs. Always provide a receipt to your patient when accepting cash. You can use a superbill, CMS 1500 form, or a cash receipt form from a stationery or office supply store.

You will not incur any additional expenses by accepting checks. However, your bank will assess fees if they bounce. You can take precautions to safeguard yourself from bounced checks. If a check lacks a printed name or is numbered less than 500, the account is new. You may want to inquire about such accounts with the patient (1). If in doubt about the check, it would be wise not to have another appointment with the patient until the check has cleared.

Consider having a policy in place for handling returned checks. Determine what your bank charges you for returned checks, then work that charge into your fee structure. It is important to place this information on your new patient information sheet and/or post a sign in the waiting room. One way to avoid returned checks and overdue accounts is to accept credit cards. This can also greatly reduce your accounts receivable.

You must pay fees to the credit card companies if you wish to accept credit or debit cards. However, the expense may be justified if accepting credit cards helps you collect payments efficiently and attracts patients who wish to pay this way. The fees affiliated with credit cards can include a percent per transaction fee, a monthly fee, and set-up fees. The same equipment you use to accept a credit card can also accept a debit card. When a patient presents a debit card instead of a check, you pay a fee. A consideration in accepting credit or debit cards is whether you accept third-party payers. When patients pay their co-pay by credit card, you receive about 1.5 to 3 percent less on the co-pay. See Chapter 3 for more information on credit cards.

Collecting Unpaid Balances

You must have a collections policy in place in the event you are not paid after an initial invoice is sent. How will you collect money from past-due accounts? Begin with a friendly phone call or face-to-face reminder to people who owe you money. Send an invoice indicating their account is past due. If these approaches are unsuccessful, send a letter stating that payment is due by a certain date or further action will be taken, and specify the action. Usually the letter will prompt payment. If not, you may want to use the services of a collection agency, but this will depend on the amount of the debt. Agencies charge a percentage of the total sum collected or a flat fee for each satisfied account. The additional fees can be added to the patient's outstanding balance. Include this in your payment policies. Ask colleagues and others in business for recommendations of a reputable collection agency.

Missed Appointments

Many practitioners have a 24- or 48-hour cancellation policy. They inform patients in advance that the patients will be charged for missed appointments. Include this in writing as part of your payment policy. This way you can collect for missed appointments (although you usually cannot enforce this policy for first-time appointments). A statement such as "Twenty-four (24) hour notice is required for cancellation of appointments or a $XX (or full) fee will apply can be added to your new patient forms.

Note that you cannot bill third-party payers—including private insurance companies, Medicare, and Medicaid—if services were not rendered. However, you may be able to bill the patient a fee for a missed appointment (2). Confirm this with each third-party payer.

If you accept credit cards, you can keep each patient's credit card number on file and bill for missed appointments. This policy should be printed on your patient information sheet and presented in writing along with your other payment policies at the first visit. Some practitioners find it helpful to have their policy printed on the bottom of an appointment card.

Setting Fees for Your Private Practice

Before starting a private practice, most registered dietitians (RDs) want to know how much to charge a patient or client. As you consider your fees, start by reviewing the fee-setting information in Chapter 3. Consider your fixed costs (rent, phone and Internet service, etc) and variable costs directly associated with each patient or client (3). How much will you need to charge to cover these expenses and earn the salary you desire?

As you think about fees, you may also want to ask consumers who have used similar services what they have paid and what they would be willing to pay. However, it is a potential violation of federal antitrust laws to discuss fees for professional services with other professionals, because this could be construed as price fixing (4,5).

A simple way to judge whether the market will bear your price is to try to gauge patients' reactions when you state your price. If most prospective patients do not balk and schedule an appointment, you know you are on target. If you receive a large number of excuses or people saying they will call back, your fees may be too high.

Consider your *perceived* value. If your rates are consistently lower than others providing the same service, you may lose clients because they feel you are not the best. On the other hand, professionals demanding the highest rates tend to have the reputation, experience, and higher levels of specialty that enable them to do so.

Although it is a questionable practice to routinely charge fee-for-service patients less than insurance patients (that is, offer a cash discount), you may occasionally discount your fees to a needy or indigent patient. You must determine how often you can afford to do this. You may also consider bartering for services, charging differently for home visits, or offering a discount for couples. If you do not deal with reimbursement, you may want to offer different fee schedules for day versus night visits. Weekend hours could bring premium rates. You may also want to offer a family rate.

In general, you will have at least two levels of service, an initial visit and a follow-up. Initial visits may take twice as long as follow-ups, so set your fees accordingly. Also, you will have greater administrative expense seeing two patients in one hour for follow-up than seeing one patient in one hour. It may be appropriate to set your half-hour fees to account for these increased costs.

When setting fees, do not start too low. It becomes difficult to catch up. You can only raise your rates incrementally at any given time. For example, raising your follow-up rate from $30 to $60 is a 100 percent increase. That increase would not be palatable to your existing patients. Take your time and carefully consider all the above-mentioned variables when setting fees.

The Basics of Third-Party Payers

Whether you decide to become a third-party payer or not, it is important to understand the basic principles and terminology of the health insurance industry, including the types of insurance carriers (referred to as "third-party payers"). Box 8.3 defines many terms important in the discussion of reimbursement (6–8).

Box 8.3 Glossary of Terms

Accept assignment: A health care provider who participates with an insurance plan. The health care provider agrees to accept the fees specified by the insurance carriers and cannot collect additional fees for the service beyond the co-payment and/or deductible.

Beneficiary: Any person who receives insurance benefits from an insurance plan.

Claim: A claim is a request for payment for rendered services.

CMS 1500: Form that health care providers use to submit Medicare and other insurance claims.

Complementary and alternative network (CAM) or complementary network (CN): A network of practitioners that includes services of different practitioners—such as massage therapists, nutritionists/registered dietitians, and chiropractors—whom are considered nontraditional. Firms sell both benefit and access services to insurance companies and employer groups to supplement existing services included in these groups' health benefits plans. Services are provided at a discounted rate of usual fees and are paid directly to the provider by the client.

(continued)

Box 8.3 *(continued)*

Co-payment/co-pay: In most health plans, the amount a patient pays for each medical service. A co-payment is usually a set amount specified by the policy that the patient pays for a service (for example, five dollars or more for a doctor's visit).

CPT (Current Procedural Terminology): Procedural codes for physicians and other health care professionals, developed by the American Medical Association. Registered dietitians and other nutrition professionals have specific procedural codes.

Deductible: The amount a person needs to pay out-of-pocket for health costs before the insurance covers costs.

Explanation of benefits (EOB): A statement from a third-party payer describing coverage for services rendered.

Explanation of Medicare benefits (EOMB): A statement from Medicare describing coverage for services rendered.

Fee for service: A health care provider provides services to an individual without submitting an insurance claim. The provider takes payment for services at the time of the visit.

Health maintenance organization (HMO): A type of health insurance plan that delivers previously determined comprehensive services to its policyholders for a prepaid sum and contracts with or employs health care providers to deliver service.

ICD-9-CM/ICD-10-CM (International Classification of Diseases, Clinical Modifications): Codes determined by the treating or primary care physician to classify all diagnostic and surgical procedures.

Medicaid: A program jointly funded by federal and state governments that pays medical assistance for certain individuals and families with low incomes and limited resources.

Medicare: The federal health insurance program for people 65 years of age or older, certain younger people with disabilities, and people with end-stage renal disease (those with permanent kidney failure who need regular dialysis or a kidney transplant).

National Provider Identifier (NPI): A unique 10-digit number required for all health care providers. This number is used to identify an individual health care provider for all health transactions. Even if you choose not to accept reimbursement from third-party payers, you should obtain an NPI.

Point of service organization (POS): A health plan that offers its members the option of receiving services from participating or nonparticipating providers. Generally, coverage is reduced for services by nonparticipating providers.

Preferred provider organization (PPO): A health care delivery system that contracts with providers and health care organizations to provide services at discounted fees to members.

Superbill: A preprinted form that itemizes and describes all services and fees. The client can submit the superbill directly to the health care insurer.

Third-party payer: Organization or company that disburses payment on behalf of an insured (the patient, which is the first party) for medical services to a provider (the second party).

Source: Data are from references 6, 7, and 8.

Reimbursement Resources

Private practitioners should stay current with all the reimbursement issues. The information is constantly changing. Fortunately, staying current is made easy through the resources available through ADA. Resources that can help you stay informed include the following:

- The Nutrition Services Coverage Team at ADA—members of the team are extremely helpful and available if you have specific questions.
- Your state dietetic association, district dietetic association, or dietetic practice group (DPG) reimbursement representative. He or she should be available to assist you with local issues.
- Mentoring services offered by several DPGs to their members.
- ADA's annual Public Policy Workshop and affiliate meetings. Participation in these meetings or online Webinars allows you to receive the latest information on policy as well as the opportunity to meet and lobby your representatives.
- Reimbursement manuals and/or materials published by some DPGs. Some sell their resources; others provide them as a free service to their members. Consult the individual DPG Web sites for a listing of materials. You can link to DPG sites through the ADA Web site (http://www.eatright.org).
- Your local library and the Internet. These are good places to research business-related information, reimbursement, and policy issues.
- Information on medical nutrition therapy on the ADA Web site (http://www.eatright.org).
- Centers for Medicare & Medicaid Services (CMS) and your Medicare Administrative Contractor (MAC) Web pages.
- Private third-party payer Web pages.

Common Types of Third-Party Payers

Private Health Insurance Companies

Private health insurance companies offer insurance plans not funded by the government. There are so many of these commercial plans, it is difficult to track them. The plans vary from state to state. Even within the same insurance company, the benefits vary from plan to plan.

Managed care organizations' plans are the most popular plans offered in the United States. These include health maintenance organization (HMO) plans, preferred provider organization (PPO) plans, and point-of-service organization (POS) plans.

To be reimbursed by these plans, an RD must be enrolled as a provider of medical nutrition therapy or other nutrition services. Many plans require some form of preauthorization, such as a referral for coverage. They may limit the number of visits annually or for the life of the beneficiary. The more plans you join, the greater potential for reimbursement.

Complementary and Alternative Medicine Networks

Another option is for the RD to join networks. These are often referred to as Complementary and Alternative Medicine (CAM) programs or Complementary Networks (CNs). Being a member of a CAM network differs from being a provider. Upon joining the network, RDs agree to provide their services at a discounted rate to members of that particular plan. In this type of arrangement offered through the CN, the member pays for the service. For example, CareFirst BlueCross BlueShield of Maryland allows patients who have not been diagnosed with an illness requiring nutrition counseling or who cannot receive preauthorization for coverage to see a dietitian at a discounted rate (9). CNs may also offer benefit CAM services, in which the employer or insurer pays for the service.

CAM networks pursue RDs to join them. Before you join, it is important to determine whether the reimbursement arrangements are a viable option for your practice. While joining this type of network can potentially increase your referral base, consider the downside. As a member of these networks, you may need to provide deeply discounted fees to members. Some networks offer set fees that do not differ by geographic region. If you practice in a city where the cost of doing business is high, it may not be worth your time to join. Also, joining these networks may associate you with other practitioners like chiropractors and massage therapists who have different levels of training and credentialing than RDs.

Medicare

RDs and other qualifying nutrition professionals are eligible for providing medical nutrition therapy (MNT) to Medicare Part B beneficiaries. Patients with diabetes or nondialysis kidney disease and those post–kidney transplant can receive the benefit.

CMS is the government agency that establishes guidelines and regulations. RDs who want to become Medicare providers must meet specific criteria. The following are some of the RDs' options:

- **Enroll:** Practitioners who meet the provider qualifications can enroll at any time to become a Medicare provider.
- **Do not enroll:** Practitioners who choose not to enroll are not able to provide MNT services to qualifying Medicare beneficiaries unless they opt out of Medicare Part B. Practitioners who have not enrolled or opted out of Medicare cannot provide and bill MNT to beneficiaries with diabetes or nondialysis kidney disease, or post-kidney transplant. Instead, these RDs should inform patients that they do not participate in Medicare and direct those patients to another RD who is an enrolled Medicare provider.
- **Opt out:** In this instance, the practitioner chooses to enter into a private contract with each qualifying Medicare beneficiary in order to provide MNT services. The private contract created for each beneficiary requires

very specific requirements as defined by CMS. The opt-out period is two years (10–13).

Medicaid

Medicaid is regulated and administered on a state-by-state basis, so coverage for MNT varies by state. Some states do not cover MNT for Medicaid beneficiaries. Further information on specific state regulations can be found at the Centers for Medicare & Medicaid Services Web site (14). Your state dietetic association reimbursement representative may also be able to provide assistance or resources on Medicaid.

Accepting Third-Party Payers or Fee for Service: What's Right for Your Practice?

You may have already decided whether to accept payment from third-party payers or only accept fee for service, or you may be in a quandary about what to do. Before making this decision, research as much as you can. Speak with colleagues on both sides of the fence. Identify whether accepting insurance reimbursement is feasible and something you want to do. Post your debate on DPG Listservs. Contact your local, state, and DPG reimbursement representatives. Be up-to-date to make an informed decision. Crunch your numbers. Compare your overhead expenses versus potential income from third-party payers and fee for service.

Many RDs believe that reimbursement will make or break their practice. This is not necessarily the case. Some RDs do not accept insurance coverage at all. This is a growing trend in medical practices.

Physicians in some major metropolitan areas are opting out of insurance plans and seeing patients on a fee-for-service basis (15). They feel they cannot practice medicine with the financial and procedural restrictions placed on them by the insurance companies. This may not be a realistic option for many private practice RDs, however. They may find it necessary to accept insurance to be successful in private practice. Especially when first starting out, accepting third-party payment can quickly build your practice. You need to make a decision. Would you prefer to make less money per patient and be busier or make more money per patient and work less? This is a decision only you can make.

An important fact to keep in mind is that all health care professionals are competing for the same reimbursement dollars and it may be difficult to get paid for services that are not in the basic realm of service. This does not mean, however, that you should throw in the towel. Some RDs might argue that the lack of reimbursement has kept them from being successful in their private practices. They are giving up too easily! RDs *are* being reimbursed for MNT.

Reimbursement policies have an impact on how you structure your fees. Handling insurance claims increases the overhead for a practice. It takes more administrative time to check on eligibility and referrals, file the claims, resubmit the claims if they have been rejected, and bill the patient when denied. Often there is a lag time between the time of filing a claim and receiving payment. The increased administrative time required contributes to the overhead costs for handling insurance claims. Submitting claims costs you time to complete the forms and reduces the time you could spend providing billable nutrition services to your clients. If you decide to use someone else to submit claims, such as a biller, this will also add to your costs. Billers' fees can range from an extra five dollars *per claim* up to 7 percent of the collected reimbursement (16).

Whether you decide to accept third-party payers directly as payment or opt to follow the fee-for-service model, it is wise to have an overview of reimbursement for MNT. Being knowledgeable about coverage for third-party payers will assist your patients and can be helpful for your own insurance issues.

Billing Options

Once you have some understanding of reimbursement, your fees established, and your accounting system in place (see Chapter 3), you are ready to determine which reimbursement policies work best for you. Table 8.1 summarizes several practice models, which are also discussed in the following sections (17).

Medicare Only

It is possible to base your practice solely on Medicare clients. Beneficiaries are required to receive a written physician referral annually. If you have a few good referral sources, you can maintain a steady stream of clients. Medicare beneficiaries can receive three hours of coverage in the first three years and two hours in subsequent years, so you will need a constant source of new referrals. With another physician referral, additional hours of MNT can be provided based on a change in the patient's medical condition, diagnosis, and treatment.

Becoming a Medicare provider requires having the necessary systems in place to comply with regulations. Some potential pitfalls of a Medicare-based practice include the possibility that the reimbursement rate may not meet your salary expectations or adequately cover your business expenses and your administrative duties are likely to increase. Your client base will be limited to the diseases and conditions Medicare covers—diabetes and renal disease—until coverage expands to include other diseases.

Payer Blend, Medicare Opt-Out

In this scenario, RDs see clients and Medicare beneficiaries who pay out-of-pocket for service. These RDs are also participating providers for one or more

Table 8.1 Selecting a Dietetics Practice Model

Model	*Pros*	*Cons*
Medicare clients	• Stable and predictable • Potential for large number of clientele • Minimal marketing • Opportunity for follow up • Good systems development • Recognition as a Medicare provider	• Reimbursement rate may not meet salary requirements • Administrative duties • Medicare clients limited to diabetes and renal disease
Self-pay clients, third-party payers, and opting out of Medicare	• Potential for higher payment rate • Broader range of clients' payment rate • Provider status with private plans	• Requires marketing and negotiating skills • May be less stable • May reduce referrals • Ramifications of opting out of Medicare
Medicare and third-party payers, plus self-pay clients	• Variety and professional satisfaction • Success with Medicare generates non-Medicare referrals • Maintains client flow • Builds skills and confidence with billing and negotiating systems • Benefit from economies of scale as a result of time and experience	• Requires up-front work to stay organized and efficient with time • Management of contracts and billing
Self-pay clients	• Potential for higher payment rate • Less administrative work • Frequently used with highly specialized practices • Registered dietitian can establish a wellness-based practice	• Requires constant creative marketing • May be less stable • May reduce referrals

Source: Adapted with permission from American Dietetic Association. *MNT Medicare Provider*. January 2004, p.2. Copyright © 2004 American Dietetic Association.

private insurance plans that directly reimburse them. They are not providers of Medicare MNT and can only provide MNT to Medicare beneficiaries through the government's opting-out regulations. Potentially, this scenario may bring higher payment rates. It also provides a more varied client population.

Consider the downsides of this model. Opting out of Medicare may reduce your referrals, and you may have to increase your marketing efforts to compensate. Also, there may be ramifications of opting out of Medicare. One such ramification is that the opt-out period lasts for two years, so opting out could potentially impact your future employment opportunities (11).

Payer Blend Including Medicare

This model encompasses all scenarios. The RD is a provider for Medicare and private insurance plans, and accepts self-pay patients. This model may offer a larger volume of clients and a greater income. Depending on the mix of self-pay and third-party payers in this model, you will see a varied range of payment for your services. Medicare and private insurance plans can provide a steady referral source.

A potential pitfall of this model is that it requires a great amount of organization to track referrals, benefits, and numerous claims and to manage contracts and billing.

Self-Pay Clients Only (Fee for Service)

This model is one in which the RD is not a provider for Medicare or private insurance plans. The RD informs patients when they call for an appointment that payment is expected at the time of the visit. The patient will be provided with a superbill or a completed CMS 1500 form and encouraged to file for reimbursement with their insurance company. Although this may deter some potential patients from scheduling appointments, individuals who choose to pay for services may potentially be more serious about implementing dietary changes.

This model does have the potential for higher payment rates and requires much less administrative work for the RD. With less time spent on administrative duties, more time can be spent seeing patients and billing for that time. RDs can become highly specialized in this case, and patients will seek them for their particular specialty niches. For example, specialists in eating disorders, weight management, or women's health may wish to build a fee-for-service practice. Along with the previously mentioned pitfalls associated with opting out of Medicare, choosing not to be a provider for private insurance companies has the potential to greatly reduce your client base and income. You also must expend extra time and effort in marketing your services.

How to Become a Third-Party Payer

To become a provider for a third party, you will need some information before you submit an application. Having this data readily available will make the process easier. Figure 8.1 provides a checklist of what you may need to complete an application to become a provider.

- ❑ Location MNT services will be rendered, office phone number, fax number, business e-mail account.
- ❑ Copy of your malpractice insurance cover sheet. Different third-party payers may request specific amounts of malpractice coverage.
- ❑ Federal tax identification number, also known as Employee Identification Number (EIN). See Chapter 2 for information on obtaining an EIN.
- ❑ NPI (National Provider Identifier) number.
  Contact information for NPI: https://nppes.cms.hhs.gov or 800/465-3203.
- ❑ Copy of your college diploma(s).
- ❑ Copy of your state certification/license.
- ❑ Copy of any other certifications.
- ❑ Copy of your Commission on Dietetic Registration (CDR) card and American Dietetic Association membership card.
- ❑ Updated resume or curriculum vitae.
- ❑ List of professional and personal references, including address, e-mail address, and phone number, if requested on the application.

Figure 8.1 Checklist for applying to third-party payers. Reprinted with permission from Ann Silver.

Private Insurance Companies

Develop a list of private insurance companies providing coverage in your office vicinity or for which you are interested in becoming a provider. You will need the name of the insurance company, mailing address, Web site, e-mail address, phone number, and, if possible, the name of the provider representative. The following are various ways to collect a list of potential insurance companies:

- Ask district and state dietetic association reimbursement representatives.
- Inquire of local colleagues who are already providers.
- Question health care providers in your community.
- Inquire of your neighbors.
- Ask your own physician.
- Check the ADA's Web page on "Private Insurance MNT Coverage Throughout the US" (18).

To request an application to become a provider, call or write the insurance company, or send an e-mail to the contact listed on the company Web site.

Medicare

Medicare's application process for providers is different from that used by private insurance. Applications are available at the CMS Web site (www.cms.hhs.gov). Complete and submit the most recent CMS Form 855I, the Application for Individual Health Care Practitioners; other enrollment forms may also be required (19). Applications can be downloaded from the CMS Web site or completed online through Medicare's online provider enrollment, called Provider Enrollment, Chain and Ownership System (PECOS) (20). Tutorials are also available to assist with completing the Medicare application (21).

Local or geographical Medicare carriers, also known as Medicare Administrative Contractors (MACs), administer Medicare. Medicare Part B is the part that covers outpatient medical services (including MNT), whereas Part A covers inpatient services such as hospitalizations. The completed application for Medicare will be submitted to your MAC. Some MACs may require you to include additional forms. RDs should contact their state's Part B MAC with any questions or concerns about enrolling in Medicare or any other issues they may have including claims, reimbursement, and customer services. You can look on the ADA or CMS Web site for your MAC or contact your state dietetic association reimbursement representative for assistance (22). Check the CMS or your MAC Web site for the most updated information on Medicare enrollment.

Medicaid

Coverage for MNT by Medicaid is determined by each state. Applications are specific to each state. Check the CMS Web site or contact your state dietetic association reimbursement representative about whether your state will recognize you as a provider and how to obtain a provider enrollment application.

Tips for Completing the Third-Party-Payer Application

Read instructions before completing applications. Complete all parts of third-party payers' applications. Enclose all requested information, or the application will either be sent back or denied. Sign the application.

Keep copies of all submitted applications. Mailing the application certified via the US Postal Service can confirm receipt of your application. You may need to follow up with the insurer to determine status of the application by phone or e-mail. You can check on your enrollment in Medicare via PECOS (20).

Realize it can take many months to become a provider with third-party payers. If your application is denied, find out why. Be persistent in trying to become a provider. Don't give up!

Now You Are a Provider: What's Next?

Obtaining Referrals and Pre-authorizations

When you accept third-party payments, you need to understand and attend to certain administrative tasks before the patient's first visit. Learn whether your third-party contracts require patient referrals and which diagnoses they will cover for MNT.

Although patients should know if they need a referral with their health insurance, many may not. You will need to know. Private insurance companies will not pay you when a referral is required and there is none in place. In this circumstance, you will not be able to bill the patient. Ultimately, you will not be getting paid for the services you rendered when a referral is not obtained.

Find out how you will receive the referral: will the patient bring the written referral to the first appointment, will it be faxed to you automatically, or will you need to retrieve it electronically? Medicare Part B requires a referral from the treating physician specifying MNT services and the patient's diagnosis (23). Make sure a referral or pre-authorization will be in place by the time of the appointment, if required.

Verifying MNT Coverage

Patients need to understand that health insurance does not guarantee the insurer will pay all fees for your services. Not all diagnoses are covered, and coverage varies. Even if a referral is in place, this does not guarantee the visit will be covered. Determine coverage before the first visit. You can call or check online to verify coverage for MNT; however, this can be time-consuming. You can place the onus on the patient by requesting they contact their insurer to confirm coverage.

When MNT is not covered or is questionable, inform the patient they will be responsible for payment. Tell the patient what the fee will be. No one likes surprise bills.

If you are rendering services to a Medicare-insured patient for a diagnosis not covered by Medicare, you must inform patients before their visit that they are responsible for payment. Ask patients whether they have additional insurance that might cover the MNT visit. You may want to complete an Advance Beneficiary Notice of Noncoverage (ABN), as shown in Figure 8.2. This form verifies that patients understand they are responsible for payment of services not covered by Medicare (24).

If patients are not covered by insurance, you may need to discuss the advantages and health cost savings they will achieve by receiving nutrition services. Even without insurance, some patients may decide to see you if they think the services you provide are beneficial.

After you interact with insurance companies for a while, you will find such interactions are not quite as daunting. You will begin to get a feel for the insurance carriers in your area that reimburse for nutrition services. You will have their Web sites bookmarked on your computer and/or their numbers in your speed dial to streamline your process.

Other Third-Party Payer Requirements

The plans with which RDs contract to provide MNT may have other requirements that affect your practice. For example, Medicare and many private insurance plans require the use of protocols. The regulation for the Medicare MNT benefit states, "dietitians and nutritionists would use nationally recognized protocols, such as those developed by the ADA." The guides, titled *Medical Nutrition Therapy (MNT) Evidence-Based Guides for Practice*, are available on CD from the ADA (http://www.eatright.org/shop).

Scheduling the First Appointment

When a patient contacts you to make their initial appointment, find out the reason for the visit and obtain the patient's insurance information. This is the time to inform patients if you know or suspect their insurance may not cover for MNT and what the fee will be.

If patients need a referral, inform them before their appointment, Also advise them to obtain a copy of their diagnoses from their physician or physician's office. Ask patients to bring their insurance card and payment for the co-pay or the office visit to the appointment. Also ask them for other information you may need for this appointment, such as a list of medications, a copy of their recent laboratory test results, and a food journal.

(A) **Notifier(s):**
(B) **Patient Name:** *(C)* **Identification Number:**

ADVANCE BENEFICIARY NOTICE OF NONCOVERAGE (ABN)

NOTE: If Medicare doesn't pay for ***(D)***_____________ below, you may have to pay.

Medicare does not pay for everything, even some care that you or your health care provider have good reason to think you need. We expect Medicare may not pay for the ***(D)***____________ below.

(D)_______________	***(E)* Reason Medicare May Not Pay:**	***(F)* Estimated Cost:**

WHAT YOU NEED TO DO NOW:

- Read this notice, so you can make an informed decision about your care.
- Ask us any questions that you may have after you finish reading.
- Choose an option below about whether to receive the ***(D)***____________listed above.

  Note: If you choose Option 1 or 2, we may help you to use any other insurance that you might have, but Medicare cannot require us to do this.

***(G)* OPTIONS:** **Check only one box. We cannot choose a box for you.**

❑ **OPTION 1.** I want the ***(D)***__________ listed above. You may ask to be paid now, but I also want Medicare billed for an official decision on payment, which is sent to me on a Medicare Summary Notice (MSN). I understand that if Medicare doesn't pay, I am responsible for payment, but **I can appeal to Medicare** by following the directions on the MSN. If Medicare does pay, you will refund any payments I made to you, less co-pays or deductibles.

❑ **OPTION 2.** I want the ***(D)***__________ listed above, but do not bill Medicare. You may ask to be paid now as I am responsible for payment. **I cannot appeal if Medicare is not billed.**

❑ **OPTION 3.** I don't want the ***(D)***__________listed above. I understand with this choice I am **not** responsible for payment, and **I cannot appeal to see if Medicare would pay.**

***(H)* Additional Information:**

This notice gives our opinion, not an official Medicare decision. If you have other questions on this notice or Medicare billing, call **1-800-MEDICARE** (1-800-633-4227/**TTY**: 1-877-486-2048).

Signing below means that you have received and understand this notice. You also receive a copy.

***(I)* Signature:**	***(J)* Date:**

According to the Paperwork Reduction Act of 1995, no persons are required to respond to a collection of information unless it displays a valid OMB control number. The valid OMB control number for this information collection is 0938-0566. The time required to complete this information collection is estimated to average 7 minutes per response, including the time to review instructions, search existing data resources, gather the data needed, and complete and review the information collection. If you have comments concerning the accuracy of the time estimate or suggestions for improving this form, please write to: CMS, 7500 Security Boulevard, Attn: PRA Reports Clearance Officer, Baltimore, Maryland 21244-1850.

Form CMS-R-131 (03/08) Form Approved OMB No. 0938-0566

Figure 8.2 Medicare Advanced Beneficiary Notice of Noncoverage (Form CMS-R-131).

The First Appointment

At the initial appointment with a new patient or client, there is information you will need to obtain and/or provide. Figure 8.3 can serve as a reminder of the administrative tasks for the first visit.

Tools for Billing

Once you have determined that the insurance carrier will reimburse for your services and you have rendered MNT, a claim must be filed. This requires either a superbill or the CMS 1500 form. Even if you decide not to accept insurance, you should provide your patients with the necessary forms so they may file a claim for reimbursement.

CMS 1500 Form

Most insurance carriers accept only a completed CMS 1500 form (Figure 8.4), especially in-network providers (25). These forms can be purchased from some office supply stores or medical office supply catalogs. Third-party payers do not accept scanned or downloaded CMS 1500 forms; to be submitted as a paper claim, the form must be an original. These forms are quite time-

- ❑ Patient registration form completed.
- ❑ Signed acknowledgement of Health Insurance Portability and Accountability Act (HIPAA) and all office policies.
- ❑ Authorization for release of information to other health care providers and third-party payers.
- ❑ Copy of the front and back of patient's insurance card(s).
- ❑ Referral or pre-authorization for third-party payer.
- ❑ Physician's diagnosis with ICD code.
- ❑ Payment of co-pay or office visit.
- ❑ Superbill and/or receipt.

Figure 8.3 Checklist for a new patient. Reprinted with permission from Ann M. Silver.

consuming to fill out and must be properly completed to the specifications of the insurance carrier. Forms that are filled out incorrectly or incompletely will be returned to the provider for completion and resubmission. It may be beneficial to purchase a computer software program that can take care of this administrative task.

Filing claims electronically (via the Internet) is becoming more common. This eliminates the need to purchase forms and mail the completed forms to insurance carriers. Some insurance carriers enable you to submit your claims on their Web sites or the insurance carrier may give their contracted providers the necessary software to enable them to file claims electronically. The software may have a fee associated with it, so check first. It is critical that you abide by the privacy standards of the Health Insurance Portability and Accountability Act (HIPAA) when filing electronic claims.

Many companies and organizations provide medical billing products, educational materials for practitioners, and other resources. Box 8.4 lists some companies and organizations that provide medical billing products (26). Check the telephone book under "insurance claim processing services" or "medical billing," search the Internet, or contact local insurance carriers or other health care professionals in your area for billers. For the RD that plans to handle a multitude of insurance claims, using one of these companies to handle insurance billing could be a wise investment.

Superbill

The superbill is a different type of claim form (see Figure 8.5). This bill is more commonly used when a patient has paid you for your services and/or if the patient will seek reimbursement from the insurance company. The RD completes the form at the end of each visit. The RD provides the patient with a superbill with the understanding that the insurance company may or may not pay for the counseling. This puts the responsibility of collecting reimbursement on the patient. The patient submits the superbill to his or her insurer. Reimbursement for the service will be dependent on the insurance company and whether the patient has out-of-network benefits. If you are an in-network provider, you cannot submit a superbill.

A superbill must have certain components (see Box 8.5). You can create your own superbill using your computer or purchase camera-ready superbills.

Diagnosis and Procedure Codes

Both the CMS1500 form and superbill use specific numeric identification to indicate the diagnosis, also known as the ICD-9-CM, or diagnosis codes. These forms also require a number; the Current Procedural Terminology (CPT) code identifies the procedure provided by the RD. Whether you are directly submitting a claim to a third-party payer or your client is submitting to their insurance company, this information needs to be specified for you to be reimbursed.

1500

HEALTH INSURANCE CLAIM FORM

APPROVED BY NATIONAL UNIFORM CLAIM COMMITTEE 08/05

PICA PICA

CARRIER

1. MEDICARE (Medicare #) MEDICAID (Medicaid #) TRICARE CHAMPUS (Sponsor's SSN) CHAMPVA (Member ID#) GROUP HEALTH PLAN (SSN or ID) FECA BLK LUNG (SSN) OTHER (ID)

1a. INSURED'S I.D. NUMBER (For Program in Item 1)

2. PATIENT'S NAME (Last Name, First Name, Middle Initial)

3. PATIENT'S BIRTH DATE MM DD YY SEX M F

4. INSURED'S NAME (Last Name, First Name, Middle Initial)

5. PATIENT'S ADDRESS (No., Street)

6. PATIENT RELATIONSHIP TO INSURED Self Spouse Child Other

7. INSURED'S ADDRESS (No., Street)

CITY STATE

8. PATIENT STATUS Single Married Other

CITY STATE

ZIP CODE TELEPHONE (Include Area Code) ( )

Employed Full-Time Student Part-Time Student

ZIP CODE TELEPHONE (Include Area Code) ( )

9. OTHER INSURED'S NAME (Last Name, First Name, Middle Initial)

10. IS PATIENT'S CONDITION RELATED TO:

11. INSURED'S POLICY GROUP OR FECA NUMBER

a. OTHER INSURED'S POLICY OR GROUP NUMBER

a. EMPLOYMENT? (Current or Previous) YES NO

a. INSURED'S DATE OF BIRTH MM DD YY SEX M F

b. OTHER INSURED'S DATE OF BIRTH MM DD YY SEX M F

b. AUTO ACCIDENT? PLACE (State) YES NO

b. EMPLOYER'S NAME OR SCHOOL NAME

c. EMPLOYER'S NAME OR SCHOOL NAME

c. OTHER ACCIDENT? YES NO

c. INSURANCE PLAN NAME OR PROGRAM NAME

d. INSURANCE PLAN NAME OR PROGRAM NAME

10d. RESERVED FOR LOCAL USE

d. IS THERE ANOTHER HEALTH BENEFIT PLAN? YES NO *If yes,* return to and complete item 9 a-d.

READ BACK OF FORM BEFORE COMPLETING & SIGNING THIS FORM.

12. PATIENT'S OR AUTHORIZED PERSON'S SIGNATURE I authorize the release of any medical or other information necessary to process this claim. I also request payment of government benefits either to myself or to the party who accepts assignment below.

SIGNED ______ DATE ______

13. INSURED'S OR AUTHORIZED PERSON'S SIGNATURE I authorize payment of medical benefits to the undersigned physician or supplier for services described below.

SIGNED ______

PATIENT AND INSURED INFORMATION

14. DATE OF CURRENT: MM DD YY ◀ ILLNESS (First symptom) OR INJURY (Accident) OR PREGNANCY(LMP)

15. IF PATIENT HAS HAD SAME OR SIMILAR ILLNESS. GIVE FIRST DATE MM DD YY

16. DATES PATIENT UNABLE TO WORK IN CURRENT OCCUPATION FROM MM DD YY TO MM DD YY

17. NAME OF REFERRING PROVIDER OR OTHER SOURCE

17a. 17b. NPI

18. HOSPITALIZATION DATES RELATED TO CURRENT SERVICES FROM MM DD YY TO MM DD YY

19. RESERVED FOR LOCAL USE

20. OUTSIDE LAB? YES NO $ CHARGES

21. DIAGNOSIS OR NATURE OF ILLNESS OR INJURY (Relate Items 1, 2, 3 or 4 to Item 24E by Line)

1. ____ . ____ 3. ____ . ____

2. ____ . ____ 4. ____ . ____

22. MEDICAID RESUBMISSION CODE ORIGINAL REF. NO.

23. PRIOR AUTHORIZATION NUMBER

24. A. DATE(S) OF SERVICE From MM DD YY To MM DD YY	B. PLACE OF SERVICE	C. EMG	D. PROCEDURES, SERVICES, OR SUPPLIES (Explain Unusual Circumstances) CPT/HCPCS MODIFIER	E. DIAGNOSIS POINTER	F. $ CHARGES	G. DAYS OR UNITS	H. EPSDT Family Plan	I. ID. QUAL.	J. RENDERING PROVIDER ID. #
1								NPI	
2								NPI	
3								NPI	
4								NPI	
5								NPI	
6								NPI	

25. FEDERAL TAX I.D. NUMBER SSN EIN

26. PATIENT'S ACCOUNT NO.

27. ACCEPT ASSIGNMENT? (For govt. claims, see back) YES NO

28. TOTAL CHARGE $

29. AMOUNT PAID $

30. BALANCE DUE $

31. SIGNATURE OF PHYSICIAN OR SUPPLIER INCLUDING DEGREES OR CREDENTIALS (I certify that the statements on the reverse apply to this bill and are made a part thereof.)

SIGNED DATE

32. SERVICE FACILITY LOCATION INFORMATION

a. NPI b.

33. BILLING PROVIDER INFO & PH # ( )

a. NPI b.

PHYSICIAN OR SUPPLIER INFORMATION

NUCC Instruction Manual available at: www.nucc.org

APPROVED OMB-0938-0999 FORM CMS-1500 (08/05)

Figure 8.4 CMS 1500 health insurance claim form.

Box 8.4 Billing Resources

Government

Centers for Medicare & Medicaid Services (CMS)

http://www.cms.gov/home/medicare.asp

http://www.cms.gov/ElectronicBillingEDITrans

As part of the Health Insurance Portability and Accountability Act (HIPAA), CMS offers program updates and publication notices through the Electronic Data Interchange (EDI) electronic mailing list. Free Medicare Electronic Media Claim (EMC) software is also available.

Nonprofit

American Medical Billing Association (AMBA)

http://www.ambanet.net

AMBA provides networking and some advocacy for small and home-based professional medical billers. Their Web site features software packages and a list of vendors with AMBA's Medical Billing Certification.

Medical Billing Network of America

http://www.medicalbillingnetwork.com

The Medical Billing Network is a trade association and school for both small and large independent medical billers. They offer several electronic medical billing software products on their Web page.

Web-Based

Medicalbillingworld.com

http://www.medicalbillingworld.com/index.html

An online outlet for medical billing books, forms, software, and customer service. Review its entire inventory at the Web site.

Source: Data are from reference 26.

Insert

Header and/or logo

Here

Tax ID # ____________ Date

NPI # ____________ Pt. ID # ____________

RD # ____________

Lic. # ____________

Patient's Name ________________________

	Code	Diagnosis		Code	Diagnosis
☐	790.2	Abnormal Glucose Tolerance Test	☐	535.4	Gastritis
☐	783.1	Abnormal Weight Gain	☐	558.9	Gastroenteritis
☐	783.21	Abnormal Weight Loss	☐	530.81	Gastroesophageal Reflux
☐	626.0	Amenorrhea	☐	648.8	Gestational Diabetes
☐	280.9	Anemia (Fe Deficiency)	☐	579.0	Gluten Sensitive Enteropathy
☐	285.9	Anemia, Unspecified	☐	274.9	Gout
☐	307.1	Anorexia Nervosa	☐	553.3	Hiatal Hernia
☐	414.0	Arteriosclerotic Heart Disorder (ASHD)	☐	042	HIV Infection
☐	715.0	Arthritis (Rheumatoid)	☐	272.0	Hypercholesterolemia
☐	493.90	Asthma	☐	643.00	Hyperemesis, gravidum
☐	307.51	Bulimia Nervosa	☐	790.29	Hyperglycemia
☐	575.10	Cholecystitis	☐	272.2	Hyperlipidemia
☐	574.20	Cholelithiasis	☐	401.9	Hypertension
☐	585.9	Chronic Renal Failure	☐	242.9	Hyperthyroidism
☐	749.20	Cleft Palate with Cleft Lip	☐	272.1	Hypertriglyceridemia
☐	428.0	Congestive Heart Failure	☐	251.2	Hypoglycemia
☐	564.0	Constipation	☐	244.9	Hypothyroidism
☐	555.1	Crohn's Disease, Large Intestine	☐	646.8	Insufficient Weight Gain
☐	555.0	Crohn's Disease, Small Intestine	☐	564.1	Irritable Bowel Syndrome
☐	277.02	Cystic Fibrosis	☐	271.3	Lactose Intolerance
☐	722.6	Degenerative Disc Disease	☐	627.2	Menopausal Syndrome
☐	715.90	Degenerative Joint Disease	☐	412	Myocardial Infarction
☐	276.50	Dehydration	☐	583.81	Nephritis and Nephropathy
☐	250.01	Diabetes Mellitus, Type 1	☐	278.00	Obesity
☐	250.00	Diabetes Mellitus, Type 2	☐	733.00	Osteoporosis
☐	648.00	Diabetes with Pregnancy	☐	332.0	Parkinsonism
☐	250.4	Diabetic Nephropathy	☐	533.70	Peptic Ulcer Disease
☐	799.9	Diagnosis Deferred	☐	270.1	PKU
☐	564.5	Diarrhea	☐	564.2	Post-Gastrectomy Syndrome
☐	562.11	Diverticulitis	☐	V22.2	Pregnancy, Normal
☐	562.10	Diverticulosis	☐	263.9	Protein Calorie Malnutrition
☐	787.20	Dysphagia	☐	791.0	Proteinuria
☐	307.50	Eating Disorder, Unspecified	☐	590.80	Pyelonephritis
☐	782.3	Edema	☐	593.9	Renal Disease
☐	646.1	Excess Weight Gain Pregnancy	☐	780.57	Sleep Apnea
☐	783.41	Failure to Thrive	☐	556.9	Ulcerative Colitis
☐	693.1	Food Allergies	☐	269.2	Vitamin Deficiency

Office Procedure:

☐ 97802 Initial Assessment
☐ 97803 Reassessment
☐ 97804 Group

Fee: ____________

Payment ____________

Balance ____________

Provider's Signature ____________

Figure 8.5 Sample superbill. Reprinted with permission from Faye Berger Mitchell.

Box 8.5 Components of a Superbill

- Provider name
- Provider address
- Provider telephone/fax numbers
- NPI number
- License number (if applicable in your state)
- Tax identification number (EIN)
- Patient name
- Date of service
- Diagnosis code from International Classification of Diseases, 9th revision (ICD-9-CM), or from 10th revision (ICD-10), when available
- Procedural code (Current Procedural Terminology [CPT])
- Fee for service
- Payment
- Balance due
- Provider signature

ICD-9-CM and ICD-10-CM

ICD-9-CM stands for the "International Classification of Diseases, Clinical Modifications, 9th edition." The *ICD-9-CM* is the manual that contains a listing of the diagnoses and their assigned numerical codes. The ICD-9-CM codes are used when submitting claims to a third-party payer. Two critical notes:

- First, it is important to obtain a correct diagnosis code(s) from the patient's physician. RDs cannot determine the medical diagnosis; this is *not* in the RD's scope of practice.
- Second, if the physician provides the primary diagnosis and diagnosis codes for co-morbidity, some health providers may receive increased coverage.

ICD-9-CM codes are periodically revised. CMS has designated October 1, 2013, as the implementation date for the 10th revision of the International Classification of Diseases, Clinical Modification (ICD-10-CM) (27). The ICD-10 codes are very different from the ICD-9 codes (see Table 8.2) (28,29). Always be sure you are using the most updated codes. You can purchase an ICD manual from the American Medical Association (http://www.ama-assn.org), an online bookstore, or a local bookstore. There are also resources on the Internet where you can obtain ICD codes.

Table 8.2 ICD-9-CM and ICD-10-CM Codes Commonly Used by Registered Dietitians[a]

Diagnosis	*ICD-9-CM*	*ICD-10-CM*
Abnormal weight gain	783.1	R63.5
Anemia, unspecified	285.9	D64.9
Anorexia nervosa	307.1	F50.0
Arteriosclerotic heart disorder (ASHD)	414.0	I25.10
Asthma, unspecified	493.9	J45.909
Bowel, irritable bowel syndrome	564.1	K58.9
Bulimia	307.51	F50.2
Celiac disease	579.0	K90.0
Cholecystitis, unspecified	575.10	K81.9
Chronic kidney disease, unspecified	585.9	N18.9
Cleft palate with cleft lip, unspecified	749.20	Q37.9
Congestive heart failure, unspecified	428.0	I50.9
Constipation	564.0	K59.00
Crohn's disease	555.9	K50.90
Cystic fibrosis with pulmonary manifestations	277.02	E84.0
Degenerative disc disease	722.6	M51.9
Degenerative joint disease	715.90	M19.90
Diabetes, gestational	648.8	099.810
Diabetes, type 1	250.01	E10.9
Diabetes, type 2	250.00	E11.9
Diabetes with pregnancy	648.00	O24.319
Diabetic nephropathy	250.4	E11.21
Diarrhea	787.91	R19.7
Diverticulitis	562.11	K57.80
Diverticulosis	562.10	K57.30
Dysphagia	787.20	R13.10
Eating disorder, unspecified	307.50	F50.9
Excess weight gain, pregnancy	646.1	O12.00
Failure to thrive, child	783.41	R62.51
Food allergy, dermatitis	693.1	L27.2
Gastritis	535.4	K29.60
Gastroenteritis	558.9	K52.8
Gastro-esophageal reflux	530.81	K21.9
Gout	274.9	M10.9
Human immunodeficiency virus disease (HIV)	042	B20
Hyperlipidemia	272.2	E78.2

(continued)

Table 8.2 *(continued)*

Diagnosis	*ICD-9-CM*	*ICD-10-CM*
Hypertension, essential	401.9	I10
Hyperthyroidism	242.9	E05.90
Hypoglycemia	251.2	E16.2
Hypothyroidism	244.9	E03.9
Impaired fasting glucose	790.21	R73.01
Insufficient weight gain, pregnancy	646.8	O26.819
Irritable bowel syndrome	564.1	K58.9
Lactose intolerance	271.3	E74.39
Loss of weight	783.21	R63.4
Malnutrition	263.9	E46
Menopausal syndrome	627.2	N95.11
Myocardial infarction	412	I25.2
Obesity	278.00	E66.9
Obesity, morbid	278.01	E66.01
Osteopenia	733.90	M89.9
Osteoporosis	733.00	M81.8
Overweight	278.02	E66.3
Parkinsonism	332.0	G20
Peptic ulcer disease	533.70	K27.7
PKU	270.1	E70.0
Postgastrectomy syndrome	564.2	K91.1
Pre-diabetes	790.29	R73.09
Pregnant state incidental	V22.2	Z33.1
Renal disease	593.9	N28.9
Sleep apnea, unspecified	780.57	G47.30
Ulcerative colitis	556.9	K51.90
Underweight	783.22	R63.6
Vitamin deficiency	269.2	E56.9

[a]Always consult the most up-to-date International Classification of Diseases to confirm the accuracy of all codes. ICD manuals can be purchased from the American Medical Association (http://www.ama-assn.org); codes are also published on some Web sites.

Source: Data are from references 28 and 29.

CPT Codes

CPT, or Current Procedural Terminology, Codes are the codes used to describe office procedural codes. The 2009 CPT manual contains specific codes for MNT counseling by RDs (Box 8.6) (30). The MNT codes are time based. Individual codes are based on 15-minute units, and group codes on 30-minute units. They can be billed in multiple units. Keep track of the amount of time you are with the patient to bill accurately. For example, if the initial MNT visit is 60 minutes, four units are billed.

Box 8.6 Medical Nutrition Therapy (MNT) Codes

- 97802: MNT, initial assessment and intervention, individual, face-to-face with the patient, each 15 minutes.
- 97803: Reassessment and intervention, individual, face-to-face with the patient, each 15 minutes.
- 97804: Group (2 or more individuals), each 30 minutes.

CMS requires the use of two new MNT codes for billing additional hours of MNT. A Medicare beneficiary can receive MNT beyond the three hours of initial episode of care in the first calendar year and beyond two hours of follow-up episode of care in each subsequent calendar year when the physician determines there is a change in diagnosis or medical condition that makes a change in diet necessary. This requires a new referral from the physician.

- G0270: MNT reassessment and subsequent intervention(s) following second referral in same year for change in diagnosis, medical condition, or treatment regimen (including additional hours needed for renal disease), individual, face-to-face with the patient, each 15 minutes.
- G0271: MNT reassessment and subsequent intervention(s) following second referral in same year for change in diagnosis, medical condition, or treatment regimen (including additional hours needed for renal disease) group (2 or more individuals), each 30 minutes.

Source: Data are from reference 30. Current procedural terminology (CPT) codes, descriptions, and material only are copyright ©2009 American Medical Association. All Rights Reserved.

Accounting and Reimbursement Issues

Be sure to set up a system to record your account receivables. Whether you accept third-party payments or not, you need to track outstanding balances. As noted earlier in this chapter, you should get into the habit of having patients pay you after their visits. This minimizes the amount of billing and paperwork you need to perform for self-pay patients and for co-payments or deductibles with insurance patients.

Tracking claims you submit to third-party payers is more involved. You will have more paperwork. Develop a system or routine that makes the task easier. Box 8.7 provides criteria to include when setting up a form to track monies owed you, both by self-pay patients and insurance. You can monitor by date of service or by third-party payers or whatever works best for you. Create a form on a spreadsheet or a table on your word processing program.

Box 8.7 Information to Include to Track Payments

- Date of service
- Patient Name (as it appears on the insurance card)
- Patient date of birth
- Third-party payer or self-pay
- Patient identification number for third-party payer
- Referral number, if required
- CPT code and number of units
- ICD-9-CM (or ICD-10-CM) Codes
- Fee for service rendered
- Co-payment or other payments made, including the date
- Date(s) billed to patient and/or third-party payer
- Communications from third-party payers

After completing and submitting the CMS 1500, follow up on every claim you submit. You will receive an explanation of benefits (EOB) from private insurers and an explanation of Medicare benefits (EOMB) from Medicare in response to your claim. If you do not receive a response to your claim submission within 45 days, resubmit the claim. Remember there is a shorter time limit on claims submission with private insurance companies than with Medicare.

Review the EOB or EOMB. Determine whether the claim was paid and how much. If the claim was denied, find out why. You may simply need to resubmit the claim after correcting any errors or providing additional information requested. If you do not understand why the claim was denied, pursue it. Do not accept *no* as the answer if you believe the claim should have been paid. Contact the third-party payer for an explanation. You can also enlist the assistance of the patient to help get the claim paid. Teach patients to advocate for themselves.

Professional Example: One RD's Reimbursement Policies

Rebecca Bitzer, MS, RD, the owner of Rebecca Bitzer, MS, RD, and Associates, has a large nutrition practice with offices in Greenbelt and Annapolis, Maryland. In private practice for 22 years, Rebecca employees six RDs and is a provider for numerous insurance companies, including Medicare. Therefore, most of her practice's patients pay only a co-pay to receive MNT.

Many of Rebecca's referrals come from physicians' offices that prefer working with RDs who participate with third-party payers. Initially, Rebecca performed all the business and insurance tasks manually, but she has incorporated technology as her business has grown. This has allowed the practice to become automated and streamlined.

Rebecca uses a billing and scheduling software package to improve office efficiency and workflow. Once data are entered on a patient, a custom template module automatically fills in the patient's information, bills the patient's insurance, and generates letters to referring physicians. This software setup also can easily and quickly generate reports for Rebecca to evaluate her business. She can determine the amount each insurance company paid, the number of patients seen, and the amount billed and collected each day, week, and month.

Before a patient is seen at Rebecca's practice, insurance is verified to establish the patient's specific coverage, including co-pay responsibility. At the time of the appointment, the patient completes a patient registration form (Figure 8.6). This form includes the patient's agreement to bill the insurance company and the office's policies.

A copy is made of the front and back of the patient's insurance cards. Each RD tracks the amount of time spent with a patient as the CPT codes for MNT are time based. A claim for reimbursement is filed electronically with the insurance company based on the CPT and ICD codes.

After the claim is submitted, Rebecca's office tracks it for payment. When claims are not paid, they are investigated to determine the reason.

Private Practice Business Decisions: A Summary

Before you start a private practice, you have many business decisions to make. If making all these decisions seems overwhelming, consider seeking the advice of professionals, such as accountants, business advisers, or other RDs. Some private practitioners are available to mentor entrepreneurs on a consulting basis. Remember, they too must be paid for their professional services. Budget accordingly, and seek professional advice when necessary (see Chapter 2 for more on selecting advisers). Additionally, keep the following points in mind:

- It is imperative to set office policies before you see patients. You must have policies in place for billing, collecting past-due accounts, returned

7219 D Hanover Pkwy.
Greenbelt, MD 20770
Tel (301) 474-2499
Fax (301) 474-5943
www.rbitzer.com

The Eating & Exercise Experts

PATIENT REGISTRATION

(Please print clearly)

Patient Name: First Middle Last			Home Phone Number:	
Home Address: Apt. No.	City:		State	Zip Code:
Occupation:	Marital Status	Date of Birth	Age:	Gender:
E-mail address:	Cell Phone:			
Employer:	Address:	Work Phone Number:		
Spouse (or parent) name:				
Spouse (or parent) employer:		Work Phone Number:		
Family Physician:	Address:	Phone:		
Referred By:	Address:	Phone:		

BILLING AND INSURANCE INFORMATION

PRIMARY INSURANCE				
	Insurance Company Name:		ID or Policy Number:	Group / Code
	Subscriber's Name:		Date Effective:	
	Subscriber's Date of Birth:	Sex:	Home Phone Number:	Relationship to Patient:

Do you have any other Insurance? Yes No (If yes, please specify)

A message: ☐ **can** ☐ **can not be left on my home phone.** (Please check a box.)

PRIVACY CONSENT

Rebecca Bitzer MS RD & Associates (RBA) requires your consent to use and disclose your protected health information to carry out treatment, payment and healthcare operations. If you would like a more detailed description of such uses and disclosures please refer to our Notice of Privacy Practices. You have the right to review our Notice of Privacy Practices before signing this Consent. The terms of our Notice of Privacy Practices of RBA may change from time to time. You can get a copy of our revised Notice of Privacy Practices by contacting our office at 301-474-2499. We will also post a copy of our current Notice of Privacy Practices in our office.

You have the right to revoke this consent in writing and the revocation will be effective except to the extent RBA has acted in reliance on your consent.

I have had an opportunity to discuss with the Registered Dietitian and/or with other office personnel, the nature and purpose of medical nutrition therapy. I understand the results are not guaranteed. I give RBA permission to send a summary note to my physician or referring doctor of my consultation here.

By signing below, you hereby consent to our use of your protected health information for treatment, payment and health care operations and acknowledge receipt of a copy of this Consent if requested.

Printed Name: ______________________________

Signature: ______________________________ **Date:** ______________

copyright 2008 Page 1 of 2 Final Registration Form

Figure 8.6 Sample registration form. Reprinted with permission from Rebecca Bitzer, MS, RD, and Associates. *(continued)*

POLICIES

Thank you for choosing Rebecca Bitzer MS, RD & Associates (RBA) as your nutrition specialist. The following rules will help facilitate a positive working relationship.

1. I hereby authorize RBA to apply for benefits on my behalf for covered services rendered. I certify that all information given is correct, and authorize the release of all information, including medical information, for this or related claims.

2. I understand RBA may bill me for services rendered upon denial of my insurance company/ Medicare—despite prior approval. I agree to be fully and personally responsible for payment.

Policies to Know:

- It is your responsibility to obtain the proper referral prior to your visit and bring it with you. If a referral is faxed, please call to verify that it was received. Please do not ask us to get your referral. **If your insurance requires a referral, you will not be seen by a dietitian without a referral unless you self-pay the fee for the entire visit ($XXX for initial visit, $XXX for follow-up appointment) upfront.** We will not submit this date of service to insurance; therefore, no refund will be given.

- Co-pays are due at the beginning of the appointment. **We do not bill for co-pays.**

- We do not submit claims to secondary insurances. If you desire to submit your receipt to your secondary insurance, we will provide a superbill for the services rendered.

- We require **24 hour notice** to cancel and/or change appointments or a **$XX fee** will be issued.

- There is a **$XX** fee for any returned checks. **All payments for a returned check and further payments will be due in cash or money order only.**

- If your account is 90 days past due, it will be sent to a collection agency. A **percentage-based collections fee** will be issued.

3. All clients need to handle any bills in a timely fashion. You will NOT be seen by your Dietitian if you have an outstanding balance.

4. We allow 45 days for your insurance company to make payment to us. Sometimes insurance companies request more information before they make a payment; please respond promptly to your insurance company or RBA with requests for further information. If you fail to respond, you will be billed and expected to pay promptly.

5. Each insurance has different guidelines as to what diagnoses are covered. We strive to stay current with all insurance coverage guidelines, but we cannot guarantee any coverage.

Thank you for your cooperation!

I have read, understand, received a copy (if requested) and agree to these policies.

Signature:______________________________________ **Date:**________________

 Page 2 of 2 Final Registration Form

Figure 8.6 *(continued)*

checks, cancellations, and no-show appointments. All patients should be informed of your policies when they schedule their first appointment and in writing at the time of their first visit.

- When setting fees, factor in your fixed and variable expenses and your desired salary, and investigate what patients are willing to pay.
- Some RDs are strictly fee for service. They inform the patient that payment is due at the time of their visit. The patient files an insurance claim for self-reimbursement. Other RDs are reimbursed for MNT by private insurance plans, complementary and alternative medicine networks, Medicare, and Medicaid.
- The RD's options for involvement in enrollment in the Medicare MNT benefit include enrolling to become a provider, choosing not to enroll, or opting out.
- The RD should use a superbill if method of payment is fee for service. If the RD is filing insurance claims, a CMS 1500 form must be used. Up-to-date ICD and CPT codes are required for successful claims processing.

References

1. Strauss SD. *The Small Business Bible: Everything You Need to Know to Succeed in Your Small Business*. Hoboken, NJ: John Wiley & Sons; 2008:217.
2. Centers for Medicare & Medicaid Services. Charges for Missed Appointments. Transmittal 1279. Pub 100-04 Medicare Claims Processing. June 29, 2007. http://www.cms.hhs.gov/Transmittals/Downloads/R1279CP.pdf. Accessed June 12, 2009.
3. Myers EF, Michael P, Duester KC. Tips for contract negotiations and establishing MNT rates. *J Am Diet Assoc.* 2001;101:624–626.
4. Federal Trade Commission. Dealings with Competitors: Price Fixing. *FTC Guide to the Antitrust Laws*. July 8, 2008. http://www.ftc.gov/bc/antitrust/price_fixing.shtm. Accessed January 21, 2010.
5. American Dietetic Association. Legal analysis: the fine line of antitrust. *Medicare MNT Provider: Part B News for Registered Dietitians*. 2010;8(10):2.
6. American Medical Association. CPT® Process—How a Code Becomes a Code. http://www.ama-assn.org/ama/no-index/physician-resources/3882.shtml. Accessed January 21, 2010.
7. US Department of Labor. Definitions of Health Terms. www.bls.gov/ncs/ebs/sp/healthterms.pdf. Accessed August 14, 2009.
8. American Dietetic Association. Glossary of Terms. http://www.eatright.org/Members/content.aspx?id=7200. Accessed April 18, 2010.
9. CareFirst BlueCross BlueShield of Maryland. Options Discount Program. Nutrition Counseling. http://www.carefirst.com/providers/html/NutritionalCounseling.html. Accessed July 13, 2009.
10. American Dietetic Association. RD Considerations for Participating in the Medicare MNT. http://www.eatright.org/Members/content.aspx?id=7236. Accessed April 18, 2010.
11. Infante MC, Michael P, Prichett E. Opting out of Medicare: a serious business decision. *J Am Diet Assoc.* 2002;102:1061–1062.

12. Centers for Medicare & Medicaid Services. Private Contracting/Opting out of Medicare. Transmittal 92. CMS Pub 100-02 Medicare Benefit Policy. June 27, 2008. http://www.cms.hhs.gov/Transmittals/Downloads/R92BP.pdf. Accessed January 21, 2010.
13. Centers for Medicare & Medicaid Services. Private Contracting—Definition of Physician/Practitioner. Transmittal 62. CMS Pub 100-02 Medicare Benefit Policy. June 27, 2008. http://www.cms.hhs.gov/Transmittals/downloads/R62BP.pdf. Accessed January 21, 2010.
14. Centers for Medicare & Medicaid Services. Medicaid home page. http://www.cms.hhs.gov/home/medicaid.asp. Accessed July 18, 2009.
15. Connelly J. Doctors are opting out of Medicare. *New York Times*. April 1, 2009. http://www.nytimes.com/2009/04/02/business/retirementspecial/02health.html. Accessed July 13, 2009.
16. American Dietetic Association. Streamlining the payment process—how a professional biller for Medicare MNT can benefit your practice. *Medicare MNT Provider Newsletter.* 2006;4(11):1–3.
17. Finding the practice model that fits your business needs. *Medicare MNT Provider Newsletter*. 2004;2(7):1–3.
18. American Dietetic Association. Private Insurance MNT Coverage Throughout the US. http://www.eatright.org/Members/content.aspx?id=7784. Accessed January 23, 2010.
19. Centers for Medicare & Medicaid Services. CMS 855I Medicare Enrollment Application—Physicians and Non-Physician Practitioners. Revision date February 1, 2008. http://www.cms.hhs.gov/CMSForms/CMSForms/itemdetail.asp?filterType=dual,%20keyword&filterValue=855i&filterByDID=0&sortByDID=1&sortOrder=ascending&itemID=CMS019477&intNumPerPage=10. Accessed July 17, 2009.
20. Centers for Medicare & Medicaid Services. Provider Enrollment, Chain and Ownership System (PECOS). https://pecos.cms.hhs.gov/pecos/login.do. Accessed July 23, 2009.
21. TrailBlazer Health Enterprises, LLC. Part B: Getting Started. How to Complete the Paper CMS-855I Enrollment Application for Solo Providers. http://www.trailblazerhealth.com/Provider%20Enrollment/PartBGettingStarted.aspx?DomainID=1. Accessed July 23, 2009.
22. Centers for Medicare & Medicaid Services. Contacts: Contact Your MAC/Carrier. http://www.cms.hhs.gov/center/provider.asp. Accessed January 24, 2010.
23. Centers for Medicare & Medicaid Services. Medical Nutrition Therapy Services—Overview. http://www.cms.hhs.gov/MedicalNutritionTherapy. Accessed July 30, 2009.
24. Centers for Medicare & Medicaid Services. Revised ABN CMS-R-131 Form and Instruction. http://www.cms.hhs.gov/BNI/02_ABN.asp. Accessed July 30, 2009.
25. Centers for Medicare & Medicaid Services. CMS 1500. Health Insurance Claim Form. http://www.cms.hhs.gov/CMSForms/CMSForms/itemdetail.asp?filterType=dual,%20keyword&filterValue=cms%201500&filterByDID=0&sortByDID=1&sortOrder=ascending&itemID=CMS1188854&intNumPerPage=10. Accessed July 18, 2009.
26. American Dietetic Association. Billing Resources. http://www.eatright.org/Members/content.aspx?id=7804. Accessed April 18, 2010.
27. Centers for Medicare & Medicaid Services. ICD-10 Statute/Regulations. Program Instructions. http://www.cms.hhs.gov/ICD10/04_Statute_Regulations_Program_Instructions.asp#TopOfPage. Accessed January 24, 2010.
28. ICD9.Data.com Web site. Free 2010 Medical Coding Data. 2010 ICD-9-CM Volume 1. http://www.icd9data.com/ Accessed January 24, 2010.
29. EcodingNow Web site. ICD-9-CM and ICD-10-CM Search Results—BETA. http://www.ecodingnow.com/OnlineCodes/codes.html. Accessed January 25, 2010.

30. Centers for Medicare & Medicaid Services. Clarification Regarding Non-physician Practitioners Billing on Behalf of a Diabetes Outpatient Self-Management Training Services (DSMT) Program and the Common Working File Edits for DSMT & Medical Nutrition Therapy (MNT). Transmittal AB-02-151. October 25, 2002. http://www.cms.hhs.gov/Transmittals/downloads/AB02151.pdf. Accessed January 24, 2010.

Chapter 9

It's All About You: How to Market Your Private Practice

While details for your private practice such as your office location and phone number are coming together, you need to begin working on your marketing plan. Your marketing plan is the way you will bring new clients or patients into your practice. A good plan will build your practice and be memorable on some level (1). You want people to remember you and what you do. Be creative and unique, but not kooky. Don't sacrifice your professionalism or ethics—they can be difficult to gain back once you have sacrificed them.

Marketing plans change. As your business develops and grows, you must regularly revisit the effectiveness of your plan. From time to time, you will revise and modify it to ensure that it is bringing in new business.

There are numerous ways to market your business. Read and even re-read Chapter 5. That chapter discusses in detail valuable information about tools and methods to consider in marketing a nutrition business, which certainly applies to your private practice. When reviewing Chapter 5, consider the approaches that can work best for you.

All registered dietitians (RDs) in private practice will not have the same marketing plan. Your plan will be specific for you. Use a combination of marketing efforts. Don't simply try one tool or method and wait to see if your phone rings. Use different approaches to find clients or patients. Ask new clients how they came to you. Track the information on a spreadsheet to determine what is working and not working. Modify or discontinue those marketing efforts that are ineffective. Almost everything you do that is related to your practice should promote your business.

This chapter focuses on specific marketing techniques for building a successful private practice. There are three components to consider when marketing: you, your referral sources, and your clients.

Promoting Yourself First

In private practice, you are the practice! When you market your business, you are ultimately marketing yourself. In marketing yourself, you are on 24/7. The way you dress, the way you speak, and the image you project in your professional and personal life send a message about you and your practice (2,3). Even when you shop for food or eat out you are promoting yourself. People who know you are an RD will watch your food selections just a little closer. If you advocate physical activity in your counseling, you should set an example by exercising. Those interested in seeing you professionally will want to know whether you practice what you preach. Keep in mind that your lifestyle is a form of marketing.

How will you pitch your practice? What will you say when someone asks you what you do? Your response needs to be quick, interesting, and leave an impression. Don't be long-winded or boring. Work on your pitch. Practice it so you are prepared when asked (1). Chapter 5 can help with this.

A phone call to your office is often someone's first contact with your practice. What is the caller's experience when calling your office? Will he or she speak with a person or hear an answering machine message? Is the voice representing your office businesslike and harried, or is it friendly yet professional? Ask friends or family members for feedback about their experiences when calling your office. You may obtain valuable suggestions.

Prospective patients and referral sources call your practice because they are interested. You want to capture that interest. Make the telephone exchange as pleasant and welcoming as possible. This can be your first (and possibly only) chance to make the "sell." When you are unavailable and a caller leaves a voice message, call back by the end of the day or within 24 hours.

You may also receive e-mails inquiring about your practice or to schedule an appointment. Check your e-mail frequently throughout the day. Reply to e-mail in a timely fashion. The amount of time it takes you to respond to phone calls or e-mails may make or break someone's decision to use your services. Delays can be lost business.

Other examples of promoting you and your practice include your business cards, your Web site, brochures, and advertisements. Always carry your business cards with you; you may find opportunities to distribute them at social or sporting events, and even while shopping. Store your business cards in a variety of places so you are always prepared. You will be pleasantly surprised how people will request your card once they learn what you do.

Direct people to your Web site. Your Web site describes you and the services you provide. Display your Web site address on your business card, letterhead, advertisement, and anywhere you can list it.

Develop a brochure. Distribute your brochures to other health care providers, health clubs, and even health food stores. Think of untapped places to leave your brochures to find your target market.

Advertising will cost you money. Make sure your ads will be worth the money you spend. Local newspapers and yellow pages are typical places you may advertise. Consider placing a display ad or even an image of your business card in newsletters, directories for schools and places of worship, or any other publication in which you can promote your practice.

Consider donating your services to market your practice. For example, Kathleen Searles, MS, RD, offered a nutrition counseling session or kitchen makeover at a fund-raising auction to a population she wanted to reach. There are limitless ways to let others know about your practice. Think of unusual or unique ways to accomplish this.

What Will You Call Yourself? The Value of the RD Credential

You are a registered dietitian! This credential indicates that you have met the academic and professional requirements to qualify as an RD (4). Some RDs use other titles, such as nutritionist, nutritionist therapist, or nutrition consultant. However, registered dietitian is the title sanctioned by the American Dietetic Association (ADA) and it encompasses all the different aspects of the field in which an RD can function, including private practice (5).

As an RD in private practice when you market yourself, you are marketing the whole profession. You also have the support of the American Dietetic Association. The ADA's Web site offers a feature called Find a Registered Dietitian, which allows site visitors to find an RD in their local area. A listing in this directory promotes you as an RD in private practice to both referral sources and potential patients.

What Else Do You Call Yourself? The Value of Licenses and Credentials

Are you a licensed or certified dietitian? You want to identify yourself as such. Your state licensure or certification sets you apart from those not practicing within the law for your state. At the end of your name, include the approved abbreviation that indicates you are qualified to provide medical nutrition therapy (MNT) within your state. In some instances, you may find it advantageous to include in your title the phrase "licensed dietitian."

Other credentials can market you and add credibility. If you have additional credentials, such as Certified Specialist in Sports Dietetics (CSSD) from the ADA or a Certified Diabetes Educator (CDE), the initials for the credential after your name. To capitalize on your credential further, especially if it's related to your area of expertise, indicate your title—such as "Registered Dietitian and Specialist in Sports Dietetics" or "Registered Dietitian and Certified Diabetes Educator"—on your business card, advertisements, even your business checking account. A word to the wise—use those credentials that will help market you. Just adding letters to the end of your name may look like "alphabet soup" and not be meaningful to clients.

Promoting Your Previous Experience

Your prior work experience can assist in promoting your practice. A description about you and your previous experience in your area of specialty or expertise can be a selling point on your Web site or brochure. Only mention relevant work experience. For example, if you plan to limit your practice to pregnant women and you worked at the Special Supplemental Nutrition Program for Women, Infants, and Children (WIC), certainly share this information.

Will You Be a Generalist or a Specialist?

To market your services, first determine whether you will work as a generalist or a specialist (6). A generalist practice will allow you to see a wide range of clients. Generalists need to be current and informed about all that is trendy and prepared for change. Generalists will rarely find their work stale or boring.

As a specialist, you will provide services in an area about which you feel passionate and where you have a great deal of knowledge. Your specialty may be a particular disease entity, an area of interest, an age group, or population. It can separate you from your competition. However, you may need to work extremely hard to stay current in areas outside your specialty.

RDs question whether a general practice or a specialized practice is right for them. The answer is, "It depends." Over time, your practice may evolve. Although you might know the answer from the start, it is likely that the answer will emerge as you begin to practice. For further guidance on this issue, see Box 9.1 (6).

For many reasons, you may need to see all types of patients when you first start your private practice. Try working with many populations. You may find that you have a knack for working with an aging population or you get frustrated and annoyed when working with children. As your practice develops, what you love will emerge, and it will most likely be what you are good at.

Marketing is easier when you have a niche. Your niche identifies something different about you and can help you define your target market (7). When developing a niche, think of where and how you can be connected with these possible clients. A practice limited to sports nutrition for women could market to health clubs (especially those exclusively for women), physical therapists, massage therapists, gynecologists, and orthopedists. Send letters to these potential referral sources introducing you and the services you provide, and include business cards and brochures. Write articles for a local newspaper's sports page and other health and sports publications, leave brochures at

Box 9.1 Generalist vs. Specialist Practice: Weighing the Pros and Cons

Specialist Practice

A specialized practice makes good sense if you have a passion for a specific area of nutrition or if you would like to offer one particular type of service or medical nutrition therapy (MNT) to your clients.

Pros

- If you specialize in one or two areas you are passionate about, you can then focus on working with clients within your realm of interest.
- You have a greater depth of information in a given area than the vast majority of other registered dietitians.
- You have likely gathered abundant resources within your specialty, which will simplify staying abreast of changes in your area.
- If you live in a market with many other food and nutrition professionals, a specialty practice will set you apart.
- Specialists can usually charge more than generalists.
- Specialists draw from a larger geographic area, as people will travel a greater distance to see a specialist.
- If you are the only specialist in your area of interest in your community, competition will be minimized.

Cons

- There may not be a great enough need for your area of practice to create full-time employment.
- Your knowledge in other areas of nutrition can become outdated very quickly (for example, if your food allergy client has diabetes and you have not kept up with the latest in diabetes management, you would need to refer him elsewhere).
- It can be challenging to find continuing professional education opportunities that pertain to your area of interest and fulfill your Professional Development Portfolio.
- Membership in specialty professional organizations (for example, Food Allergy Network, American Academy of Allergy, or the American Association of Diabetes Educators) may be expensive.
- If other local practitioners specialize in your area, competition will exist. Do a SWOT analysis (Strengths, Weaknesses, Opportunities, and Threats) for you and your competitors.

Generalist Practice

If you don't have a specific area of interest or you enjoy the challenge of keeping current with a broader base of nutrition specialties, creating a more flexible practice may better suit your needs. However, are you confident that you have the energy and expertise to do everything, including MNT and more?

(continued)

Box 9.1 *(continued)*

Pros

- You can consistently use and hone a broad range of skills, including coaching, counseling, business, fitness, marketing, public speaking, teaching, and writing.
- You can keep your approach fresh by dabbling in many different areas.
- Your business can constantly change and evolve as new opportunities arise or needs surface.
- Having a wide area of expertise gives you access to a broader base of clients, which is important in starting a business.
- Frequent new challenges are intellectually stimulating.

Cons

- You may find it challenging to keep current with nutrition updates in many different specialty areas.
- If you have only traditional experience, you may need additional training.
- Even if you have previous experience, you may still need to fine-tune skills.
- There may be several RDs in flexible practice in your area, which increases competition. Do a SWOT analysis (Strengths, Weaknesses, Opportunities, and Threats) for you and your competitors.

Source: Indorato D. Specialized or general practice? In: *Nutrition Entrepreneurs Toolkit 2009.* Chicago, IL: American Dietetic Association Nutrition Entrepreneurs; 2010. Adapted with permission from American Dietetic Association Nutrition Entrepreneurs. http://www.nedpg.org.

sporting goods stores, or make a presentation at a local Road Runners club meeting.

Getting Referrals

A steady flow of referrals from a variety of sources can keep your practice busy. Look for referrals from people you already know, and invest time and resources in building new contacts.

Referrals from Your Existing Network

As you begin your search for possible referral sources, start with those who know you and the quality of your work. For example, reach out to physicians, physicians' assistants, nurse practitioners, mental health specialists, and other health care professionals from prior work settings. These potential referrals are easy to tap. Let them know you are in private practice and ready to help their clients/patients. They may even refer your services to their colleagues. Think of it as word of mouth among professionals.

Referrals from Local Health Care Providers

Go through the phone book or do an online search to develop a list of appropriate health care professionals near your office and inform them of your practice. As they will not be familiar with you or the quality of your counseling, it may take some time for them to feel to comfortable referring clients to you. They may need to hear about you from a variety of sources. This can even include satisfied clients.

There are no absolutes about how to market to health care professionals. You can begin by sending a letter of introduction, including a description of your credentials, work experience, and practice, and how your services will benefit their patients and their practice. You may want to include your curriculum vitae or resume. In the letter, offer to meet the health care professional or their office manager. Include some business cards and brochures. Follow up with a phone call.

Referrals from Third-Party Payers

When you are a provider, third-party payers can be another source of referrals. Your practice information will be listed as an in-network provider. To limit out-of-pocket expenses, people with insurance will most likely seek the services of an RD who accepts their insurance.

Referrals from Other RDs

Learn about colleagues in your area. Remember, fellows RDs in private practice are your colleagues and friends, not your foes. Learn how these RDs, even those in the same town, can be assets if you handle the situation appropriately. Their target market might be a different population, or you may refer patients to each other when one practice accepts a type of third-party payment and the other does not. When you are on vacation, they can cover for you, and vice versa. Build bridges, don't burn them. Working together can have its rewards.

Other Referral Sources

Think creatively to identify other referral sources. For example, Christine M. Palumbo, MBA, RD, has cultivated image consultants as a referral source. Image consultants often have relationships with large corporations that wish to groom up-and-coming professionals for their next career advancement. They are often in the position to refer clients to RDs for weight loss and general improvement in eating. Milton Stokes, MPH, RD, CDN, has found having coffee or tea with psychotherapists to be an effective way to increase referrals in his practice specializing in eating disorders. Wedding planners can refer brides and/or grooms who wish to lose weight for their big day.

Maintaining Referral Sources

Once you have established a referral source, you want to keep it and maintain it. To expedite the process for busy medical offices, provide them a preprinted pad with tear-off pages to complete when referring patients.

Acknowledge your gratitude for the referral. A simple thank-you note for a referral, without mentioning the patient's name, will suffice. To a referring physician, a follow-up letter about a patient is an excellent form of ongoing marketing (see Figure 9.1). In this letter, let the referring physician know the nutrition services provided to his or her patients and include business cards and a flyer or a brochure, if possible. (It is important to note that you must have your patients sign a release to allow you to send a follow-up letter. Refer to Chapter 7 for more information on client privacy issues.)

Another way to perpetuate referrals is to send a holiday gift or other gift any time of the year to those who have provided referrals in the past. Choose gifts that are appropriate and are in theme with your practice. A subscription for a health or cooking magazine is a gift that lasts all year and is an ongoing reminder of you.

Marketing Directly to Patients and Clients

In addition to referrals, you will want to market directly to potential patients and clients. Start by thinking about who will be your clients or patients. Are they a particular age group or sex, or do they have a specific disease? Once you have identified the population you want to concentrate on, learn everything you can about these potential patients or clients. Understanding all aspects of your interested population will assist you in marketing to them. What are the demographics of this group? What are their socioeconomic backgrounds? Where do they go for medical services? For example, if you want to specialize in pediatrics, your marketing plan will be more directed to parents but with an appeal to children, pediatricians, and family practitioners.

What will you call the people who receive your services: clients or patients? These terms can affect your marketing and signal to individuals whether you are the right nutrition professional for them. You may choose to use "clients" if your practice is wellness based or specializes in eating disorders. "Patients" is a preferable term for RDs who provide MNT.

People need to hear your name repeatedly from a variety of sources to believe you are reputable and they can trust you (1,7,8). Remember that before a prospective patient finally calls you for an appointment, he or she may find your listing in the yellow pages, look at your Web site, listen to your presentation at the local library, and hear about you from a neighbor.

Date:

Re: ______________________

Dear ______________________:

Thank you for allowing me the pleasure of seeing this patient for medical nutrition therapy. ______________________ came to see me concerning ______________________.

_______________ stands ___________ tall and weighs _____________ pounds, with a body mass index (BMI) of __________. His/her healthy weight range is __________ to __________, with a BMI of __________.

A complete nutrition assessment indicated to me that ____________________________

____

I reviewed this with _______________ and provided him/her with a written summary of these findings. Together we established goals for medical nutrition therapy.

A follow-up appointment has been scheduled in ___________ weeks time.

Thank you again for this kind referral.

Sincerely,

______________________________ , RD

Figure 9.1 Sample follow-up letter. Reprinted with permission from Faye Berger Mitchell, RD.

Clients/patients may go to online directories to find a nutrition professional. Listing with these directories can be helpful. Perform an Internet search to find these directories. Some are free, while others charge a fee annually or monthly for a listing. When paying a fee to list on a directory, make sure it is worth your investment. Inquire of colleagues or post on a dietetic practice group Listserv to learn about directories you are considering.

There is no limit to the amount of money you can spend to market your practice, especially to patients and clients. You can end up wasting valuable marketing dollars. A tip: to determine whether you are spending your money wisely on marketing, figure out how many people you would have to treat to pay for the cost of the advertising. Ask yourself whether the amount is realistic.

When you promote your practice, you may attract inappropriate clientele or unrealistic requests. Be prepared. Don't be surprised by a phone call asking you to mail a copy of your diet to lose weight. You may receive a random e-mail with a food record inquiring whether it is healthy or which supplements to purchase. While you want business, you do not want to give your professional services away for free! Use these situations to market your practice. Your conversation can be something like this: "It's difficult for me to determine what will best for you to do nutritionally without knowing anything about you. If you'd like, let's make an appointment for me to review you medical, nutrition and other information and for us to develop a plan specific for you." Of course, at times you want to give back to the community and provide your services at a reduced fee or free. However, you do not want to give away your professional services to everyone who asks. Be sure that you make the decision when you want to provide community service.

There are circumstances—such as when a physician refers individuals to you or they find you through their insurance—in which you may feel promotion of your practice directly to patients and clients may be unnecessary. Not so. Think big. The doctor and insurance company may present patients with choices of RDs. The patients may then check these names in the telephone book and on the Internet. If they find nothing about you but find information about the other recommended RDs, this will affect their decisions about which RD to see. Remember, the patient needs to learn about you from a variety of sources. This is why your marketing needs to be multifaceted.

There is no better publicity than a satisfied client or patient. Your patients are your best marketing tools. How you speak to and treat your clients will influence their willingness to say, "I have this great registered dietitian who I highly recommend."

It's All About You: A Summary

You will need to market your practice to have a practice. This will be an ongoing process. As your practice grows, you will need to continually update your marketing approach. Consider the following when marketing your practice:

- You are your practice. Promoting yourself will be promoting your practice.
- Be creative in finding ways to develop referrals for your business. Once you establish a relationship with a referral source, sustain it by sharing your appreciation.
- Prospective clients need to hear your name repeatedly from a variety of sources. Reach out to patients in multiple ways.
- Your best advertising is word of mouth.

References

1. Strauss S. *The Small Business Bible: Everything You Need to Know to Succeed in Your Small Business*. 2nd ed. Hoboken, NJ: John Wiley and Sons; 2008.
2. Stein K. Good or bad: what you see isn't always what you get. *J Am Diet Assoc*. 2006;106:1022–1024.
3. Peregrin T. Clothes call: your professional image can have a big impact on your career. *J Am Diet Assoc*. 2009;109:395–397.
4. American Dietetic Association. Frequently Asked Questions: What Are the Qualifications of a Registered Dietitian? http://www.eatright.org/Public/content.aspx?id=6713. Accessed April 18, 2010.
5. American Dietetic Association. Should ADA consider changing the title, Registered Dietitian, to something else? http://www.eatright.org/Members/content.aspx?id=10195&terms=january+2008+and+nebraska, Accessed April 18, 2010.
6. Indorato D. Specialized or general practice? In: *Nutrition Entrepreneurs Toolkit 2009*. Chicago, IL: American Dietetic Association Nutrition Entrepreneurs; 2010.
7. Tyson E, Schell J. *Small Business for Dummies*. New York, NY: John Wiley and Sons Publishing; 2008.
8. Lesonsky R. *Start Your Own Business*. Irvine, CA: Entrepreneur Media; 2007.

Chapter 10

Repeat Visits: Getting Your Patients to Return

Many private practitioners find that attracting patients is fairly easy, but keeping their business is more difficult. To generate follow-up sessions, which in business terms translate into repeat business, you may need to reconceive of your professional purpose, transitioning from the traditional role of nutrition educator to that of a nutrition therapist. This chapter explores the distinction between these two roles and offers guidance to help you sustain a successful nutrition practice.

From Educator to Counselor

Registered dietitians (RDs) employed in traditional settings, such as hospitals or outpatient clinics, typically have a difficult time envisioning how to counsel patients in a private-practice setting. Many RDs wonder: How do you structure the session? What do you do in follow-up sessions? How do you encourage patients to return?

One reason that RDs in traditional settings ask these questions is that they have been taught a medical model of patient care. This model is appropriate in the hospital and clinical settings where RDs have historically practiced (see Table 10.1) (1). The traditional medical model relies on short-term nutrition intervention. The RD generates goals for the patient, focusing on what the patient needs to learn. Typically, the RD needs to develop only a superficial relationship with the patient. In this model, nutrition counseling includes assessing the patient's status, planning necessary diet changes, and then providing information. Counseling, in this sense, is really educating (1–4).

Table 10.1 Medical Model vs. Nutrition Therapy Model

	Medical Model	*Nutrition Therapy Model*
Scope of intervention	Short-term intervention primarily of an educational nature	Long-term care
Patient-provider relationship	Minimal relationship	A significant relationship in and of itself is a key part of the therapeutic process
Type of treatment plan	Quickly determined, often standardized plan of action	A treatment plan that is highly individualized and evolves over time

Source: Data are from reference 1.

Generally, inpatient consultations are brief. A diet consult may be requested when the patient is about to be discharged from a hospital. The patient may be preoccupied with other issues at this time. The consult may take place in a setting that is not private, so it is unlikely that the patient can be completely candid. In an outpatient setting, you might have more time with the patient, but you still seize the opportunity to teach the patient instead of actual counseling, as you may never see the patient again. For the RD practicing in a clinical setting or an outpatient department, the nutrition therapist rarely emerges. Rather, the RD serves a useful but quite different function as a nutrition educator.

Thus, traditional nutrition counseling, by necessity, is very different from the nutrition therapy process that can be used in a private-practice setting. Nutrition therapy is a dynamic relationship between the RD and the patient and often between the RD and other health care providers. Although clinical nutrition principles are incorporated into the nutrition therapy process, the techniques used to impart the information and the pace at which information is shared are different. Some believe that nutrition therapy is the future of the profession as a whole. Writing in the *Journal of the American Dietetic Association* in 2002, Julie O'Sullivan Maillet predicted that "in 2017, much [will have] changed . . . the role of the clinical dietitian [will] become that of a nutrition therapist" (5).

Nutrition therapy is a client-centered approach that focuses on beliefs, emotions, and behaviors, particularly as they relate to food and eating. It results in the formation of a long-term relationship with your patients and with a psychotherapist, if one is involved. Treatment plans are highly individualized and evolve over time (3).

Nutrition therapy is a widely accepted approach in the eating disorders arena, where RDs have learned that simply educating a client about dietary changes does not mean that the client will be able to implement the changes. To see real change in individuals with eating disorders, you need to incorporate nutrition therapy and nutrition education skills. In fact, the nutrition therapy approach can be useful, even necessary, to your development as a skilled counselor working with *any* patient population (2). For example, this approach can be very useful in helping patients with diabetes make the necessary dietary changes to achieve blood glucose control.

Although some of your patients' goals will be accomplished merely by providing them with factual information, it is unlikely that you will be able to build a practice based on one-time nutrition education sessions. As your patients fail to make life-long changes, you will get frustrated and look for ways to help your patients become more successful. A nutrition-therapy approach will enable you to better help your patients. Your success will be measured by your clients' success. You will have more follow-up visits, and your satisfied clients will help you to build your practice.

Becoming a Nutrition Therapist

The transition from nutrition educator to nutrition therapist is a process that happens over time and through experience. This process takes training and practice.

Training and Education

Making the transition to a nutrition therapist requires learning basic counseling skills. Typically, RDs do not receive much training in counseling skills, and it is recommended that those who will be working with patients on an ongoing basis seek additional training (4). You can benefit from attending formal counseling courses and reading counseling books. Two of ADA's dietetic practice groups, Behavioral Health Nutrition (BHN) and Weight Management, offer counseling-skills workshops as part of their annual symposia or devote columns in their newsletters. Other resources are listed in Box 10.1 and Chapter 14.

Box 10.1 Resources for the Emerging Nutrition Therapist

- **Renfrew Center for Eating Disorders** (http://www.renfrewcenter.com): Publishes quarterly newsletter addressing counseling topics. Holds annual symposium.
- **MollyKellogg.com** (http://www.mollykellogg.com): Resource for supervision information and a monthly newsletter. Two publications: *Counseling Tips for Nutrition Therapists Volumes 1 and 2.*
- **Bulimia.com** (http://www.bulimia.com): A comprehensive listing of books, periodicals, and resources about treatment and prevention of eating disorders and other food issues.
- **Nourishing Connections** (http://www.nourishingconnections.com/moving_away_diets2.htm): Book and handouts based on the non-dieting approach.
- **Motivational Interviewing Web site** (http://www.motivationalinterview.org): Resources and information on motivational interviewing. General information about the approach, links, and training resources are provided.

Incorporating Nutrition Therapy Skills

There is no protocol for developing nutrition therapy skills when counseling patients. While formal education is often the first step, some RDs may not have the formal training yet they intuitively use these skills without realizing it. Other RDs who do not feel confident with the concept of nutrition therapy can gradually introduce these skills into their counseling style.

Effective Listening Skills

Our role as educators often preempts us from listening to our patients. We sometimes feel we don't have the time to listen. However, what clients actually want from the session is sometimes very different from what they need, and you need to listen to hear the difference. Being a good listener will require you to be flexible in your approach. What you think a patient may be ready to address in your session may very well not be what he or she is ready to do (6).

You may feel uncomfortable if there is silence in the room, but there will be times when your response should be silence. For example, during a nutrition therapy session a patient may tell you she does not cook much since her spouse died. She then becomes tearful. Your role is to sit with her and her sadness, not to jump in and try to fix it. You may also be surprised by what you learn from your patient when you allow silence to fill the room. As awkward as it may seem initially, silence will help provide your patient with time to divulge more information. This process may be very valuable to the patient's overall success.

A good listener should be able to paraphrase what a patient says. Referred to as "mirroring" or "reflective listening," this allows the patient to have an opportunity to review the topics discussed in the session and can help clarify any misunderstandings (7).

Empathy and Support

When your patients respond to questions, you need to assume a nonjudgmental stance. They may never have felt safe enough to realize how food is intertwined with the rest of their lives and talk openly about it. When patients realize that you are not there merely to provide the latest diet information, they may be more willing to share their feelings about the difficulty they face in making important and necessary diet changes. You can validate those feelings and be knowledgeable about how and when they can make any changes.

Care and Trust

Nutrition therapists must be caring and genuinely interested in helping their patients. These are attributes you cannot fake. Your patients must feel safe to talk freely about food and the issues around food. Listen to their concerns and respond in a caring manner. Refer to Box 10.2 for a list of the qualities patients seek in a nutrition therapist (1).

Box 10.2 Personal Traits of a Skilled Nutrition Therapist

People with eating disorders want a nutrition therapist with the following traits:
- Flexible
- Understands the client's fears about food and weight
- Will work at a pace the client can handle
- Caring and nonjudgmental
- Patient
- Has realistic expectations

Source: Data are from reference 1.

Learning Advanced Techniques and Building Networks

When you are first attempting to make the shift from educator to counselor, you may find it difficult, daunting, and unnatural. There are many strategies you can use to expand your work into the counseling arena, improve outcomes with your patients, and generate repeat visits.

Coursework

Consider expanding your studies. Take a psychology class that includes information about personality disorders, cognitive behavioral interventions, family systems theory, and different counseling styles. You can also take courses on counseling techniques.

Networking

Discuss your interests with professors, colleagues, friends, and others who can enhance your knowledge in counseling techniques related to your particular area of interest (such as eating disorders). Perhaps you can find a mentor who can aid you in this process.

Exploring the Benefits of Supervision

You might want to discuss your own relationship to food, weight, exercise, and body image with a therapist. This work will give you the opportunity to experience what a counselor-client relationship is like and discover what techniques, approaches, and counseling styles you prefer.

As stated in the American Dietetic Association Code of Ethics, "The dietetics practitioner assumes a life-long responsibility and accountability for personal competence in practice, consistent with accepted professional standards, continually striving to increase professional knowledge and skills and to apply them in practice" (8). To advance as a nutrition therapist, supervision may be necessary and beneficial.

Supervision is a concept widely used in the psychotherapy world. As RDs, we may be unfamiliar with it. On her Web site, Molly Kellogg, RD, defines "supervision" as follows (9):

> When one or a group of nutrition therapists contract with an experienced professional to help them advance their counseling skills. It includes such things as discussion of cases, exploration of the therapists' own issues that come up in client sessions, practice of new skills, advice on what to try next with a particular client, support for limit-setting, handling burnout, etc. The emphasis is on the *process* of counseling rather than on the content. It is assumed that participants have other sources of information on disease states, diet recommendations, etc.

Consider being supervised by a health professional you respect who is a skilled therapist or counselor. You can receive supervision from an experienced RD, a psychotherapist, or a psychiatrist. Look for a professional counselor with whom you connect well and who shares your philosophies. Another option is to form a mixed-peer supervision group. Consider including psychotherapists, psychiatrists, and nutrition therapists in the same group. This allows professionals from different disciplines to learn from one another while gaining further insight on how the team approach works.

Supervision is not mentoring. Mentors do not expect reimbursement, but when you engage in a professional supervision relationship with any health professional, you should expect to pay for that service.

Motivational Interviewing

Training in Motivational Interviewing (MI) skills can also improve your counseling skills. The Motivational Interviewing Web site defines MI as "a client-centered, directive method for enhancing intrinsic motivation to change by exploring and resolving ambivalence" (10). MI is a very effective counseling style in which the clinician collaborates with the client to help promote dietary behavioral change (11).

Respecting Professional Boundaries

As you move beyond the role of nutrition educator, you must be completely informed of ADA's Code of Ethics and Standards of Professional Practice (8,12). Behaviors play a role in how, what, why, and when we eat. Our work as RDs will always be grounded in food. To truly motivate a patient to change, the boundaries of nutrition therapy and psychotherapy will sometimes feel blurred. You should never assume that you are the psychotherapist . . . simply the nutrition therapist. You need to understand what your domain is and what should be referred to a psychotherapist. Generally, the goals in nutrition therapy are related to medical conditions, food behaviors, and possibly the patient's relationship with food and his or her body. Psychotherapy focuses more on mood, relationships, treating mental illness, and healing from trauma (13). If you are in a state that requires licensing, become familiar with the scope of practice. Always be knowledgeable of and respect the ADA Code of Ethics.

Either because of personal prejudices, a need to be confrontational, or misconceptions about mental health counseling, some RDs may hesitate to make referrals to mental health professionals. However, the ADA Code of Ethics requires that RDs know how and when to make appropriate referrals (8), and this will be necessary in your expanded role as a nutrition therapist.

To make good referrals, you need to know who is in your community. Keep your network up to date (see Chapter 5). Mental health professionals need to know about you, too. They need to know what you do and what to expect when they refer a patient to you. Networking allows you and others to supplement your respective practices.

Getting Patients to Return for Follow-Up

Many RDs who are new to private practice have difficulty with getting patients to return for follow-up appointments. They are not sure what, in addition to a therapeutic approach that conveys trust and a desire to help patients, are the actual mechanics that bring patients back. There are some useful techniques to use to encourage follow-up compliance (see Box 10.3).

If you do your own scheduling, you can set the stage from the first inquiry about your practice. Share your philosophy. Let the prospective client know that there is a process involved in making change—and that change

Box 10.3 How to Get Patients to Return: Words of Wisdom from Registered Dietitians

Milton Stokes, MPH, RD, CDN

"After the first visit, I assess whether I want the patient to return. I make sure the relationship is a good fit. I don't throw the kitchen sink at them on the first visit. Instead we come up with one to three goals to work on. I tell them up front that the purpose of the first visit is to build rapport and get to know one another so we have a direction to go. I also stress that it usually takes a few visits to change habits and eating patterns. Finally, I send a very brief and simple handwritten thank-you note to the patient."

Ashley Harris, RD, CD

"When my weight-loss patients have reached their personal goals, they think they are done. I explain that maintenance is the hardest part, so I pitch them a 'health insurance policy' or 'extended warranty,' if you will. The accountability and support will help them maintain their weight for life. I create a package of four follow-up sessions (of 30 minutes each) at my regular rate, and schedule a session every three months through the next year. This ensures that clients return and maintain their weight."

Cathy Leman, MA, RD

"At the initial session, I ask my clients what they would like to accomplish during their work with me. We list their goals, and the clients assign the order of importance. As we strategize about possible ways to meet their objectives, we discuss the fact that it's impossible to tackle everything in a couple of sessions; this gives them a better sense of the time and financial commitment required. Because they participate in creating the "big picture," they become invested in seeing it through. If they have budget concerns, we outline a plan for session length and frequency that supports their goals yet leaves them feeling comfortable. I then send every new client who has come through my door that week a thank-you postcard; it lets them know that their trust and confidence in me is appreciated, and that I value their business!"

takes time. You might share how you structure your sessions. For instance, if you are using the first session to provide a thorough assessment, it is important to inform the patient of this so they do not expect that first session to include in-depth counseling.

With some types of patients, a technique referred to as "previewing" may be helpful. Previewing allows prospective patients to know, or preview, some of the topics you hope to address together. Weight-management programs often use previewing by outlining topics that will be covered in subsequent sessions.

If you choose to outline goals with your patients, make sure that you break the goals down into achievable "baby steps." It is in an RD's nature, as a caregiver and a teacher, to provide patients with as much information as time allows. As a result, the patient may leave a session suffering from information overload. This technique backfires because it does not allow patients to break the information down into a usable form. Instead, practice providing information in small manageable messages, or "sound bites." Patients are much more likely to return if they feel they are making progress. They are also much less likely to feel overwhelmed.

You might find it useful to enter into a contract with a patient, outlining what you both hope to accomplish. This type of previewing encourages follow-up because the patient has a clear sense of what will be covered in subsequent sessions. When setting up a plan with your patients, be prepared to modify it on the basis of their needs and readiness to use the information. A simple technique to assess your patient's readiness to change is to ask during initial intake, "Do you want to change your eating habits?" You may be surprised at the answers you receive.

Learn how and when to end sessions. Sometimes a patient will have more to discuss than time allows in that session. If a patient brings up a topic as the session is ending, acknowledge the importance of the topic and let the patient know you will be happy to discuss it at the next appointment. Although the patient may feel unsatisfied, it is important that he or she understands and respects your need to adhere to a schedule. Be sure to explain to the patient your desire and intention to answer the questions, allowing the time they warrant. Patients will appreciate your ability to manage your time.

To encourage a patient to return for a follow-up session, close the session with an open-ended question: "When would you like your next appointment?" or "I'd like to see you in one week, what are your thoughts?" as opposed to "Do you want to come back for follow-up?" (14). Open-ended questions encourage the patient to assume an active role in treatment. Be sure you allow time at the end of a session to schedule the follow-up appointment rather than asking the patient to call you. Box 10.4 provides further insight into how to get patients to return.

Box 10.4 Determining Your Client's Readiness to Return

Clients are most likely to come back if they . . .

- Are at least somewhat ready to change
- Know that real change happens gradually over time and in stages
- Believe you understand their concerns and care about them
- Believe you have the skills and knowledge to help them reach their goals
- Are not significantly triggered to resist change in the first session

Source: Adapted with permission from Kellogg, M. *Counseling Tips for Nutrition Therapists: Practice Workbook Volume Two*. Philadelphia, PA: Kg Press; 2009.

Some RDs find it helpful to provide patients with a written form or card at the end of the session that indicates the follow-up appointment date and time (Figure 10.1). Consider putting the appointment reminder on the back of your business card. If you employ a receptionist, you may want to have a policy where he or she places a follow-up call or sends a reminder e-mail or postcard (Figure 10.2). Generally, patients who receive a reminder postcard, telephone call, or detailed information in a behavioral contract may be more likely to return for follow-up.

Jane Doe, MS, RD
Registered Dietitian
555 Fictitious Street • Chicago, Illinois 55555
(555) 555-5555

Mon. ____ AT ____ Tues. ____ AT ____

Wed. ____ AT ____ Thu. ____ AT ____

Fri. ____ AT ____

Figure 10.1 Follow-up card.

You've been missed . . .

Your last nutrition appointment was ___________

Please call or e-mail the office to schedule your next appointment.

____

Jane Doe, MS, RD
(555) 555-5555
email@net.net

Figure 10.2 Reminder card.

Bundling sessions and giving patients discounts for multiple sessions may also encourage follow-up. If you use this technique, it is advisable to require payment up front. By using this technique to encourage follow-up, you can also give patients a "preview" of topics that may be covered in subsequent sessions. Patients may focus on the need to cover specific topics in the sequence that best meets their needs. This ensures that the sessions' goals are the patient's goals, not the RD's goals for the patient.

Selling Nutrition Therapy

The success of your practice depends on you—and how well you can sell yourself. If you are going to sell yourself as a nutrition therapist, referral sources and prospective clients must be aware of your approach. Be prepared to address preconceived ideas of what you will do as an RD. For example, patients and their families may believe you will focus on nutrition education and expect quick results. In such cases, you may need to help them understand nutrition counseling as part of a longer therapeutic process (see the case study in Box 10.5).

Box 10.5 Case Study of D.J.: Communicating Nutrition Therapy to Patients and Their Families

D.J., a 14-year-old girl, was referred for nutrition counseling because she was a "picky eater." Her parents were frustrated with her limited food choices and thought a nutrition consultation to "tell her what to eat" was in order. In the first visit, an intake session without D.J. present, the nutrition therapist explained to the parents that she would first need to establish a relationship with the daughter, whom they described as "sassy," to determine why she didn't eat certain foods before instructing her about what she needed to eat.

D.J. was extremely thin, had not yet started menstruating, and had always been a picky eater. She informed the nutrition therapist that she "knew all about the Food Pyramid," so the session would probably be a waste of time. As D.J.'s relationship with food was explored, it was clear that she had been a restrictor since the age of eight because she was afraid of becoming fat. With RD input and further medical evaluation, she met the diagnostic criteria for "eating disorder, not otherwise specified." The RD conveyed her findings to the physician who was then able to make the diagnosis.

Upon diagnosis, D.J. was referred to a family therapist and a pediatrician skilled in working with adolescents, and she had subsequent sessions with the nutrition therapist. With this professional help, she explored the struggles she was having with food. She is now a healthy, recovered, 21-year-old college student who has a normal weight and eats a wide variety of foods. Had the nutrition therapist merely instructed her what was necessary for her to eat during a single visit, the eating disorder would not have been then diagnosed.

Similarly, physicians may refer their patients to you with the expectation that you will "teach" a prescribed diet. Although you may ultimately do this, nutrition therapy may involve many other steps in between. Therefore, you will need to educate referring physicians about your philosophy, style, and broader therapeutic approach. Develop a one-page handout or letter to inform them of your approach. Help them understand that patients may not initially lose weight, reduce their blood pressure, or have greater control over their diabetes. Goals for their patients may not be immediate or measurable in the conventional way. Patients may take small steps toward resolving issues that have kept them from achieving long-term dietary compliance. It may take time for them to reach their ultimate goals. That goal in the end may be different from the physician's original thought. For instance, a healthier lifestyle without dieting may be a more appropriate goal for a chronic dieter who is depressed. If the physician is using weight loss to assess progress, he or she may need to appreciate the much larger goals you have helped the patient achieve (see case study in Box 10.6).

Box 10.6 Case Study of S.D.: Communicating Nutrition Therapy to Physicians

S.D. was referred by his physician for nutrition counseling for hypertension and obesity. During the initial visit to assess intake, the nutrition therapist learned that S.D. had recently lost his job, was forced to move back with his family, and was overeating in response to the stress. S.D. wanted to improve his diet, lose weight, and begin exercising. However, the nutrition therapist and S.D. agreed that his precious health care dollars would at that point be better spent working with a therapist to help him deal with the other stresses in his life.

The nutrition therapist communicated this to the referring physician, who at first was disappointed that his patient would not be tackling his obvious nutrition problems. After the nutrition therapist explained the overall goals to the physician, he had more realistic expectations for S.D. and agreed to monitor his weight and blood pressure. He also agreed to provide encouragement to S.D. to work through his personal problems and then to return for nutrition therapy.

Nutrition therapy may be hardest to sell to some managed care providers. Managed care visits are most often arranged with a predetermined number of visits. You may be able to impart dietary advice with this arrangement, but you may never see real change unless your patient can communicate the need to have additional visits with you. It may take some effort, but it is possible to work with managed care providers to increase the number of covered visits.

If your practice is going to largely be sourced by referrals from managed care health plans, your financial success may depend on high volume. You may need to see many patients for brief visits, and your number of visits with patients may be limited. Your role as a nutrition therapist may be compromised. Your role may need to be more of the traditional model of nutrition educator. This is a need that must be filled in private practice, too. Ideally, you will be able to help those patients *and* assist them in lobbying their insurance plans to allow the necessary number of visits with you to achieve the identified nutrition goals.

Repeat Visits: A Summary

A flourishing private practice may require a change in the traditional approach to dietetics. To encourage follow-up visits, you must position yourself as a nutrition therapist. Successful patients are your best form of advertising. Success will be defined in many ways, but one absolute measure will be whether your patients feel satisfied. It may also be necessary to educate referral sources as well as patients on more acceptable measures of success.

Keep the following key points in mind:

- Staying in business means developing a practice where the need for repeat business, or follow-up sessions, is a reality.
- You will be more successful with your patients when you learn how to transition your approach to a counseling style appropriate for long-term relationships.
- Through course work, individual work, and specialized training, you will gradually become more comfortable with your role of nutrition therapist. There are numerous resources available to the RD, but implementing counseling techniques into your practice is the most useful way to make the transition.
- Certain techniques related to scheduling, running, and concluding appointments will encourage patients to return.
- Communicating your counseling approach to your referral sources and potential patients is necessary to avoid misunderstandings and to set expectations about what nutrition counseling will achieve.

References

1. Reiff D, Reiff K. *Eating Disorders: Nutrition Therapy in the Recovery Process*. Gaithersburg, MD: Aspen Publishers; 1992.
2. Rosal M, Ebbeling C, Lofgren I, Ockene J, Ockene I, Hebert J. Facilitating dietary change: the patient-centered counseling model. *J Am Diet Assoc*. 2001;101:332–341.
3. Cairns J, Milne RL. Eating disorder nutrition counseling: strategies and educational needs of English-speaking dietitians in Canada. *J Am Diet Assoc*. 2006:106:1087–1094.
4. Coste-Saloff C, Hamburg P, Herzog D. Nutrition and psychotherapy: collaborative treatment of patients with eating disorders. *Bull Menninger Clin*. 1993;57:504–516.

5. Maillet JO. Dietetics in 2017: what does the future hold? *J Am Diet Assoc.* 2002;102:1404–1406.
6. McCaffree J. Client satisfaction: turning referrals into regulars. *J Am Diet Assoc.* 2002;102:340-341.
7. Kellogg M. *Counseling Tips for Nutrition Therapists Practice Workbook Volume 1.* Philadelphia, PA: Kg Press; 2006.
8. American Dietetic Association. Code of ethics for the profession of dietetics. *J Am Diet Assoc.* 2009;109:1461–1467.
9. Kellogg M. Professional supervision. Molly Kellogg, RD, LSC, Web site. http://www.mollykellogg.com/supervision.html. Accessed August 18, 2009.
10. Motivational Interviewing Web site. http://www.motivationalinterview.org. Accessed August 17, 2009.
11. Glovsky E, Rose G. Motivational interviewing: a unique approach to behavior change counseling. *Today's Dietitian.* 2007;9(5):50. http://www.todaysdietitian.com/newarchives/tdmay2007pg50.shtml. Accessed August 10, 2009.
12. American Dietetic Association. Standards of professional practice. *J Am Diet Assoc.* 1998:98:83–5.
13. Kellogg M. *Counseling Tips for Nutrition Therapists Practice Workbook Volume 2.* Philadelphia, PA: Kg Press; 2009.
14. Kellogg M. Tip #60: open and closed questions. Molly Kellogg, RD, LSC, Web site. http://www.mollykellogg.com/archive07.html#60. Accessed August 18, 2009.

Section 3

Beyond Private Practice

Chapter 11

Breaking into the Writers' Market

Perhaps you've always aspired to author a weight-management book with a unique approach, or you dream of writing your own nutrition advice column in a magazine or on a Web site. In whatever medium your written words and name may appear, your vision is to be recognized and to earn money by writing.

As a registered dietitian (RD), you may have a variety of reasons for writing. It can be a way to promote your business or private practice. You may want to contribute to the profession. Writing can also be a way to supplement your income. Although writing may come easily, getting your words published can be difficult, and making an income from writing can be even more challenging (1). Don't quit your day job just to write. The paychecks are irregular. This chapter will guide you on how to break into the writers' market and be paid for writing, whether you want to be an author or freelance writer.

There is no single way to become a successful writer and have your work published. Explore every route and opportunity that you can. You never know what just might work.

Writing prospects include newspapers, magazines, books, educational material, newsletters, Web sites, and blogs. Words on paper are being replaced more and more by electronic formats (2,3). Be creative in thinking about where you want your written words to appear.

Become familiar with the media you would like to write for. Examine the format of written pieces and the tone. Are there advertisers, and who are they? Survey the topics covered in these media. Realize that nutrition topics that are timely today can be old news a year from now, when your piece might be published. Note the authors and their credentials. Check to see if there are writer's guidelines. These guidelines will provide you with the information an editor seeks. They may specify such details as topics, word count, tone, use of visuals, and deadlines. *The American Directory of Writer's Guidelines* is one helpful resource (4). Also, keep in mind that you must write for the audience that will read your material. Consider their demographics. For example, an article on bone loss may not be of interest to a men's magazine (5).

Freebies First

As a nutrition writer, you may have to start by writing for free. The goal is to get your name out there and begin developing samples of your published work. These samples will establish your ability and credibility as a writer. Your first published sample might be a simple letter to the editor of a newspaper in response to a nutrition or health article. You can build from that point. You can also add to your portfolio by writing articles for your community's newspaper or other local publications, even those distributed for free (6). Volunteer to write an article or review a book for a dietetic practice group (DPG) newsletter. Consider writing for your local hospital, senior center newsletter, or corporate newsletters. The opportunities exist; you need to search for them. Your goal is to get your name out there.

Traits of Effective Writers

Writing can be a lonely process (1). You have to take pleasure in that process. Consider whether you are the type of person who enjoys working alone. There are opportunities to interact with others, but they can be limited.

Self-discipline is a necessary quality of writers. No one will stand over you and remind you of deadlines. If you have a contractual deadline, you may want to develop a timeline with smaller deadlines or goals to help you along to the final goal (7). Box 11.1 provides suggestions for staying on track to meet deadlines (8).

Some people struggle to find time to research and write. You have to balance your work, time for family and friends, and time for yourself. Some writers designate specific times of day when they will write (3). Determine your most effective time of day for researching and writing. Do you work best at the crack of dawn or burning the midnight oil? Other writers squeeze in writing as their day permits or make an appointment to write. There is no right or wrong time to write. It's what works best for you (7).

Where you write can influence your creativity and writing ability. What type of physical space and environment works best for you? Do you need a quiet, nondistracting setting, or do you work better in a stimulating

Box 11.1 Meeting Your Writing Deadlines

Identify which of the following goals you can fulfill. "X" equals your goal. Be realistic in selecting your "X."

- X number of hours spent writing per day (or week)
- X number of pages produced per day (or week)
- X number of queries submitted per week or month
- X number of projects (articles, stories, or chapters) written per month or year

Source: Adapted with permission from Allen M. Setting effective writing goals. Writing World.com Web site. 2001. http://www.writing-world.com/basics/goals.shtml. Accessed June 23, 2009.

environment with noise and a lot going on? The question you have to answer is what kind of situation fosters you to write (9).

Your choice of topic affects your writing. Writing is easier if you have an expertise or passion about your subject. However, you are not limited to topics you know. Exploring something new may spark your interest and excitement about writing. If you have little to no knowledge about a topic, you will need to research it before your write. In fact, writers must research to write effectively, whether the topics are new or familiar. It helps to be a quick study (10).

Some disappointments are inevitably part of the writing process. Be prepared for rejection. It comes with the territory and you should not take it personally. Instead of looking at rejection negatively, use it constructively. Understand why your proposal or manuscript was not accepted. Incorporate any suggestions (2). Perseverance can pay off.

Many writers write to be recognized. Imagine the pleasure from the recognition of seeing your name in print. You will relish the feeling of accomplishment and love being paid for your work.

Generating Ideas

Sometimes, the hardest part of writing is getting started. You want to write, but you can't seem to come up with an idea that you think will sell. Or, you have a great topic and have developed an outline, but you can't get your creative juices flowing.

Experienced writers develop ideas in a variety of ways. Provide yourself opportunities to think. This entails time alone. Take a shower, a long walk, or a drive. For some, a distraction helps. Cook, garden, or do the laundry. Ideas and creativity can just appear, seeming to develop from nowhere. Allow your subconscious to work, and just be. Sometimes pressuring yourself can hinder ideas (5,11).

Read, read, and read some more. Read everything, including books, magazines, newspapers, newsletters, journals, online material, and even junk mail. You never know where an idea may come from. Talk and listen to people. This means family, friends, friends of friends, colleagues, and people you meet in a variety of settings. Hear their stories and experiences. Even your own experiences may trigger a subject (12).

Depending on your writing ability and ambition, even unusual approaches may be ways to provide information on food or nutrition. For example, you could consider writing a poem or screenplay about food.

How to Query

At some point when becoming a writer, you will write a query letter, which is a traditional and effective way to get your written material published. The purposes of a query letter are as follows (4):

- Selling your idea of an article or book proposal
- Explaining how you will develop the material
- Showing your familiarity with the publication
- Explaining why you are the right person to make this proposal work

Research the publication you want to query. Make sure your query letter is addressed to the correct person. Determine who the proper editor is for your proposal. Do not write "Dear Editor." Instead, identify the editor by name, and make sure you spell the name correctly if you want your query read. Verify the editor's gender to address the query letter properly. You can obtain this information online at Literary Market Place (13).

Mail your query to different publications at the same time. You don't want to mail your queries one at a time while waiting for a response that may never come. Increase your chances of receiving a response. However, make sure to write your query specific to the publication. Do not write generic queries (10).

The query is basically a single-spaced business letter written on letterhead stationery in a plain font, such as 12-point Times New Roman (see Figure 11.1). Include your contact information and enclose a self-addressed, stamped envelope or self-addressed stamped postcard to improve the likelihood of a response (10). If you enclose a postcard, print check-off boxes to make it easier for the editor to respond quickly. The postcard options may include something like, "Thanks, but no thanks" or "We're considering your proposal but will get back to you." A query may also be sent as an "e-query," if the publisher accepts them. Check first. The "Author's Tool Kit" in *The American Directory of Writer's Guidelines* is an excellent resource when writing your query (4).

October 28, 2009

Jackie Plant
Woman's Day
1633 Broadway, 42nd Floor
New York, NY 10019

Dear Ms. Plant:

Vegetarianism: What to Do When Your Tween Goes Meat Free

It's one of those rare evenings when the entire family is at the dinner table together. You've made your famous marinated steak tips, and all is right with the world. Until, that is, your 11-year-old son announces he's become a vegetarian. A what? This from the boy whose carrots you hid in spaghetti sauce when he was a child. Once over the initial shock, you realize you're in desperate need of some "Cliffs Notes" on vegetarianism. You're more than happy to let him explore this new lifestyle but want to ensure he gets the proper nutrition. So where to begin?

Know you're not alone. According to a new survey by the Centers for Disease Control and Prevention, as many as 1 in 200 kids are vegetarians. "While a vegetarian diet can be totally safe, some nutrients are more challenging to get and are easily missed by children and teens," cautions Keri M. Gans, MS, RD, a spokesperson for the American Dietetic Association. In addition, according to a recent study, while teen and young adult vegetarians may be considered healthier than nonvegetarians in many ways, they are also more likely to have problems with binge-eating and extreme unhealthful dieting.

In "Vegetarianism: What to Do When Your Tween Goes Meat Free," I'd like to help *Woman's Day* readers manage this trend when it happens in their own home. I'll discuss the challenges vegetarians face, nutritionally speaking, and help your readers ensure their children consume the correct balance of nutrients required for healthy growth and development. I'll also address cautions to look out for and provide ideas for how to incorporate vegetarian-friendly meals into a family of carnivores. This piece also lends itself well to a sidebar describing the various types of vegetarianism, including the recently labeled "flexitarian." I plan to interview Dawn Jackson Blatner, RD, author of *The Flexitarian Diet*.

Not only am I a freelance writer, I'm also a registered dietitian and, most importantly, mom to two young children. I've counseled countless families on how to feed their family more healthfully, and I practice what I preach daily when caring for my own children. My latest book, *The Complete Idiot's Guide to the Superfood Cookbook*, was released last year. In addition, my work has been published in newspapers; magazines such as Today's Diet and Nutrition, Fitness, and Family Circle; cookbooks; and Web sites. As a past spokesperson for the American Dietetic Association, I've been quoted as a nutrition expert in hundreds of magazine articles and television broadcasts. I look forward to working with you on "Vegetarianism: What to Do When Your Tween Goes Meat Free."

Sincerely,
Heidi McIndoo, MS, RD

Figure 11.1 Sample query letter. Adapted with permission from Heidi McIndoo, MS, RD.

You want the editor to read your query. Begin with an interesting opening. Fascinate the editor. A question, a story, or an unusual or unknown fact can be your "hook." Then the editor will then be more interested to read the rest of your query.

Explain to the editor why you chose this publication. Be specific in presenting your idea. Provide a creative title and the key points for your book or article. Explain how your material will help the reader and how it is going to be different. Promote yourself. Include your credentials and why you are the right person to write this article or book. Describe what resources you may use in your research.

Editors are busy people. Be clear and to the point. Come across as confident, self-assured, and passionate. Show you know how to write. If your query sounds like a form letter or is too long—longer than one page—it may be tossed. However, that's not to say you can't break the rules by sending longer queries. A longer query that is well researched can demonstrate you know what you are talking about (10). Your query is a sample of your work. This is not the time to discuss money. Wait until you've been given the job to ask how much you will be paid.

Which Comes First—The Proposal or the Manuscript?

When you are starting out as a writer, you may think you should first write the article or book and then find someone to publish it. On the other hand, you may not want to spend hours researching and writing a manuscript, only for it to be rejected. Thus, the question is which should you do first, write the proposal or the manuscript? This is a difficult call, especially for the first-time writer with no published work. A well-written proposal with information that convincingly sells your idea and your ability to write may be all an editor needs to say yes. However, because you lack a proven record as a writer, you may decide or may be asked by an editor to write on speculation, or "on spec," which means you submit a finished manuscript for consideration by a publisher. When an editor requests a manuscript written on spec, this means they are interested. However, it does not mean your work will be published (4).

Writing on spec may be a good risk to take if you want to write a newspaper or magazine article that does not require a big investment in time. However, writing a book on spec is a different story, because it involves a lot more time. What happens if you don't find a publisher after you have exerted the time and energy to write it (1)? You may choose to explore self-publishing (discussed later in this chapter).

Your Copy Rights

According to US copyright law, you own the rights to your original words (14). This copyright is guaranteed for 70 years after your death. After you sign a contract with a publisher, however, you may no longer own the copyright to the material you wrote. Similarly, when you write as an employee, your employer can own the copyright. Always establish copyright ownership before you submit your work for publication (see Box 11.2) (15), and be aware that you may be in violation of copyright laws if you sign over the copyright to your material and then reuse it in another format. Think twice before signing over copyright if you can anticipate ways to repurpose material in future money-making ventures.

Box 11.2 Your Rights As a Writer

- **First serial rights:** You give a publication permission to be the first to publish your material. All other rights remain with you, the writer.
- **One-time rights:** You sell your material to more than one publication. Each publication can use your material only once. They have nonexclusive rights.
- **Second serial rights** (or reprints rights): Your material appeared elsewhere, but you allow it to be reprinted. The publisher has non-exclusive rights.
- **All rights:** You sell all your rights to the material you wrote. In other words, you no longer own your material. "All rights" are the least desirable rights for a freelancer.
- **Electronic rights:** You sell rights to use your material electronically. Electronic uses can include Web sites, online magazines, and CDs. You will want to specify which electronic rights you are assigning. Any unspecified rights remain with you.

Source: Adapted with permission from Provost G. The writer's guide to money. In: *Craft & Business of Writing: Essential Tools for Writing Success*. Cincinnati, OH: F+W Publications; 2008:49.

Traditional Publishing Media

In which medium do you want your writing to appear? You may feel pressure to write a book for a variety of reasons. However, not everyone who writes must write a book. Pieces in a newspaper or magazine are much shorter and easier to accomplish. Many writers are content to write as freelancers for newspapers, magazines, and newsletters (1).

Newspapers

Newspapers may be your first step into the world as a paid writer. Most likely your first published article will not be in the *New York Times, Washington Post*, or *Boston Globe*. Instead, your first article may appear in your local town's weekly newspaper. Look for opportunities to write for regular specialized sections or columns on food and nutrition, or perhaps you can weave something about nutrition into another section; for example, you could write tips in the travel section on sticking to a diet while traveling.

When you write for a newspaper, it is especially important to be reliable and accurate, and deliver on time no matter what. As you build a reputation for meeting these expectations, more writing opportunities may come your way.

Read the newspaper you want to write for a couple of weeks. Newspapers worldwide are available online (16,17). Learn the trends of the newspaper. Note the days of the week that food or nutrition articles may be appropriate. Determine whether they use staff writers or freelancers, also identified as specialized writers.

Breaking into the world of freelancing for newspapers can depend on who you know. Contacts are very important. Your first contact can be the editor of a newspaper. Introduce yourself via phone call or e-mail. When you develop a contact, maintain that contact. Keep in touch regularly. And as with anything else, if at first you don't succeed, try, try again. Persistence can have its rewards. You never know when a newspaper may choose to fill empty space with your article. Being in the right place at the right time can pay off.

Magazines

Writing for magazines can be similar to writing for newspapers. You may have to start with the smallest publications and climb the ladder to the next level. Your articles may first be published in a local magazine, then over time you may move on to a regional magazine, and if you are successful, a national magazine (5).

Identify which publications you would like to write for. *The American Directory of Writer's Guidelines* is helpful for magazines. The directory specifies what editors are looking for in articles from freelancers. Magazines may be more open to new writers when the publications are newer, smaller, older and under new ownership, or going through a facelift (4).

Submit your proposals to more than one magazine. Obtain previous copies of the magazines from your library and study each publication. Tailor your query specifically to each magazine.

Become familiar with all aspects of the magazine. Examine the topics covered and the length of the articles. Identify the style of writing in the articles. Look at the publication and notice if there are illustrations, photos, or sidebars. Review their advertisers and writers. Develop a sense of what the editor may look for (5,18). Understand who reads the publication. Research the demographics of its readers.

Books

Authoring a book is different than writing an article. On the one hand, writing a book requires more organization and a greater volume of research and writing than an article for a newspaper or magazine. On the other hand, a book may provide greater recognition and credibility, and more business opportunities. Observe the reaction of people you know when you say you are writing or wrote a book. They will be impressed.

As a nutrition professional, you will likely write a nonfiction book. These are easier to get published than a novel. More people purchase nonfiction books, and more publishers publish them. A well-written proposal can sell a nonfiction book (1).

Choosing a Topic

The process in getting a book published is somewhat similar to writing for newspapers and magazines. First, you need to identify the topic or idea that will be your subject. Your topic can be an area of expertise or one you are passionate about. If you can learn, you can even write about something about which you initially know nothing. Writing a book will take longer and can be more of a challenge than writing an article. Keep in mind it can take more than one year for the book to appear after you start writing it, and probably longer. Consider whether the topic will still have appeal then.

Market Research

After you identify a topic, the next step is doing market research to see what has already been written on your subject. At your local library, review the annually updated, multivolume reference *Books in Print* published by R.R. Bowker Company (also available online by subscription). This "bible" lists all current books in print as well as books to be published. You may also find information on competitive products from online research, by visiting bookstores, and through your library. Once you have identified the books written on your topic, study them. Is there something missing in these books? Can you do a better job? Does your topic take a different approach? Look at the titles of these books. Who will buy these books? How will you market your book to these potential readers? Take careful notes. Some of these books that you may view as competition can become references in your book (1).

Publishing Options

Before you sit down to write your book query, you have a decision to make. Who will publish your book? Explore your publishing options. There are basically two choices: someone else publishes your book or you do it yourself. There are different types of publishers, and each provides a different level of service (19). *The American Directory of Writer's Guidelines* (4) provides information on the types of books publishers are looking for. Box 11.3 describes the different types of publishers (1,19–27). Table 11.1 compares the use of a traditional publisher versus self-publishing (2,3,19,23,25,28).

Box 11.3 Options for Publishing

- **Traditional publishers:** These large publishers purchase the rights to publish your book, handle all aspects of your book, and pay you royalties. You usually incur no costs. Highly selective, they are only interested in books that sell and sell big. They typically work with well-known authors with established track records for selling or names in the limelight that will sell. This is not necessarily where you will start unless your food or nutrition book will have a large appeal and sell many books.
- **Niche, specialized, or medium-sized publishers:** These are smaller and more specialized publishers. They tailor distribution to the markets they know would be interested in particular book genres. When you conduct your research to find other books written on your topic, take note of these sorts of publishers. Those that have published books that are the same genre as yours may be especially receptive to your query, and they are more likely to recommend you to another publisher if they are not interested themselves.
- **Vanity publishers:** They will publish any book, but you pay all publishing costs. The book is your property.
- **Subsidy publishers:** These publishers will publish your book and perhaps provide other services, such as distribution and promotion, but you will foot the bill. The publisher retains ownership of your book until they are sold, and you are paid a royalty.
- **Print on demand (POD) publishers:** Similar to vanity publishers, except the POD publisher owns your book. The publisher will print the book on demand as sales come in. You are paid a royalty when books are sold.
- **Literary agents:** A question you may ask is, "Do I need a literary agent?" Literary agents represent authors in their negotiations with publishers, especially the large publishing houses. They know what publishers are looking for. Literary agents are selective about who they chose to represent and will only take on writers they know will sell. Their fee is a percentage of what you receive. Publishers are accustomed to dealing directly with nonfiction writers, so you will most likely not need a literary agent.
- **Self-publishing:** At one time frowned upon, self-publishing is now a respectable way to be guaranteed your book will be published. You will not need to write a query, proposal, or find a literary agent. You will be in charge of getting your book published, including all costs. Many nutrition colleagues have been quite successful at self-publishing. Self-publishing does not mean you have to do everything yourself. You can contract out those activities you can't or don't want to do. Self-publishing involves a great deal of work, and you will learn a lot about publishing. If you want to sell your book in bookstores or through online vendors, you will need to name your publishing company and obtain an International Standard Book Number (ISBN) for the book. A book's ISBN is a unique number that booksellers use to identify the book by publisher, title, author, and edition. Additional information on ISBNs is available from the ISBN Web site (http://www.isbn.org).

Source: Data are from references 1 and 19–27.

Table 11.1 Traditional Publishers vs. Self-Publishing

	Traditional Publisher	*Self-Publishing*
Query or proposal	Required	Not required
Cover design and title	Publisher controls	You control
Copyright	Publisher owns	You own
Costs of publishing	Publisher pays	You pay
Speed of publishing	Slower	Faster
Marketing	You and publisher market the book	You market the book
Author's profit per book	Less	More

Source: Data are from references 2, 3, 19, 23, 25, and 28.

Other Writing Opportunities

In addition to newspapers, magazines, and books, there are many other writing opportunities available to the nutrition professional. For example, you can write for marketing products, advertising agencies, and public relations firms.

Newsletters

Writing articles for newsletters is one option to explore. Associations, corporations, nonprofits, and charities are organizations that distribute newsletters. Newsletters may be sent via e-mail or postal service. They may be sent to subscribers for free or a subscription fee. Some organizations may use in-house writers for articles, but others contract freelance writers. You can find newsletter-writing opportunities by searching the Internet and online databases, contacting organizations directly, or by volunteering. Compensation can vary (1).

Blogging

Blogging can be an outlet for your writing on the Internet. Blogs are written on an ongoing basis, often daily. As a blogger, you can write about personal experiences, topics of interest, or any information you want to share. You can allow only select readers to read your blog or open it up to everyone. In addition, your readers can respond and provide feedback to your blog postings. Learn more about blogging in Chapter 6.

Ghostwriting

If you love to write and do it well, you may want to share your skill as a ghostwriter. Ghostwriters usually remain anonymous but may obtain writing credits. They write for those who are unable to write due to lack of skill or time. A search on the Internet can identify possible opportunities (1).

Making Money Writing

The final reward of writing is making money. Realize one thing about writing. The amount of time and energy you put into writing may not be reflected in your compensation. You will not be paid based on the number of hours it took to complete the project, the number of items you wrote, or the quality of your work. In general, writers are underpaid (1).

From your research for one newspaper or magazine article, you can find ways to make more money. You can rework the information in the article. For example, you can adapt your research for an article about how to eat healthfully in restaurants to an article on feeding children in restaurants when on vacation. If you own the copyright, you can resell your article if magazines buy reprints or second serial rights. If you write a book, perhaps you can include the article. Adding photos, graphics, or a sidebar to an article can increase the amount you are paid when writing for a magazine or newspaper. Think of it as added value.

Nutrition entrepreneurs want to know how much they will likely be compensated. Here are some numbers to provide you an idea. This is not set in stone. In each situation, you will need to negotiate your payment, which may differ from the amounts listed here. These amounts are guidelines only.

Newspaper and Magazine Articles

Newspapers typically compensate less for articles than magazines. The distribution of a newspaper reflects their ability to compensate. A small-town newspaper might pay you 10 percent of the amount a large city paper offers.

Compensation for your magazine article will depend on the magazine's circulation. Magazines make most of their money from their advertisers. A national magazine obtains a larger fee from advertisers, and in return it may pay writers more than a regional or local magazine. An article in a national magazine may receive twice or more the compensation of a regional magazine. There are magazines that have no advertisers but can still pay well. Don't assume that a publication that has no advertisers doesn't pay.

Payment for articles can be by either the word or a flat fee. Rates can range from a few cents to a few dollars per word (1). The book *The Renegade Writer* advises writers to not accept less than one dollar per word (10). The flat-fee payment per article will depend on the article and publication (1). Negotiate your compensation.

Look at what will work best for you to make the most money. If a flat fee pays you $500 for a 1,000-word article, figure out the math. How many hours would it take to write the article? If you want to earn $100 per hour, you must spend only five hours. Can you conduct the research and produce an article in five hours? This can provide a sense of whether it is worth your time (5).

Books

With a traditional publisher, book authors are usually paid either an advance or a royalty. Most likely, you will not be offered an advance because the author needs to attract a large enough audience for the sales to cover the advance and publishers will not take this risk on an unproven writer. Royalties typically range from 5 to 10 percent of retail price or 5 to 15 percent of the net price (2).

If you self-publish a book, you may make more money. You are in charge of everything. The net revenues will depend on your expenses in publishing the book and your effectiveness in marketing it. You will not make as much money with a vanity or subsidy publisher as you would if you self-published. The costs of using a vanity or subsidy publisher are greater than in self-publishing, and more of the profits will go to the publisher (29).

Firsthand Accounts of Successful Writers

As noted earlier in this chapter, there is no one route to becoming successful as a writer. Note this as you read the stories and tips of these three dynamic RDs who have succeeded as writers.

Nancy Clark, MS, RD, CSSD

Nancy is a sports nutritionist in private practice in the Boston area and author of the best-selling Nancy Clark's Sports Nutrition Guidebook, *4th edition (Human Kinetics, 2008).*

When I first started working as a sports nutritionist, I had a very quiet office. To bring that office to life, I knew I had to exist in the media. Therefore, I called editors at *Runners' World*, the *Boston Globe*'s sports editors, and contacts at other fitness publications in hopes that they would welcome my wonderful ideas for sports nutrition articles. Although I was willing to write as a means to teach others, I was actually more interested in the credit line that would accompany the article. My goal was to get free advertising—"Nancy Clark, Boston-area sports nutritionist"—so my phone would ring off the hook with new clients!

I quickly learned that I generally needed to make several calls before I found the right gatekeeper. I also learned the importance of networking and being visible. For example, I met the editor of *Runner's World* at a road race; I befriended a columnist for the *Washington Post* at FNCE [the American

Dietetic Association Food and Nutrition Conference and Expo]. My efforts paid off, and I received payment for writing for runners, golfers, cyclists, and even sports medicine doctors. The sports world was hungry for nutrition information.

If you want to become established as a writer, I suggest you identify your niche, use Google to find appropriate publications or Web sites that might welcome your expertise, and start fishing! Also, attend conferences and make a special effort to meet members of the media who might be in attendance. Without a doubt, being in the right place at the right time can help bolster your career!"

Victoria Shanta Retelny, RD

Victoria is a Chicago-based writer, media spokesperson, speaker, corporate wellness coach, and nutrition therapist.

Writing is my passion. With a degree in both communications and dietetics, I started my nutrition communications business as a sidebar to my job as a clinical outpatient RD. In the beginning, I pitched any and all types of publications—from trade and general health magazines, to DPG newsletters, to newspapers—because I was determined to get published. And it paid off—my first writing assignment came while I was still in my nutrition program. For a class paper, I interviewed the editor of a national restaurant publication, and as a follow-up I sent her a copy of my paper. A few weeks later, she asked me to write an article for her magazine—and was going to pay me to do it! It was a dream come true. Since then, I have written for numerous publications, including *Self*, *Women's Health*, *EatingWell*, the *Chicago Tribune*, *IDEA Fitness Journal*, *ALL YOU*, *Today's Dietitian*, and *Today's Diet & Nutrition*. The bottom line: if you want to write, do not take no for an answer, turn editors' rejections into opportunities to pitch other ideas, and keep all your writing clips to showcase what you've done for future assignments. Your due diligence will pay off one day—I promise.

Bonnie Taub-Dix, MA, RD, CDN

Bonnie lives in the New York metropolitan area and is a successful writer and spokesperson. Among her publications is the forthcoming book, Read It Before You Eat It *(Plume, 2010), which teaches consumers how to decipher food labels and shop for the healthiest foods.*

Even after three decades of being in the nutrition business, I still take pride in reflecting on the journey that brought me to where I am. The scope of my practice has included consulting to private clients, corporations, restaurants, health clubs, and media outlets. As a national spokesperson for the American Dietetic Association, I'm often called upon to talk and write in sound bites, but when writing about my career, being concise is not a simple task! So here's a slice of my pie of experience: I am a nutrition consultant for the Cartoon Network, an advisory board member of *Family Circle* magazine, co-author of a cookbook called *Kosher By Design Lightens Up* (Artscroll, 2008), a blogger for *USA Today*, a contributor to MSNBC.com, a columnist for Kosher.com, a blogger for several other corporate sites, and a journalist for various magazines, newspapers, and Web sites.

Although these days my keyboard is busier than ever, it wasn't always that way. The first and perhaps one of the most meaningful writing positions I had was as a columnist for *Newsday*. The salary was less than memorable, but the experience was invaluable. It taught me to open my eyes and ears to nutrition news and food trends, and to paint a picture with words. For those of you who are starting out, never sell yourself short, but remember that money isn't the only benefit you get out of a job. My best advice to you: always carry a pen and paper with you because you never know when a brilliant thought may come to mind.

Breaking into the Writers' Market: A Summary

Here are the main points you should take away from this chapter:

- As you get started in writing, you may need to write for free as you gather your portfolio.
- You should consider whether you have the traits required to become a successful writer.
- Extensively research topics you want to write about. Make sure the subject matter will be timely when it is published.
- Determine what media you will be writing for and if you need to send a query letter. When writing a query, be sure it is sent to the correct editor and sells you and your proposal.
- You may not make as much money as you would like, but your writing can create other opportunities.

References

1. Camenson B. *Careers in Writing*. New York, NY: McGraw-Hill; 2008.
2. Shur R. *How to Publish*. Garden City Park, NY: Square One Publishers; 2001.
3. Poynter D. *Writing Nonfiction: Turning Thoughts into Books*. Santa Barbara, CA: Para Publishing; 2005.
4. Mettee S, Doland M, Hall D. *The American Directory of Writer's Guidelines*. Sanger, CA: Quill Driver Books/Word Dancer Press; 2007.
5. Ruberg M, ed. *Writer's Digest Handbook of Magazine Article Writing*. Cincinnati, OH: F+W Publications; 2005.
6. Sagan D. Break into Writing for Newspapers: How to Get an Article Published. Suite 101.com Web site. July 21, 2007. http://writingnonfiction.suite101.com/article.cfm/writing_for_newspapers#ixzz0GujB17G6&. Accessed May 29, 2009.

7. Clark N. Finding time to write. *Nutrition Entrepreneurs DPG Ventures Newsletter.* 2007;(Winter):8–9.
8. Allen M. Setting effective writing goals. Writing World.com Web site. 2001. http://www.writing-world.com/basics/goals.shtml. Accessed June 23, 2009.
9. Estrin J. For a writer, a home with a hideout. *New York Times* (Real Estate section). July 12, 2009. http://www.nytimes.com/2009/07/12/realestate/12habi.html?_r=1. Accessed July 12, 2009.
10. Formichelli L, Burrell D. *The Renegade Writer: The Totally Unconventional Guide to Freelance Writing Success.* Oak Park, IL: Marion Street Press; 2005.
11. Tedesco A. Overcoming writer's block. In: *The Craft & Business of Writing: Essential Tools for Writing Success.* Cincinnati, OH: F+W Publications; 2008:25–28.
12. Daugherty G. Where to get great article ideas. In: *The Craft & Business of Writing: Essential Tools for Writing Success.* Cincinnati, OH: F+W Publications; 2008:179–182.
13. Literary Market Place Web site. http://www.literarymarketplace.com. Accessed July 1, 2009.
14. US Copyright Office. Copyright Basics. http://www.copyright.gov. Accessed June 21, 2009.
15. Provost G. The writer's guide to money. In: *Craft & Business of Writing: Essential Tools for Writing Success.* Cincinnati, OH: F+W Publications; 2008:49.
16. OnlineNewspapers.com Web site. http://www.onlinenewspapers.com. Accessed June 21, 2009.
17. Newspapers—USA and worldwide. Refdesk.com Web site. http://www.refdesk.com/paper.html. Accessed June 21, 2009.
18. Swann L. How to get your article published. In: *Nutrition Entrepreneurs Toolkit 2009.* Chicago, IL: American Dietetic Association Nutrition Entrepreneurs; 2010.
19. Poynter D. *Self-Publishing Manual: How to Write, Print and Sell Your Own Book.* Santa Barbara, CA: Para Publishing; 2007.
20. What can your publisher do for you? Writer's Digest Web site. June 2, 2009. http://www.writers digest.com/article/what-can-your-publisher-do-for-you. Accessed June 23, 2009.
21. Self-publishing definitions. Writer's Digest Web site. February 11, 2008. http://www.writers digest.com/article/Self-Publishing_Definitions Accessed June 23, 2009.
22. Science Fiction and Fantasy Writers of America. Writer beware: what is a print-on-demand self-publishing service? http://www.sfwa.org/for-authors/writer-beware/pod. Accessed June 23, 2009.
23. Frishman R, Spizman Freedman R. *Author101—Bestselling Book Proposals: The Insider's Guide to Selling Your Work.* Avon, MA: Adams Media; 2005.
24. Writers Digest. *The Craft & Business of Writing: Essential Tools for Writing Success.* Cincinnati, OH: F+W Publications; 2008.
25. Jacob D. *Will Write for Food: The Complete Guide to Writing Cookbooks, Restaurant Reviews, Articles, Memoir, Fiction and More.* New York, NY: Marlowe; 2005.
26. International Standard Book Number Web site. http://www.isbn.org. Accessed July 1, 2009.
27. Beyer J. *You Can Write A Book.* Auburn, MI: NutraConsults; 2009.
28. Reiss F. *The Publishing Game.* Newton, MA: Peanut Butter and Jelly Press; 2003.
29. Lichten J. Do you want to publish a book? *Ventures: Enterprising News and Ideas for Nutrition Entrepreneurs.* 2009;25:6–7.

Chapter 12

Becoming a Media-Savvy Registered Dietitian: Public Speaking and Media Consulting

Some registered dietitians (RDs) dream of being in front of an audience and seeing their name in print. Their goal is to speak to large groups, appear on television, or be quoted in newspapers, magazines and other print media. Others shudder at the thought of being in the limelight. For those that have aspirations of speaking in public or consulting to the media, this chapter is for you.

Communication Skills

Regardless of the venue, communicating to large audiences is very different from speaking to one patient or client. You must be able to deliver your message in a clear and concise manner while maintaining the interest of your audience. You must appear calm, cool, and collected even if you are nervous or suffering from a little stage fright. If you are speaking about nutrition topics, you have the added challenge of translating complex scientific information into a message that the audience can understand.

All of these skills require practice. Consider volunteering to speak in front of audiences to gain experience before trying to land a paid speaking engagement or media placement. Volunteer at local senior centers, places of worship, community centers, and other similar venues. Join the local Toastmasters club. Most of the members are there because they want to become comfortable speaking to an audience. You can even attend workshops to perfect your communication skills. Chapter 14 lists many excellent resources for aspiring public speakers and media moguls.

Communicating through the print media is slightly different, but it is still essential that you have good communication skills. If you are being quoted, you must make your point in a way the reader can understand and make every word count. You must paint a verbal picture.

Public Speaking

Many RDs across the country have combined their nutrition expertise with public speaking skills and are hitting the speaker's circuit. The venues vary and the possibilities are endless. Some RDs pursue a full-time career as professional speakers. They earn a substantial amount of their income from public speaking, focus on developing exceptional speaking skills, and understand the ins and outs of the speaking industry. For those at the top of their field, a career in public speaking can be lucrative, with speeches commanding high fees.

In contrast to these professional speakers, other RDs can be considered "professionals who speak" (1)—these RDs speak occasionally on subjects or research they know well as a sideline to their primary career or to promote themselves. They may or may not always earn money from their presentations. Usually, RDs who have made it to the top of the ranks as public speakers started small and worked their way up.

Getting Started

As a nutrition expert, you can find ample opportunities for public speaking. Many clubs, schools, colleges, religious institutions, sports teams, and senior citizen centers provide programs, and these organizations are always on the lookout for interesting speakers. Before you seek paid speaking engagements, consider volunteering to give presentations whenever the opportunity arises. These unpaid presentations will allow you to polish your skills.

Getting Paid to Speak

Once you feel comfortable speaking in front of an audience and you have paid your dues by providing free presentations, you can then market your speaking services to clubs and organizations. At this point, when contacted to give a presentation, you can ask the amount of the honorarium. You may still receive requests to provide your services for free. Evaluate each situation individually. Continue to speak for free if you consider the presentation a good marketing opportunity.

If you have a specific area of expertise within the field of nutrition, consider submitting a proposal to speak to your district or state dietetic association. Whether your area of expertise is in clinical nutrition, foodservice management, or medical billing, look for opportunities to present to your colleagues.

Corporations hire RDs to present lunch-and-learn sessions to their employees as an employee benefit. They also hire nutrition experts to give lectures or presentations and even keynote addresses at major meetings.

Becoming a Professional Speaker

If speaking becomes your passion (and you are great at it), you may want to take it to the next level and become a professional speaker. See Box 12.1 for an example of how one RD turned her love of speaking into her primary income source.

Giving Memorable Presentations

Almost anyone can get up and speak, but it takes a special talent to give a great presentation. A memorable presentation can lead to positive feedback, which ultimately will lead to more jobs. Box 12.2 gives tips on how to be an effective speaker (2).

Organizing Your Presentation

To maintain and entertain your audience, it is important to present your information in an organized manner. Typically, you will want to organize an informational talk as follows (3):

- Introduction: present an overview of the topic.
- Body of the talk: present all the facts you want to include. This is really what the audience wants to hear.
- Conclusion: summarize all the information presented.

The introduction should give your audience an "agenda" or a set of goals for the body of your talk. The introduction is the first part of your talk, but you may want to write it last, after you have a clear idea of what you talk will cover and in what order you will present topics. It is important to establish rapport immediately with the audience. Consider beginning with a question. For example, if you are presenting the topic of incorporating more fruits and vegetables into one's diet, you could begin by asking the audience, "How many of you ate fruit with your breakfast this morning?" You could

Box 12.1 How One Registered Dietitian Became a Professional Speaker

Cindy Heroux, RD, was in private practice and teaching at a local college. The school received a request from a local women's group for a speaker on nutrition, and Cindy thought speaking to the group would be a great way to attract new patients so she accepted the invitation. Not only did Cindy find new patients, she found a new career! The presentation was so well received that she soon had several requests to speak to other organizations. She started offering nutrition and wellness seminars at local markets, schools, and health clubs. Public speaking was far more fun for her than working with patients; it contained all the elements she loved about teaching; and it was much more lucrative than either private practice or college instruction. In a very short time, Cindy was earning more for giving a 1-hour talk than for teaching an entire 17-week course as an adjunct professor. Speaking enabled her to spend more time with her young children, do something she thoroughly enjoyed, and earn an excellent living doing it. It was a perfect fit.

Cindy believed that her performance was her best "calling card," so she spoke every chance she could. She prepared a speaker's packet and made sure to network aggressively before and after each presentation. These efforts expanded her range of contacts and built market awareness for her speaking business. Her first big break came when a major insurance company contacted her to speak. After hearing about Cindy from someone who had attended one of her seminars, the insurance company hired her to do a one-time lunch-and-learn program titled "Packing Power Lunches" for the employees of one of its major customers. Offering health-related seminars was an added service benefit that helped the insurer differentiate itself from its competitors. The audience was so thrilled with the presentation that Cindy was able to convince the insurance company to purchase a series of lunch-and-learn classes on a variety of health and wellness topics. It was a win-win outcome for everyone involved. The customer was pleased by their employees' interest in improving their own health; the insurance company was pleased with the positive feedback from their customer, and Cindy had found a way to increase her speaking opportunities in corporate wellness services.

Cindy provides these tips for aspiring professional speakers: If you want speaking to be a major part of your career, then you need to master presentation skills as well as skills for promoting and managing a business. One of the best ways to become a better speaker is to join your local chapter of the National Speakers Association. Most offer a Speaker's Academy for those interested in becoming a professional speaker. Another organization that offers opportunities to develop your delivery skills is Toastmasters. The Nutrition Entrepreneurs Speakers Specialty Group provides a wealth of knowledge and support. Attend conferences and conventions in a variety of industries, and listen to as many speakers as you can. Watching others will help you find your own voice, identify your personal style, and determine what kind of speaker you want to be. Videotape yourself every time you talk and ask for evaluations. Feedback lets you know how well you connected with your audience, and the video enables you evaluate and improve your performance. It's also an important marketing tool. Finally, practice, practice, practice!

Box 12.2 The Ten Habits of Highly Effective Speakers

1. Have a passion for your subject(s). If you are not excited, the audience will be bored.
2. Be persistent in your quest to be an excellent speaker. You must communicate your expertise.
3. Have the patience to succeed. No one is an overnight success.
4. Speak from your heart. Be authentic, vulnerable, and truthful.
5. Connect quickly with your audience. You have 30 seconds to make your connection.
6. Prepare 24/7. Look for material everywhere you go and in everything you do.
7. Speak to the ways people learn—auditorily, visually, and through their senses. Use a combination of techniques to keep the audience's attention.
8. Support your main points with stories. People learn best and retain your message from stories.
9. Make your presentation fun. Inject humor along the way.
10. Have reverence for the work you do. Remember, it is a privilege to be on the platform.

Source: Adapted from Schrift S. The ten habits of highly effective speakers. Sandra Schrift, Executive Speech Coach, blog. June 22, 2005. http://www.schrift.com/blog/2005/06/ten-habits-of-highly-effective.html. Accessed March 12, 2010. Adapted with permission from Sandra Schrift (www.schrift.com).

also begin with a startling statistic, a story, or a quote. Make sure you know this part of your presentation well so you do not have to glance at your notes.

The body of your talk is typically the easiest part to put together. Basically, you are giving the information and facts that relate to the title of your talk. Most attendees will probably remember a only handful of key points. Make a short list of key points you want to communicate and keep them in mind while you prepare the body of your talk.

The conclusion of your talk can be the hardest part to write. It should summarize key points in a way that sticks in the audience's memory, deliver the take-home message, and provide the audience with a lasting impression of you. When you are nearing the end of your talk, let the audience know you are about to wrap up. This will pull in the people who may not be paying close attention. "I would like to make one last point" or "I'd like to leave you with one more important message" will signal to the audience that they should pay close attention. Box 12.3 provides techniques to help you end your presentation with a bang (4).

Box 12.3 Tips for Closing Your Presentation

- **Summarize:** Reiterate your main points.
- **Use strong language:** Action words, vivid imagery, and alliteration will create a strong closing.
- **Remind them you are right:** If you have not only informed them but have drawn conclusions, use forceful, positive language.
- **Make an emotional appeal:** Put out a call for action, close with a moving poem, or recount a moving story.
- **Let the audience know how to get more information:** Remind them of handouts in their packets and give them your contact information.

Source: Adapted with permission from Smith SS. *The Everything Public Speaking Book*. Avon, MA: Adams Media; 2008.

Using Visual Aids: Handouts, Slides, and Videos

Visual and audio aids are not necessary, but they can spice up your presentation. Many motivational speakers do not use visual aids; they rely on their charisma and presentation skills. Most speakers, however, do incorporate visual aids. The most common visual aids are handouts, computerized slide presentations, and videos.

You should always provide a handout when speaking. Consider it a marketing opportunity. You may want to wait to distribute the handouts until the end of your presentation to ensure that your audience is paying attention to you instead of flipping through the handouts. Other alternatives include placing a handout at every attendee's seat or including it in a conference packet. There are many handout formats. They can be brochures, article reprints, fact sheets, or a copy of your slides. No matter what the format, always include you contact information on every page. If you have a logo, be sure to print it on materials you distribute. This helps with brand identification.

Public speakers often use computerized slide presentations. They are easy to put together using Microsoft PowerPoint, Apple Keynote, or other software. Most audiences are familiar with the conventional formats, graphics, and features offered in these software packages, so making your visual presentations unique can be a challenge (3). You can customize your presentation by using your own graphic or logo on the slides. If that seems too complicated, consider hiring someone to do it for you.

Videos can be incorporated into your slide presentation or you can show them at strategic times during your talk. Perhaps you want to give an example of a cooking demonstration, show one of your media clips, or demonstrate counseling techniques. If you use video clips, make sure the quality of the video is good enough to show in the venue.

Marketing While Speaking

If you have a product or service to market, find a way to get attendee names and contact information for future marketing. Offer something to attendees if they provide their business card, or send a list around asking for contact information. If you raffle off a copy of your product, a free or discounted consultation, or a free newsletter, you have automatically generated a targeted marketing list.

Remember to mention your product or services in the body of your talk when appropriate. You can even flash a graphic of your product on the screen as part of your visual presentation. For example, if you have been asked to present based on information contained in a book you wrote, refer to something mentioned in the book while showing a shot of your book cover. Do be careful of shameless advertising. That could turn the audience off and may be prohibited in some venues.

Media Matters

The major media outlets are inundated with food-, nutrition-, and health-related stories. You'll find some type of nutrition-related article in every women's, children's family, health, beauty, or even business magazine. In your local newspaper, every section has some content related to food or nutrition, as do many local and national TV news and magazine programs. RDs are therefore in the unique position of being *the* experts on a topic that is of great interest to the public. Nutrition is hot, and RDs can and should capitalize on the public's interest.

Working with the media encompasses a broad range of opportunities. Just as there is a differentiation between full-time professional speakers and professionals who speak occasionally, media consultants can also be divided into those who have taken their talent and aspirations and turned them into an income stream and those who work with the media on occasion to share their knowledge and expertise but are not compensated. The latter group consults with media because they love it, they have media skills and confidence, and it helps them with marketing and name recognition.

Types of Media Outlets

The term "media" refers to print, radio, and television. Print includes newspapers, magazines, and Web content. Radio is still alive and well and presents many opportunities, including satellite radio. Television includes news programs and talk shows. The same story concepts may appeal to all media outlets, but the delivery of information differs, and each outlet has its own nuances. Also, be aware that deadlines are very different depending on the outlet.

Newspapers

Depending on where you live, newspapers vary tremendously in size. While most newspapers are daily publications, many cities and towns have local small papers that come out on a weekly basis.

Generally, the larger the city, the larger the newspaper, and the more reporters it has. Usually, most reporters cover specific topics known as a "beat." Identify the reporters who cover health, science, medicine, fitness, or other related topics. They may be open to interviewing you as a nutrition expert.

Magazines

Some RDs seek to be quoted in magazine articles. Others write articles for placement (see Chapter 11). Ultimately, the magazine editor decides which stories to include in each issue.

There are many types of magazines, including trade, consumer, and business publications. Many are geared specifically toward food, fitness, and health, and they are always looking for fresh ideas and new experts to quote.

Radio and Satellite Radio

Many Americans consider radio their primary news source because it allows them to multitask while they listen (3). The opportunities for becoming a guest on radio talk shows are plentiful and include national, syndicated, and local shows. Some talk shows are general interest, while others have specialized focuses.

Television

The on-air opportunities in television include newscasts, community calendar announcements, public service announcements, public affairs shows, and entertainment talk shows (5). Most TV programs have a producer who coordinates the program and makes the final decision on which stories to cover. Be aware of the visual element of television as you think about the opportunities you may want to pursue.

Developing Media Skills

It takes time and perseverance to become media savvy. Some people are born naturals, while others need to work a little harder to master the skills. Many dietetic association meetings offer sessions on media training, and those are a great place to begin to learn the ropes. You can also take media training courses or hire a media training coach, but they can be quite costly. The American Dietetic Association (ADA) provides media training to their spokespersons. If you have the opportunity to take this training, jump on it immediately.

Keeping Tabs on the Media

If you want to get into the media game, start by doing your homework. Become familiar with the various media outlets and what they are covering. Watch television, read newspapers and magazines, and listen to the radio. Pay attention to differences in coverage among types of outlet, identify the locations and audiences of each outlet, and observe the styles of the reporters. Take note of the types of stories covered and which experts they use. Look for regular segments within a newscast or feature columns in newspapers or magazines. Once you familiarize yourself with media coverage, you will have a better sense of what information you can provide to the media and who will be interested.

Your homework also includes keeping up-to-date on issues in food and nutrition. Sign up for the ADA's Daily News and Journal Review e-mails (subscribe at http://www.eatright.org), attend continuing-education programs, and peruse major medical journals, the *Journal of the American Dietetic Association*, and other ADA publications. In addition to staying abreast of scientific and professional developments, familiarize yourself with what the public is reading, viewing, and hearing. Follow the buzz on professional Listservs and check the covers of popular magazines. Visit your local bookstore to see what cookbooks, diet books, health, and self-help books are in the public eye (5). For more information on following trends, see Chapter 5.

Once you have done your homework, create and regularly update a list of your media contacts. The ADA publication *Working with the Media* (5), which can be found in the members-only section of the ADA Web site (http://www.eatright.org), has media contact sheets you can download and use. In fact, you can download the entire publication for free. It is an excellent resource for those who want to get into the media game.

Generating and Pitching Newsworthy Stories

Reporters are always on the lookout for unique and interesting stories. Potentially, you can make their job easier by providing such stories. You can help them look good by providing story ideas along with pertinent credible information related to the story. This is referred to as pitching a story. To create a pitch, start by identifying those stories that you think will appeal to the public (see Box 12.4) (6). A reporter's job is to provide stories that the public will like, so your job is to put yourself in the shoes of the audience and determine what they want to know.

As you think about story ideas to pitch to the news media, remember the "five Ws": Who, What, Where, When, and Why (plus How) (5). Before you contact a reporter, know the answers to these questions so you can provide all

Box 12.4 Elements of a Newsworthy Story

- **Conflict:** Every story has two sides. What is the other side of the story you are telling?
- **Human interest:** Can you relate the story to individuals or groups of common interest to the reporter's audience? Does it strike an emotional cord?
- **Newness:** Is this the first time the topic has been covered? If not, can you put a new twist on an old story?
- **Prominence:** Does the story involve a celebrity or someone well-known?
- **Proximity:** Does the story have a local angle? Will it affect people in the area?
- **Significance:** How much impact does the story have on the audience who will read, see, or hear it? How important is the story in comparison to other news that's happening that day, week, or month?
- **Timeliness:** How recently did the event occur or how soon will it occur?
- **Unusualness:** Is there anything strange or out of the ordinary about this story?

Source: Adapted from *Telling Your Story: Control the Questions*. Rosemont, IL: Dairy Management Inc; 2008:5, with permission from the National Dairy Council.

the information he or she needs. These reporters have editors who make the decisions about which stories to cover, and often many reporters are competing to have their story run. If you provide reporters with a good story and supporting information, they can then pitch to their editor.

Your story idea will need a hook, something to draw reporters and their audiences to the information you provide. Three hooks that are sure to grab the attention of the public and therefore the media are "health, heart, and pocketbook" (5). Food and nutrition messages are often about health, so our profession lends itself to providing an automatic hook. Pitching a story about how to provide low-cost healthy dinners appeals to the pocketbook (and health!), while a story about gathering the family for regular meals can appeal to the heart.

Keep in mind that the public does not want to hear from experts who only offer facts, figures, or scientific data. They want to know how you can help them. Providing tips will catch the public's attention. Stories such as "how to slim down while eating your favorite foods" or "ten foods you can eat to boost your energy" will provide the audience with concrete information that they can use.

Once you have your newsworthy story idea, it is time to contact a reporter and make your pitch. Keep in mind that reporters are always busy and working on deadline. Timing is everything. In television, your story's chances improve if you pitch it on a slow news day (7). Also, the time of day you pitch your story can be crucial. Avoid pitching your story immediately before a newscast or print deadline.

Types of Pitches

The 30-Second Telephone Pitch

One way to pitch your story is to call a reporter to explain your story idea. Before you call, prepare and practice a 30-second speech. You may speak directly to the reporter or you may need to leave a voice mail. Either way, begin by introducing yourself, give your credentials, and describe your idea. For example, "Hello, my name is Jane Doe. I am a registered dietitian, and I have a story idea. Do you have a minute?" If the answer is yes, provide one or two sentences to describe your idea. To begin building a relationship with a reporter, follow the stories he or she covers. If you particularly like a story, give a compliment and then suggest another story idea (7,8). When you leave a voice mail, be sure to say your phone number slowly. If a reporter has to replay the message to get your contact information, you are history (7). If you do not get a call back, try again later. Reporters get busy, and a polite reminder may help.

The E-mail Pitch

Some reporters like to get story pitches by e-mail, while others do not. Some do not want to open attachments for fear of getting computer viruses (7). If you can get in touch with reporters, you can ask whether they prefer e-mail, a fax, or "snail" mail. Otherwise, use a catchy title in your subject line to pique the interest of the reporter. Your e-mail should be no more than 250 to 300 words (5).

The Pitch Letter

Another way to contact reporters is to send a pitch letter. Just like an e-mail pitch, keep your pitch letter to less than 300 words. Get to the point quickly and explain why the reporter's audience will be interested in the story. Don't forget the Who, What, Where, When, Why, and How, as well as "Who cares?" (5). Do not use the following words: basically, essentially, actually, really, nice, past, future, located, presently, and currently. They are unnecessary (5). Paint a visual picture with your words. Reporters tell stories with such images (7).

Press Releases

A press release is your pitch on paper (7). If you make your pitch by phone, the press release can be a supplement to your called-in pitch so that the reporter has the facts on paper. Alternatively, you can send one instead of making a phone call. Reporters like to have the facts on hand.

When preparing a press release, make it punchy and short. One double-spaced page is the maximum length. Be sure to include relevant contact information. Make the press release memorable by being creative. The ordinary and mundane will not attract attention. For guidance on creating a press release, refer to Box 12.5.

Box 12.5 Guidelines for Creating a Press Release

- Provide newsworthy content. Your release must have an angle or "hook" to get read at all. The headline should sum up the purpose of the release.
- Start strong. Your first sentence and your first paragraph must tell the story. It should tell the reader who, what, when, where, why, and how of the story. The reader may not read beyond that first sentence. Subsequent paragraphs can provide more details.
- Use the active voice. Be concise and to the point. Avoid clichés and stick to the facts. Every word counts.
- Limit the release to one page.
- Include a release date at the top of the press release. FOR IMMEDIATE RELEASE should appear at the top of your press release.
- Do not use press releases to make sales. They should not scream "buy me."
- Include your complete contact information.
- Proofread and check grammar. Spelling counts! Proofread again.

Even if you follow the guidelines in Box 12.5 and send the perfect press release, the media may not pick up your story. Keep in mind it is not the format of the press release that sells the story; rather, the story sells the story (7). Don't spend too much effort deciding what kind of paper to use or which colors will work best in your press release. A great story sells itself, and the very first sentence is much more important than the layout or the type of paper used for your press release (7). This does not mean you should skip the press release altogether. The news industry still considers the press release an important way to pitch a story. See Box 12.6 for a sample press release.

Press Kits

A press kit is generally used to promote the launch of a new product, new company, news conference, or other large events. It is a prepackaged collection of promotional company information and articles intended to address questions from the media, investors, potential clients, and others. Consider creating a press kit when you are trying to promote something to many media outlets at once. For example, if you run a corporate-wellness company that has been hired to plan and implement a health fair with speakers, cooking demonstrations, and multiple health screenings, you may find a press kit helpful for media outreach.

Box 12.6 Sample Press Release

The Veggie Queen™
For Immediate Release
Janine Gregor
(707) 573-1700
Janine@theveggiequeen.com

Pressure's On—In a Good Way: The Veggie Queen™ Reports Pressure Cooker Use Is on the Rise

Santa Rosa, Calif., January 2009—When things get hot, people say you're in the pressure cooker. When it comes to cooking, that can be a good thing. Using a pressure cooker saves time, money, and energy, and it also preserves nutrients. Americans are finally getting over their fear of pressure cooking, as would be expected with the modern, sleek, and safe spring-valve pressure cooker.

Jill Nussinow, aka the Veggie Queen™, the registered dietitian who cooks well under pressure, author of *The Veggie Queen™: Vegetables Get the Royal Treatment* and the upcoming book *The Veggie Queen™ Cooks Under Pressure: The New Fast Food*, has been teaching home and professional cooks the art of pressure cooking for 13 years. Nussinow emphasizes using beans as an inexpensive protein source, a strategy that certainly helps families eat well in today's depressed economy. One of Nussinow's students determined that the money she saved in a year by cooking her own beans instead of buying them in cans would more than pay for the brand-new, safe, stainless-steel pressure cooker that cost her about $100. This investment will pay itself off for years to come.

The pressure cooker allows you to easily and quickly cook inexpensive cuts of meat and turn them into tender and delectable edibles. Nussinow uses modern spring-valve pressure cookers, without mishaps, in classes she teaches at Santa Rosa Junior College in California. Students are amazed at how quickly the food cooks and how great it tastes. Vegetable soup cooks in just three minutes at pressure.

"If you can boil water and twist a lid, then you can successfully use a pressure cooker. In the past 13 years, I've shown thousands of people how to do it. Once you learn to use your cooker, you'll constantly be thinking about what to put in it next. This time of year, you can enjoy lots of winter squash and root vegetables—think Curried Pumpkin Soup, Three Sisters Stew, Moroccan Root Vegetable Stew, and more," says the Veggie Queen™. She continues, "Not only do you get great-tasting food fast, but you reduce energy usage by at least 50%, and you retain more nutrition. It's a winning combination."

Nussinow produced a DVD, *Pressure Cooking: A Fresh Look, Delicious Dishes in Minutes*, that comes with a 16-page recipe booklet to help people learn how to use a pressure cooker.

Jacques Pepin, TV personality and author of *More Fast Food My Way*, says, "Pressure cookers are designed today so they can't explode. I use an electric one and a standard one that sits on a burner. I use them often, especially when cooking beans or stews, because it cuts the cooking time so dramatically." His latest cookbook, *More Fast Food My Way*, a companion to his PBS series, contains a few recipes produced in the pressure cooker, including chili con carne and lamb curry. But, as Pepin states, bean cookery makes the pressure cooker a modern marvel.

For more information contact Jill@theveggiequeen.com.

The press kit can have many components (see Box 12.7) (5,9–11), and you can find templates for developing press kits online. While a press kit should be a comprehensive, detailed package, be careful not to include every promotional piece you or your company has ever produced. The documentation in each press kit should be targeted to the audience receiving the packet.

Box 12.7 Items to Include in a Press Kit

- Cover letter or letter of introduction. This letter should grab the reader's attention and provide an overview of the contents in the kit.
- Information about the company.
- Short, one-page biographies of company officers or speakers.
- Copies of recent press releases and positive press coverage (articles).
- Sample news story.
- Company newsletter.
- Photographs or camera-ready artwork of logos, charts, or other graphics.
- Company fact sheet.
- Recent awards.
- A DVD or CD of audio and video files of radio or TV interviews, speeches, performances, and any other media-covered events.

It is not necessary to include all of the above items. Carefully consider the recipient and choose those that you think are most appropriate.

Source: Data are from references 5, 9, 10, and 11.

Preparing for the Interview

Once you have successfully pitched a story, it is time to prepare for the interview. Do your research. You must know your subject so you can answer questions with credibility. You may want to prepare a list of questions that the reporter is likely to ask and plan how to answer them. Find out the reporter's first name so that you can use it conversationally during the interview.

Before the interview, investigate who your audience will be. This will allow you to tailor your answers appropriately. Take some time to educate yourself about the specific media outlet you will be dealing with. If you are being interviewed for a print publication, read it to get a feel for the targeted audience. For television and radio interviews, watch or listen to the program and speak with the show's producer, if possible. Ask who will be interviewing you, and if you have time, review the interviewer's work to get a sense of his or her style. Find out if the interview will be taped or live and how long it will last (if it is a TV or radio interview).

Limit your message to three key points. Decide which message you most want the audience to take away and formulate your points to support that message. No matter what questions you are asked in the interview, you should always steer your answers back to those three key points.

Regardless of the type of media, certain interview skills and techniques are helpful. As you gain more experience, these skills will become second nature. Box 12.8 provides practical tips for conducting media interviews (12).

Box 12.8 Interview Tips and Advice

- Be prepared. Being interviewed takes preparation and thought on your part. The more you prepare, the more confident and at ease you will feel, and the more effective you are likely to be.
- Spend time before the interview thinking about brief and bright ways to express your messages. Anticipate questions.
- Limit messages to three key points.
- Keep your sentences short—no more than about 25 words, if possible.
- Visualize one person (real or imaginary) whom you want to know. Be clear about what you're saying in the interview and "speak" to that person.
- Match your message to the audience. A "media pro" thinks about the audience, while the amateur thinks about the topic.
- Tell the truth. Always. Don't mislead or lie. Maintain professional ethics at all times. Don't evade questions. Be direct. Avoid exaggeration or speculation. Stick to the facts.
- Get the important facts out first, especially in a live broadcast interview.
- Use anecdotes and personal experiences to lend context or "color" to your main points.
- Keep cool, even if the interview strays off topic or seems like it's becoming confrontational. Don't be intimidated, argue, or lose your composure.
- Avoid saying "no comment." The reporter and audience may assume you are hiding something. If you don't know the answer, it is okay to say "I don't know."
- You will express yourself best if you keep these "Six Cs" in mind: Be clear, candid, concise, conversational, correct, and compassionate.

Source: Adapted with permission from American Dietetic Association Nutrition Entrepreneurs. *Nutrition Entrepreneurs Tool Kit: Interview Tips and Guidelines.* Chicago, IL: American Dietetic Association Nutrition Entrepreneurs; 2005. http//www.nedpg.org.

Techniques for Conveying Your Key Messages

In the course of an interview, the reporter may ask a question that does not relate to the topic. Some hostile interviewers do this on purpose, as they are trying to throw you off track or get you to say something you should not. More often than not, however, the off-topic question is not asked maliciously. Sometimes, reporters do not do their homework and do not ask the appropriate questions, and other times they just get sidetracked in the conversation. Do not panic. You can use tried-and-try techniques to get the interview back on topic and deliver your key points. These techniques are bridging, hooking, and flagging.

Bridging

Bridging helps you transition the interviewer from an off-topic question back to your topic. You answer the question briefly and honestly but then segue into the answer that you want to give. For example, you are filming a segment on the importance of including calcium in children's diets, and the reporter asks, "Why do you think there are so many overweight kids in America?" You could "bridge" from one topic to another by saying, "While it is true that we do have a problem with childhood obesity in this country, we also know that kids are not getting enough calcium in their diets. Let me give you some tips on how to make sure your kids get enough calcium." Other examples of bridging are:

- "I am not sure about that, but what I do know is ..."
- "Yes, and in addition ..."
- "We used to think that, but now we know ..."

Hooking

Hooking steers the interviewer to the question you want him or her to ask. Perhaps you are speaking with a reporter about how important it is to include more fruits and vegetables. You could say, "You will never believe what a recent study by the Department of Agriculture discovered." This will lead the reporter to ask, "What did they find?" Further examples of hooking include:

- "You'll be surprised to hear what our panel of experts recommended."
- "The most important thing for parents to remember is ..."
- "You'd probably be interested in some of the programs we are running."

Flagging

Flagging is a way to make sure the audience and the reporter remember your most important key point. Here are some examples:

- The most important thing you need to remember is ..."
- The bottom line is ..."
- The real issue is ..."

All of these techniques are critical parts of your media toolkit. Keep them in mind before you begin your interview.

Lights, Camera, Action: The Art of the TV Interview

A television interview presents a particular set of challenges. Because of the visual components of TV, there are many details to attend to before your interview. In addition to being well versed in your topic, you need to present a professional appearance and be very aware of your body language.

Dressing for Success

The most important thing to remember when dressing for television is to look professional. Women should wear a jacket, blazer, or cardigan so they have somewhere to clip the microphone. Bright colors show well on television. Avoid large or dangling jewelry, and wear more makeup than usual as the camera can make you look washed out. Men should usually wear a dark suit in conservative colors. Solid colors appear more authoritative (5). Do not wear stripes or patterns; they appear busy on the screen (3). Make sure your hair is neat and away from your face. These are general guidelines. Depending on the type of newscast, when it airs, and who the viewers are, you may want to dress more casually. If you are not sure, ask the producer.

Body Language

TV viewers do not pick up meaning just from the words you say. They also interpret your tone of voice and body language. Therefore, it is important to appear relaxed and confident when you are on TV. When you are being interviewed, sit attentively and lean forward slightly to convey interest. Cross your feet at the ankles and do not bounce your feet. If you are standing during your interview, stand straight but do not appear too rigid. Make sure your hands are open and maintain eye contact with the interviewer. Do not look at the camera unless there is no host. Use gestures to emphasize your point, but keep your hands below your face. Have a slight smile on your face, even when you are talking.

Perhaps all of these instructions are making you nervous. A little bit of stage fright is perfectly normal. The more interviews you conduct, the more natural all of this will become. Remember to relax and have fun with each interview. Box 12.9 provides an encouraging example of how one RD consults to the media.

Following Up on the Interview

After you have completed the interview, remember to follow up. If the interview is for a radio or television piece, be sure to thank the reporter for giving you the opportunity to work with him or her. Compliment the story after it airs and share feedback you have received about it. If you were interviewed for a magazine or some other type of weekly or monthly publication, the piece will not run immediately. Contact the reporter within a day or so after the interview and offer to assist with further information or clarification. Once

Box 12.9 One Registered Dietitian's Media Success

Lisa Drayer, MA, RD, decided she wanted to combine nutrition counseling with a career in journalism because she had always enjoyed writing. She chose to obtain a master's degree in science, health, and environmental reporting so she could pursue a career in health reporting and the media.

After completing her journalism degree, Lisa was hired as a full-time editorial manager for a weight-management Web site that needed a nutrition professional who also had writing skills. She wrote and edited content for the site, including feature articles, news articles, an expert column, recipes, and more. During this time, Lisa frequently received calls from local and national networks, including CNN, to appear as an on-air nutrition expert for specific news stories. A few months and several segments later, she pitched a weekly segment to CNN titled "Breakfast with Daybreak" for the network's *Daybreak* show. A year later, the segment became a reality. When she left her full-time job, Lisa became a freelancer with CNN and CNN Headline News, as well as WCBS-TV in New York.

Lisa provides the following advice for those who aspire to work with the media:

- Learn as much as you can about writing and reporting.
- Keep in mind, when you are in a reporter's role, you are not stating your opinion. Rather, you are creating a story based on hard facts that typically involve two sides of a story. This is not the same as giving your expert opinion as an RD.
- Consider a master's degree in communications or journalism. If you cannot commit to a degree program, consider taking a few classes.
- If your goal is to appear on camera, it is important to look and sound polished—wardrobe, makeup, hairstyle, and dialect are all important.
- Consider becoming a spokesperson. This work can be very rewarding, especially if you are passionate about the company you represent. Communication skills are key for these roles, as is maintaining a professional appearance.

the story runs, which could be several months after the interview, send a note or e-mail to let the reporter know you liked his or her work. The follow-through is essential to establish an ongoing relationship.

Becoming a Media-Savvy Registered Dietitian: A Summary

RDs who have aspirations of speaking in public or to the media should remember the following points:

- You must have excellent communication skills to speak to large audiences, regardless of the venue. These skills take practice.
- If you want to enter the speaking arena, it may be beneficial to practice your skills through volunteer work. As you become more experienced,

you may choose to seek paid speaking engagements or even make public speaking your career.

- Food and nutrition are hot topics, and RDs are in the unique position of being the experts in the field. Media outlets do want to hear from you. They are always looking for story ideas, and you can potentially make their jobs easier if you provide fresh, timely, and interesting ideas.
- It takes time, practice, and patience to become media savvy. Ensure your success by learning how to monitor the media, develop relationships with reporters, pitch news stories, and conduct interviews.

References

1. Heroux C. Professional speakers vs. professionals who speak. *Ventures*. 2009;25(4):9.
2. Schrift S. The ten habits of highly effective speakers. Sandra Schrift, Executive Speech Coach, blog. June 22, 2005. http://www.schrift.com/blog/2005/06/ten-habits-of-highly-effective.html. Accessed March 12, 2010.
3. Yaverbaum E. *Public Relations for Dummies*. Hoboken, NJ: Wiley Publishing; 2006.
4. Smith SS. *The Everything Public Speaking Book*. Avon, MA: Adams Media; 2008.
5. American Dietetic Association Public Relations Team. *Working with the Media: A Handbook for Members of the American Dietetic Association*. http://www.eatright.org/Members/content.aspx?id=9624&terms=%22working+with+the+media%22. Accessed March 12, 2010.
6. *Telling Your Story: Control the Questions*. Rosemont, IL: Dairy Management Inc; 2008:5.
7. Crilley J. *Free Publicity*. Dallas, TX: Brown Books Publishing Group; 2003.
8. Brown D. Becoming a media-savvy registered dietitian. *J Am Diet Assoc*. 2006;106:1163–1164.
9. Lautenslager A. The ingredients of a press kit. Entrepreneur Web site. http://www.entrepreneur.com/marketing/publicrelations/prbasics/article57260.html. Accessed March 12, 2010.
10. Artists Foundation. Writing a press release, PSA, calendar listing and creating a press kit. http://www.artistsfoundation.org/art_pages/resources/resources_arts_presskit.htm. Accessed March 12, 2010.
11. How to create a press kit. eHow Web site. http://www.ehow.com/how_8794_create-press-kit.html. Accessed March 12, 2010.
12. American Dietetic Association Nutrition Entrepreneurs. *Nutrition Entrepreneurs Tool Kit: Interview Tips and Guidelines*. Chicago, IL: American Dietetic Association Nutrition Entrepreneurs; 2005.

Chapter 13

Endless Possibilities: More Business Opportunities Beyond Private Practice

Once you have decided to go into business for yourself, consider all of the options and opportunities available to you. The possibilities truly are endless! Registered dietitians (RDs) have exhibited creative ways to use their education and skills that have resulted in opportunities, positions, and ultimately, money. This chapter explores various avenues of consulting and ways to branch out from private practice.

RDs across the country have taken the risk and left their jobs to become self-employed. In the American Dietetic Association (ADA) Dietetics Compensation and Benefits Survey 2009, 8 percent of the RD respondents reported that they were self-employed, 8 percent worked in consultation/business, and 5 percent were owners or partners in their practice. Furthermore, those who were self-employed earned substantially higher median wages than those in other dietetics-related positions. On the downside, median wages of those in private practice were reported as one of the few areas of dietetics that did not keep pace with inflation since the 2007 survey (1). While starting a consulting business or a private practice in the field of dietetics is clearly a viable option for those RDs willing to take the plunge, many choose to diversify beyond private practice to increase their earning potential.

Defining the Word "Consultant"

Throughout this book, the terms "private practice" and "consulting" have been differentiated. The difference is based on what one does in one's business. If you are setting up shop to provide individual nutrition counseling, you are in private practice. For the purposes of this book, all other entrepreneurial endeavors have been referred to as consulting. In this chapter, however, a consultant is defined as someone who is self-employed, who is not an employee of any organization or company, and who is paid to provide a specific service. In this regard, RDs in private practice *are* consultants, and many RDs work in private practice while simultaneously pursuing other consulting opportunities.

The Internal Revenue Service has very specific criteria that one must meet to legally be considered a consultant for tax purposes (see Box 13.1) (2). You may wish to consult with an accountant or business adviser to determine your status.

Consulting Opportunities

Years ago, most consultant RDs were either consulting to health care facilities or providing individual patient counseling. This is no longer the case. Now the types of opportunities are endless. RDs have taken their skills and expertise and developed opportunities for themselves that once would not have been considered "dietetics" at all. For example, some RDs are personal trainers, lactation consultants, registered nurses, or professional speakers. Some hold dual degrees or certificates, and others obtain different types of additional training. The goal of this chapter is to provide as many ideas and examples as possible to enable you to map out your game plan, branch out, or supplement your private practice.

As you formulate your ideas, you will probably consider the need to have various arrangements simultaneously. Earning income from just one type of consulting is quite a challenge. To figure out what you enjoy and what you do not, try your hand at various types of consulting. What are you best at? What is your forte? You may even combine consulting positions with those that are not consulting, particularly if you need to earn extra income or retain some benefits. For example, consider accepting a part-time position as a clinical RD in a hospital while you develop your business.

In some cases, you may need to provide your services for free. Before you do so, always ask yourself, "Is it a marketing opportunity?" For example, if you are building a private practice and plan to specialize in child and adolescent nutrition, you may agree to speak at a PTA meeting for free, yet decline

Box 13.1 Internal Revenue Service Criteria for Independent Contractor Status

Behavioral Control

An independent contractor decides the following:

- How, when, and where to do the work
- What tools or equipment to use
- What assistants (if any) to hire to help with the work
- Where to purchase supplies and services
- Which methods will be used to perform services (training is not provided)

Financial Control

According to the following criteria, the independent contractor controls business aspects of the work:

- Contractor has a significant investment in the facilities used for the work.
- Contractor is not reimbursed for most expenses.
- Contractor can incur a loss or realize a profit.

Business Relationship

For the independent contractor, the following are true:

- Employee benefits such as health insurance, paid sick and vacation leave, retirement investments, to name a few, are not provided to the contractor.
- A written contract may indicate independent contractor status.
- An independent contractor usually has a less permanent relationship with a company than an employee would have.

Source: Data are from reference 2.

an invitation to speak to a group of senior citizens. See Chapter 5 for more information on marketing.

Diversification from Private Practice

Many private practitioners find they need to diversify once their private practices are established. RDs who provide one-on-one counseling may seek new opportunities to avoid feeling burned out. If you are working full time as a counselor, schedule frequent breaks. Vacation or mental health days can help refresh you, even if you spend your "time off" catching up on paperwork or cleaning out the office.

Another reason for diversification is to increase income. When you see patients by the hour and bill by the hour, your income is limited. When you don't see patients, you don't make money. A full-time workweek generally consists of 25 to 30 billable hours. The remainder of the "typical" 40-hour week is reserved for paperwork, telephone calls, professional interaction, and down time. Most RDs in private practice find that diversification just happens. Once established in private practice, they begin to receive calls for other types of nutrition-related jobs.

Opportunities to Consult for Health Care Facilities

Many facilities—such as nursing homes, dialysis centers, group homes, hospices, health maintenance organizations (HMOs), day treatment hospitals, and certain types of rehabilitation facilities—do not have the budget to pay an RD's salary on a full-time basis. However, state, federal, and other regulatory agencies require the services of an RD for these facilities to maintain their licenses. Therefore, they contract RDs as part-time consultants. Of course, regulations vary from state to state. If you are interested in pursuing this type of consulting, check the regulations in your state.

Many RDs have successful consulting businesses in which they consult to numerous facilities (also referred to as "accounts"). In this type of arrangement, the RD is under contract to provide nutrition consultation to acute-care and long-term-care facilities, health agencies, home-care companies, and even the foodservice industry. Hence, an entire category of consulting opportunities—consulting for health care facilities—is open to the RD.

Among the many resources available to RDs who want to begin to consult to health care facilities is the ADA Dietetics in Health Care Communities dietetic practice group (DPG). With nearly 4,800 members, this group provides a wealth of information. Members receive a quarterly newsletter, *The Consultant Dietitian*, and the DPG sells many excellent products, including manuals and standards of practice. Refer to Chapter 14 for a listing of more resources in this area.

Public Relations Opportunities

Food companies pay big bucks to promote their products. These companies hire public relations (PR) firms to market their products. More and more often, firms are looking to involve a food and nutrition expert in their campaigns, as they now realize the value and knowledge the RD can bring to the table. Many larger PR firms that represent food companies have full-time RDs on staff. Other firms contract with RDs to do the following:

- Lend credibility to marketing campaigns.
- Serve as a media spokesperson.
- Verify the accuracy of messages in marketing materials, including press releases and ad campaigns.
- Write nutrition articles for company Web sites and blogs.
- Write consumer education and marketing brochures.
- Research and develop research reviews and white papers for health professional audiences.
- Represent products at trade shows.
- Conduct product demonstrations in malls or supermarkets.

Many RDs dream of consulting to a PR firm, in part because these firms pay generous fees. If this is your dream, keep in mind that these firms demand experienced and polished RDs with excellent communication skills (see Box 13.2). If you do not have media experience, become active in your professional organizations to get contacts and begin building your media portfolio with local television, radio, or newspaper interviews (see Chapter 12). Your state dietetic association is a great place to start. Apply for the position of state media representative. This will pave the road to being hired for spokesperson jobs. Once you have some experience, send your biography and samples of your media work directly to staff RDs on PR firms. They may be able to open doors for you.

Box 13.2 Sage Advice about Public Relations Consulting

Janet Helm, MS, RD, chief food and nutrition strategist, North America of Weber Shandwick, a global PR firm, provides this advice:

We frequently hire registered dietitians as consultants, writers, and media spokespersons for various public relations programs for our food and beverage clients. To be considered for these opportunities, it's critical to be a good communicator. That means understanding what's newsworthy and being skilled at translating science into sound bites. You need to be familiar with both traditional and new media and know how the media works and what they need.

I think it's especially important for the RDs we hire to be aware of the business objective and strategies that drive a communications plan. You need to fully understand who we are targeting and what we're trying to communicate. We want solution-oriented dietitians who can help us find creative ways to communicate our key messages, raise awareness of a product, or generate media attention for a campaign.

If your goal is to become a spokesperson or work in another aspect of PR, take some time to reflect on your personal ethical boundaries. It is always wise to determine in advance whether you have strong views about certain products. Make sure you believe in the product you will be promoting. Be true to yourself. Do not sell out!

Opportunities with Corporations

To keep employees healthy and bolster their reputations as good employers, large companies often provide unique employee benefits, such as employee-wellness programs. For these programs, companies may contract an RD to do the following:

- Teach classes, such as brown-bag seminars (see Box 13.3 for sample topics).
- Write brochures or nutrition tips for employee newsletters.
- Provide individual counseling.
- Set up a group weight loss, diabetes, or cholesterol management program.
- Consult with cafeterias to create healthful cafeteria menu items.

Box 13.3 Topics for Seminars or Classes

- Eating on the run
- Healthy snacks
- Healthy restaurant meals
- Proper portions
- Fad diets
- Surviving the holidays
- Eating awareness
- Nutrition 101
- Weight-management strategies
- Endurance eating
- Menopause myths
- Feeding your family
- Packing healthy lunches
- Alternative nutrition
- Carb loading for athletes
- Label reading
- Negotiating the grocery store
- Food safety

Some RDs make corporate wellness their primary source of revenue. If you have multiple corporate clients, you can recycle your lessons, perhaps tailoring them to the audience. You can even purchase ready-to-go seminars geared toward employee health and wellness. Many of them have been developed by successful corporate RDs.

Opportunities at Fitness Centers

Glance through any newspaper and you will see that health clubs and gyms throughout the country are competing for members. They want to offer as many services to their members as possible. Nutrition and fitness go hand in hand, so the opportunities for consulting work in these facilities abound. You can capitalize on this fitness boom by offering the following services to a health club:

- Teaching classes to members. Consider teaming up with a personal trainer or good exercise instructor and create a package of services. It can be a series of classes or single-topic classes. Perhaps the club can provide space to offer individual counseling to club members who request it.
- Writing articles or providing nutrition "bites" for a newsletter or bulletin board.
- Providing a nutrition-related handout for the front desk.
- Setting up an "Ask the Nutrition Expert Day" that will benefit members and increase your visibility.

To find consulting opportunities with fitness centers, offer informational sessions to the trainers. Inform them of your services and assure them you are not there to provide exercise advice. Because their clients tend to take their advice very seriously, trainers can greatly affect your credibility (either positively or negatively). Win them over by demonstrating how you can complement (not replace) them.

Consulting to health and fitness clubs presents unique payment issues. Some clubs may be willing to pay you as a consultant to provide elite services to their members. Too often, however, health clubs cannot afford that. They may request that you charge separately for your services. The challenge is to get the members to pay for extra services that are not included in their club membership. This prospect may seem troubling, but do not let it deter you. You may have to provide some free services to market yourself, but it is possible to pitch your services to this venue. Plenty of RDs successfully consult to health and fitness clubs!

Opportunities to Consult with Physicians and Allied Health Professionals

Some physicians and allied health professionals find it beneficial to hire an RD as a consultant to see their patients, particularly if the physician or allied health professional's specialty area has a strong nutrition-related component. Endocrinologists who treat patients with diabetes, doctors who run weight-management programs, and psychiatrists who treat patients with eating disorders are a few examples. These physicians do not have time to answer nutrition questions or provide patient instruction, so they contract with an RD to provide those services. Some RDs prefer this arrangement to private practice because the physician or allied health professional's practice is responsible for billing patients and other administrative duties. Often the RD is paid a consulting fee to see the patients who are scheduled for them, but the specifics could be worked out differently.

Sometimes a physician who has a nutrition-related practice will contract an RD as a consultant to perform administrative duties. One RD held a consulting position as the program coordinator of an eating-disorders program for a psychiatric practice. Her duties included talking to all potential patients over the phone; performing intake evaluations on all new patients to recommend a treatment plan; and marketing the program by speaking at schools, health fairs, employee assistance programs, and parenting groups. She was also responsible for placing advertisements in local newspapers.

Another RD held a consulting position as the nutrition education director of a large weight-management program in a physician's office. Her duties included developing educational materials to give to patients and working with the staff nutritionists. If this type of position appeals to you, try to target a practice that can use your expertise and go pitch your services. Tell them how your services can complement theirs.

Opportunities with Grocery Stores

Grocery store chains compete for consumer dollars, and they, too, want to be innovative in the services they provide. As consumers become more health conscious, large grocery store chains are implementing nutrition education programs and contracting with RD consultants to develop and conduct these programs. Many of grocery chains rely on RDs to do the following:

- Write pamphlets and other marketing material in the form of nutrition handouts and recipes.
- Provide grocery store tours.
- Perform product and cooking demonstrations.
- Work in the consumer relations department.
- Develop healthful prepared foods.

Even local stores in small towns use guest speakers and cooking demonstrations, not to mention many of the other services previously listed. It is possible to purchase ready-to-go information on how to conduct supermarket tours. For example, Supermarket Savvy (http://www.supermarketsavvy.com) provides presentation kits and tools for RDs to help them organize and conduct tours.

Consulting Opportunities on the Internet

The Internet is a rapidly growing market for consultants. RDs are writing for "e-zines" (online magazines), contributing nutrition-related content to virtual health education programs, and writing content for technical and nontechnical nutrition-related sites. Some RDs have created excellent Web sites to provide public education and sell their products. Some provide online counseling to groups and individuals. See Chapter 6 for more information on technology and Chapter 11 for further information on writing.

Coaching Opportunities

Professional, personal, and health and wellness coaching became popular in the late 1990s, and RDs interested in this field can develop their skills in a training program. Many types of programs are available; the one you choose will depend on your career goals. If your goal is to become a professional or personal coach, you can find a list of accredited coach training schools on the International Coach Federation Web site (http://www.coachfederation.org). If, on the other hand, your goal is to learn coaching skills primarily to complement your work as an RD and better help clients make sustainable changes in health and fitness, you may be interested in a health or wellness-coach training program, such as the one offered by WellCoaches Corporation (http://www.wellcoaches.com). Box 13.4 provides an example of how one RD used her coaching skills to take her business in a new direction.

Box 13.4 Jean Caton MS, MBA, RD: Putting Coaching to Work

Never one to settle for a just a job, I have advanced through several exciting, challenging, and rewarding careers by periodically asking the question "what's next?" In my early career, I worked as an RD, rapidly progressing from a clinical position into department management and leading a dietetics internship.

An MBA degree positioned me for a career path in the business world and ultimately over 20 years working in corporate America, where I had career and life opportunities beyond my wildest imagination. When I accepted my first corporate job, I had to relocate from Boston to Chicago. Watching my life's possessions get loaded onto the van, boarding the plane, and taking off to my new life in Chicago was a bit scary, but one of the most important career decisions I have made.

Several years ago, the answer to the "what's next" question was to become a leadership, business, and life coach. That was quite a stretch for the student who entered college to study dietetics because chemistry was her favorite subject in high school. Starting my own business was something I often considered. I decided I was finally ready when I realized to stay on my business marketing career track would require yet another relocation. The coaching business

(continued)

Box 13.4 *(continued)*

was clearly my calling. I had always recognized the importance of mentoring and developing staff and colleagues, enjoyed doing it, and found it was a natural strength.

I returned to school (virtually) and after well over 100 hours of coach training was ready to call myself a coach. The logical first niche I chose was a combination of my coach training, my master's in nutrition, and my RD credential. I opened the doors of my business under the name My Food Coach. I soon discovered my passion was not coaching individuals who wanted to lead healthier lives. Instead, my ideal clients were businesswomen in the health care, science, and technology industries, including, of course, RDs who wanted to advance in their careers.

I am able to leverage my successful career path and empower women to achieve their potential to have successful and fulfilling careers and businesses by developing skills and confidence, overcoming barriers, and earning the income they deserve. My original business vision of coaching individuals has now expanded to include group coaching, an assessment component, professional speaking and training, and product sales.

Other Opportunities

Box 13.5 provides some additional consulting opportunities you may wish to consider. There are so many other opportunities available to RDs it is impossible to list them all. To create your own opportunities, think of unconventional as well as conventional directions you could explore.

Box 13.5 **Potential Consulting Opportunities**

- Alternative and complementary care practices
- Athletic teams
- Universities
- Restaurants
- Private schools
- Culinary schools
- Spas and day spas
- Camps
- Day-care centers
- Correctional institutions
- Group homes
- Dental offices
- Home health agencies

Professional Examples

What it is really like to have your own business and work as a nutrition consultant? To explore this issue, we contacted a number of dynamic, thriving entrepreneurs and asked them the following questions:

- What do you call yourself?
- What jobs do you do under the title of "consultant"?
- What are your primary income sources?
- How do you spend a typical day?
- How would you describe your profession?
- Can you provide a biographical statement explaining what you do?

The profiles that follow are developed from their answers. You may notice that these successful professionals describe their work in similar ways. Common threads exist, and perhaps you will recognize them as traits that constitute a successful entrepreneur. As you will see, successful entrepreneurs rarely put all their eggs in one basket; rather, they work on multiple projects simultaneously and regularly vary the types of consulting they pursue. Successful entrepreneurs are always thinking of the next project.

Hope Warshaw, MMSc, RD, CDE, BC-ADM

Hope Warshaw refers to herself as both an RD and diabetes educator, as she has dual credentials as an RD and certified diabetes educator (CDE). The focus of her work is in diabetes education and diabetes management. She does, however, wear a number of hats, including freelance writer, media expert, insulin pump trainer, and corporate consultant. She has learned to be flexible with titles and work with clients to meet their objectives. Short-term and long-term projects make up the patchwork quilt of her consulting business.

When she thinks of her work as a "consultant," Hope is referring specifically to her consulting and advisory work to corporations. This includes coordinating advisory boards, offering guidance on new products, being part of PR and marketing efforts to support nutrition- or diabetes-related products, and writing content directed to health care professionals or consumers.

Hope's primary income streams are consulting for corporations and freelance writing. At this point, she has several regular corporate clients that she has worked with for many years. In addition, through the course of the year she usually picks up several short-term projects for a number of corporations, including serving as a spokesperson, providing immediate expertise, or writing a few blog pieces. Currently, her freelance writing includes regular contributions to diabetes magazines as well as serving as a diabetes expert reviewer for consumer magazines and a Web site. She also receives royalties for the numerous books she has authored or coauthored.

Hope's life varies from day to day, which is one thing she loves about her work. One day she might update her Web site, the next create a slide presentation, the next write a magazine article, and the next provide insulin pump training. She works hard and relatively long days. She works out of her home office, which provides flexibility for her family and herself.

Hope's biographical statement is as follows: Hope Warshaw is a nationally recognized and respected RD and diabetes educator. She applies nearly 30 years of experience and expertise in her business, Hope Warshaw Associates, LLC. She works as an author, freelance writer, media spokesperson, consultant, and diabetes educator. She offers practical solutions for healthier eating during individual counseling sessions or to millions through varied communication vehicles.

Hope is the author of numerous books about diabetes management and healthy restaurant eating, including several published by American Diabetes Association, such as *Real Life Guide to Diabetes, Diabetes Meal Planning Made Easy*, and *Guide to Healthy Restaurant Eating*. She is also the author of *Eat Out, Eat Right* (Surrey Books). Hope is a contributing editor for *Diabetic Living* as well as *Better Homes & Gardens* magazine and Web site.

As a nutrition and diabetes consultant, Hope has worked with companies such as McNeil Nutritionals, LLC, a Johnson & Johnson Company; National Starch Food Innovation; PRESENTdiabetes.com; Can-Am Care; Amylin Pharmaceuticals; and others.

Tracy Fox, MPH, RD

Tracy Fox refers to herself as a "nutrition policy consultant." Her official title, however, is president of Food, Nutrition and Policy Consultants, LLC. Tracy works on a variety of projects related to food, nutrition, and physical activity policy at the federal, state, and local levels.

Tracy provides analysis and advice to clients and other entities such as the Institute of Medicine, tracks policy issues related to nutrition and physical activity with an emphasis on obesity prevention, and provides expertise to clients on how certain policies affect them and how they can influence policy. For example, she works with the Robert Wood Johnson Foundation Center to Prevent Childhood Obesity in its initiatives to address childhood obesity. Tracy uses evidence and research from many programs funded by the foundation to educate legislators and other policy makers on policies and programs that promote sound nutrition and physical activity.

Tracy speaks to health and nutrition audiences—including state and local health department professionals, dietetic associations, and at national nutrition meetings—on a variety of policy issues, such as efforts to promote environments where healthy eating and physical activity are the norm. She also meets with members of Congress and staff to advocate and educate on health and nutrition issues and is working on a number of educational and policy projects at the national level, including with the US Department of Agriculture (USDA) and Head Start. These activities complement the numerous board and volunteer positions she holds, such as serving on Institute of Medicine committees related to obesity prevention in children, and as president of the Society for Nutrition Education.

Tracy's primary income sources come from nonprofit organizations, federal agencies, other consultants and consulting companies, public relations firms, and the food industry. When she is not traveling or meeting with government officials in and around Washington, DC, she spends most of her day working in her home office in DC.

Tracy's biographical statement is as follows: Tracy Fox, president of Food, Nutrition & Policy Consultants, LLC, has worked in the federal government and private sector for over 20 years and has extensive experience in federal nutrition policy and the legislative and regulatory process. Her clients include federal, state, and local agencies; public relations firms; food manufacturers; and nonprofit organizations, where she provides advice and expertise on policy and nutrition initiatives. She is an advocate for children and dedicated to promoting healthy food and beverage choices in and out of school. Areas of expertise include child nutrition and school health; federal, state, and local nutrition policy advocacy; and government relations. She has presented and spoken at national, state, and local venues across the country, and she is quoted and appears regularly in print, radio, and TV outlets on subjects such as school nutrition, children's health, obesity, physical activity, and nutrition policy.

Nadine Fisher, MS, RD

Nadine calls herself an Internet entrepreneur, technology specialist/consultant, and RD. Her current consultant roles are primarily technology related. In the past, she has also provided consultant nutrition services to individuals as well as long-term-care and institutional facilities.

Nadine has managed to pursue her entrepreneurial endeavors while maintaining a salaried position. She earns her base income as a county government manager overseeing maternal and child-health programs that primarily serve needy families. In that position, she has the opportunity to develop Internet-based communication and social marketing venues for the programs she oversees and for emergency-preparedness operations in the county. She loves her government job and cannot justify giving it up, as she will soon be eligible for paid retirement.

Nadine also loves her private business operations, which focus exclusively on technology and the Internet. She provides private consultations—usually by personal referral—on using technology, Web development, and Internet communications. Most, but not all, of her clients are involved in nutrition or health, and she consults to both individuals and organizations. She is also paid to speak and provide Webinars for state dietetic associations on technology and related topics.

A typical day for Nadine consists of rising early to work with private clients via her home-office computer. Later, she travels a short distance to her government office and works there until late afternoon. She returns home in the evening and generally does not work after 7 PM. This is a rule she set when she found she was working too late into the evening. She often works on weekends, during her government vacation time, and on holidays. She has a lot of time off and flexibility with her schedule. Nadine enjoys her consulting work so much that she does not mind working "overtime."

Nadine's biographical statement is as follows: Nadine is a master's-prepared, licensed RD located in the Midwest. In her private practice, Nadine provides nutrition and technology consultations, specializing in Web site design and development as well as emerging business technologies for health-focused programs. Many RDs know Nadine from her previous role as Internet and business technology chair of the Nutrition Entrepreneurs Dietetic Practice Group. In addition to owning Nutrition Networks Web Solutions, Nadine is a writer and editor for a variety of nutrition-related publications, including the *Ventures* newsletter, the Iowa Dietetic Association *Bulletin*, and the monthly e-zine *Tech Talk*. Nadine also coordinates and hosts live teleconferences for Nutrition Entrepreneurs members on various technology-related topics. You can learn more about Nadine by visiting her Web site (http://www.nutritionnetworks.com).

Kate Geagan, MS, RD

Kate calls herself a nutrition consultant, speaker, "green eating" expert, and author. Her business has evolved over the past five years. She has specialized in corporate wellness, but now she focuses on media communications, consulting on the "green space" of food and nutrition for companies, motivational speaking, and serving as a spokesperson for foods or products that fit with her message and core beliefs. Kate generates her income through her media communications contracts, spokesperson work, speaking, and writing.

It is difficult to describe a "typical" day for Kate. She feels that different times of year have different elements. In the fall she is busy pitching proposals to speak at spring or fall meetings, lining up or executing work around the ADA's Food and Nutrition Conference and Expo (FNCE), and investing in the strategic direction of her business for the upcoming year. Consulting, speaking, writing her column, and spokesperson work continue throughout the year.

Kate's biographical statement is as follows: An award-winning RD, Kate is a nationally known nutrition and health expert who is in demand when the topic is smart eating for busy people. Her message is simple: clean, healthy food is the best way to a lean and healthy body. Kate is the author of *Go Green, Get Lean: Trim Your Waistline with the Ultimate Low-Carbon Footprint Diet* (Rodale, 2009). Kate is also the nutrition columnist and an advisory board member for *Pregnancy* magazine, where she dishes on the latest health and nutrition info for moms-to-be. For more than a decade, Kate has worked as a speaker, counselor, and nutrition consultant; her clients include dozens of leading companies, such as GE Aircraft, Sun Microsystems,

Reebok International, Yankee Candle, Pricewaterhouse Coopers, Boston Scientific Corporation, Citistreet, Nova Biomedical Corporation, Tufts Health Plan, and Harvard Pilgrim Healthcare. Companies and groups hire Kate to motivate, educate, and inspire their members to improve their performance, navigate the fast-food landscape, and feel their best. While living in Boston in 2004, Kate was named Recognized Young Dietitian of the Year in Massachusetts by the American Dietetic Association.

A trusted media expert, Kate has been widely quoted in top media publications including *O, the Oprah Magazine; Time; The Wall Street Journal; Boston Globe; Chicago Tribune; Atlanta Constitution; Self; Prevention; Health; Family Circle; Woman's Day; Body & Soul Magazine*; and MSNBC.com. Kate has also appeared on the *Dr. Oz Show, Martha Stewart Radio*, and NBC, ABC, CBS, Comcast, and FOX affiliates across the country. Kate graduated magna cum laude from Middlebury College and received her master's degree in nutrition and health promotion from Simmons College, where she was awarded the Outstanding Student Award. Kate also spent over a year working at the Mangia cooking school in Florence, Italy, where she honed her culinary skills and love of all things Italian. In April 2006 she partnered with Field to Plate to cohost an Exchange Forum on Childhood Obesity and School Lunch in Challans, France.

Kate is a member of the American Dietetic Association, the Utah Dietetic Association, the Nutrition Entrepreneurs DPG, the Dietitians in Business and Communication Practice Group, and the Hunger and Environmental Nutrition Practice Group. She has held several leadership positions in local, state, and national dietetics. She enjoys skiing, hiking, and mountain biking with her husband and two children while living in Park City, Utah.

Mitzi Dulan, RD, CSSD

Mitzi refers to herself as an author, spokesperson, speaker, and sports nutritionist. Under the title of "consultant," she provides sports nutrition counseling to Kansas City's professional football and baseball teams and pursues writing and spokesperson work. Mitzi's primary income is generated by spokesperson and consulting work. A typical day depends on whether she is traveling or not; she travels about 15% of the time. On a typical day in her home office, she answers e-mails and works on her never-ending to-do list, which is an extension of her business's strategic plan. She might spend about 30 minutes a day on her blog (http://www.nutritionexpert.com), 1½ hours per day answering e-mail, 1 hour at the gym or playing tennis, 2 hours moving different projects forward, and 1 hour reading. Sometimes she makes conference calls or meets with professional athletes. The great thing about her job is that no two days are ever the same. Mitzi also spends considerable time answering media requests for magazines and newspapers.

Mitzi's biographical statement is as follows: Mitzi Dulan, RD, CSSD, is a highly regarded expert in the field of nutrition, exercise, and wellness. A frequently requested speaker, she is an RD, Board Certified Specialist in

Sports Dietetics, and Certified Health Fitness Specialist through the American College of Sports Medicine. Mitzi is coauthor of *The All-Pro Diet* (Rodale, 2009) with NFL player Tony Gonzalez. For several years Mitzi was in private practice in San Francisco, where she specialized in sports nutrition, personal fitness, and wellness. She now resides in Kansas City. Mitzi is currently the nutritionist for the Kansas City Chiefs football team and the Kansas City Royals baseball team. She has been a sports nutrition consultant to the Golden State Warriors basketball team and the San Jose Sharks hockey team. Mitzi was also the University of California, San Francisco, sports nutritionist and the director of nutrition services for the San Francisco Bay Club. In Kansas City, Mitzi acts as a media spokesperson and provides nutrition counseling for clients that range from CEOs to stay-at-home moms to professional athletes. She also speaks to organizations throughout the country that want to help their employees improve their health and performance. As "America's nutrition expert," Mitzi has conducted over 200 television interviews. She appeared on the Emmy Award-winning television show *Starting Over* as the nutrition expert for the houseguests. She has also frequently appeared on the nationally syndicated "Dr. Dean Edell" segments and across the country on CBS, NBC, ABC, and FOX affiliates in major media markets. Mitzi has been featured on Discovery's Science Channel, in-flight videos for United Airlines, and National Public Radio. She has appeared on television in Paris, France.

Mitzi has served as media spokesperson for many clients, including the National Honey Board, Hass Avocado Board, Fiji Water, Horizon Organic, Cherry Marketing Institute, Wild Blueberries, and Green Giant. She has been quoted in numerous publications, including the *Wall Street Journal, Newsweek, Family Circle, Men's Fitness, Glamour, Fitness*, and *Walking Magazine*, and online at ESPN.com and Glamour.com. She has consulted for public relations companies, including Edelman (New York), Ogilvy (New York), Porter Novelli (New York), Publicis Dialog (Seattle), Weber Shandwick (Chicago), Boasberg/Wheeler Communications (Kansas City), Fineman Associates (San Francisco), and the Kotchen Group (Hartford).

Lauren Swann, MS, RD

Lauren refers to herself as a nutrition consultant to the food industry, specializing in food labeling and marketing communications. She also calls herself a freelance writer.

Lauren's specialties include food labeling regulations, marketing communications, and "cultural foodways" (ethnic dietary practices). She assists food companies in ensuring their package labels comply with government requirements, and she helps with the strategy and positioning for products as well as for public health educational efforts, such as social marketing campaigns for her food company clients. She has also created a niche specialty that focuses on the effect of culture and ethnicity on food choices.

Most of Lauren's income is generated from food labeling work, including nutrient analyses of products, recipes, and menus as well as ingredient research, government liaison work, competitive label reviews, and industry and trade practice assessments. She is involved in speaking, writing, and delivering presentations about food labeling regulations and laws. An additional income source is marketing communications projects, including freelance writing, media work, and public speaking about nutrition trends and communications strategies. This can also include advising food companies on marketplace positioning and fanciful labeling or ad copy.

Lauren likes to start her day to with a cardiovascular workout or brisk power walk with her dog. Next, she grounds herself by reviewing relevant news trends from e-bulletins and newsletters. She contributes links to and participates in discussions on professional Listservs and targeted online social media, including LinkedIn, Twitter, and Facebook. She then does her client project work, such as running product nutrient calculations, researching regulations, reviewing articles, or writing reports. She tries to get the daily news and trends briefing done early in the day before conventional business hours start and clients begin to e-mail and call. Lauren makes it a point to respond to requests for fee quotes and project proposals as quickly as possible. She usually spends at least one hour a day on volunteer professional association work.

Lauren's biographical statement is as follows: Creatively applying the dynamics of strategic marketing communications to food and nutrition, Lauren's uniquely diverse background spans the full range of nutrition communications, from expertise in highly technical food labeling regulations to writing for consumer, trade, and professional audiences. Lauren also specializes in cultural dietary practices. In 1990 she founded Concept Nutrition, Inc., to meet industry and public health needs for effective delivery of accurate nutrition and food messages. Among her most notable accomplishments, Lauren established the regulatory affairs department for Vlasic Foods world headquarters and has developed food label copy for competitive marketplace positioning as well as government compliance for hundreds of food items, including novel ingredients and formulas, gourmet award winners, and Kraft Foods' first fat-free products.

Lauren regularly writes feature articles for numerous trade and popular publications, including *Prepared Foods* and the *Philadelphia Inquirer*. She has served as contributing nutrition editor for *Heart & Soul* and *Food Processing* magazines, and coauthored the country's first healthy soul food cookbook, *The Black Family Dinner Quilt*. Lauren has delivered dozens of presentations at professional conferences, appeared on CNN, BET, and all major TV networks, and guest lectured at many major universities. Lauren is a recipient of the distinguished Outstanding Entrepreneur Award from the Nutrition Entrepreneurs DPG of the American Dietetic Association and has served as the DPG's chair. She has also served on the board of directors and chaired committees for affiliate chapters of the Pennsylvania Dietetic Association,

American Marketing Association, and many other food and nutrition associations. Lauren is a member of the American Society of Journalists & Authors, National Speakers Association, and Les Dames D'Escoffier.

Are You Ready Now?

There are so many interesting, intense, innovative entrepreneurs across the country. The professionals highlighted in this chapter are only a few of the successful food and nutrition entrepreneurs. It was very difficult to decide which RDs to include. We hope these examples inspired you with ideas that you can incorporate into your marketing plan. You can combine some or all or the various aspects of consulting to create your dream job. Now is the time for you to chart your course and control your career path.

Endless Possibilities: A Summary

Here are the main points you should take away from this chapter:

- RDs nationwide are trading in their traditional jobs to start their own consulting businesses.
- The Internal Revenue Service has a list of criteria that determines whether someone is defined as a consultant for tax purposes. You should understand these criteria before striking out on your own.
- Consulting and home-based businesses are a growing market trend. Economic downturns tend to promote an increase in small home-based businesses.
- The benefits of self-employment in the field of food and nutrition include increased job satisfaction, scheduling flexibility, and higher salaries.
- Traditionally, most self-employed RDs were in private practice. It is becoming more common for RDs to begin many types of nutrition-based businesses that are unrelated to private practice.
- Private practitioners often diversify and branch out into other areas of consulting, such as public speaking, writing, media and spokesperson work, health and fitness work, and corporate wellness.

References

1. Ward B. Compensation & Benefits Survey 2009: despite overall downturn in economy, RD and DTR salaries rise. *J Am Diet Assoc.* 2010;110:25–26.
2. Internal Revenue Service. *Employer's Supplemental Tax Guide.* Washington, DC: US Department of Treasury; 2009. IRS publication 15A.

Chapter 14

Resources for Success

Publications for Starting and Staying in Business

Leonsy R. *Start Your Own Business*. Irvine, CA: Entrepreneur Media; 2007.

Litt A, Mitchell FB. *Be Your Own Boss Starter Kit*. Self-published. 2008. Available at: http://www.fayethenutritionist.com.

Stanny B. *The Secrets of Six-Figure Women*. New York, NY: HarperCollins Publishers Inc; 2002.

Strauss SD. *The Small Business Bible: Everything You Need to Know to Succeed in Your Small Business*. Hoboken, NJ: John Wiley & Sons; 2008.

Tyson E, Schell J. *Small Business for Dummies*. 3rd ed. New York, NY: Wiley Publishing; 2008.

Nutrition Resources and Products

Nutrient Analysis Software

The Food Processor
ESHA Research, Inc.
http://www.esha.com

Foodworks
The Nutrition Company
http://www.nutritionco.com

Nutribase
CyberSoft, Inc.
http://www.nutribase.com

Organizations Providing Nutrition Education and Counseling Resources

American Dietetic Association
http://www.eatright.org

Dietetic Practice Groups of the American Dietetic Association

Members of the various practice groups receive free resources, such as monthly newsletters and access to electronic mailing lists. Most DPGs sell resources to both members and nonmembers. Consult their Web sites for further benefits (DPG sites are linked to the ADA Web site, http://www.eatright.org). Key DPGs include the following:

- Dietetics in Health Care Communities (http://www.cdhcf.org)
- Dietitians in Business and Communications (http://www.dbconline.org)
- Nutrition Entrepreneurs (http://www.nedpg.org)
- Sports, Cardiovascular, and Wellness Nutrition (www.scandpg.org)
- Weight Management (http://www.wmdpg.org)

The Center For Mindful Eating
http://www.tcme.org

Food and Health Communications
http://www.foodandhealth.com

Gurze Books (educational resources on eating disorders)
http://www.bulimia.com

Nasco Nutrition Teaching Aids
http://www.enasco.com/nutrition

National Dairy Council
http://www.nationaldairycouncil.org

National Eating Disorders Association
http://www.nationaleatingdisorders.org

Nutrition Counseling Education Services Publications (NCES)
http://www.ncescatalog.com

Produce for Better Health Foundation
http://www.fruitsandveggiesmorematters.org

The Vegetarian Resource Group (VRG)
http://www.vrg.org

Wheat Foods Council
http://www.wheatfoods.org

Newsletters and Periodicals

Registered dietitians in private practice need to stay current and be well-informed about general nutrition issues and topics of interest to patients. The following are newsletters and periodicals that cover hot topics and new trends.

American Institute for Cancer Research Newsletter
http://www.aicr.org
Subscription is free; past issues online.

Consumer Health Digest
http://www.ncahf.org/digest/chd.html
Free weekly e-mail newsletter; past issues archived and available online.

Cooking Light Magazine
http://www.cookinglight.com
Periodical published 11 times per year; articles available online.

Eating Well: The Magazine for Food and Health
http://www.eatingwell.com
Periodical published quarterly.

Environmental Nutrition
http://www.environmentalnutrition.com
Newsletter published 12 times per year.

FDA Consumer Magazine
http://www.fda.gov/fdac
Periodical published six times per year.

Harvard Health Letter
http://www.health.harvard.edu
Monthly newsletter; past articles online for subscribers only.

Mayo Clinic Health Letter

http://www.mayohealth.org
Eight-page monthly newsletter.

Nutrition Action Healthletter

http://www.cspinet.org
Newsletter published 10 times per year.

Today's Dietitian

http://www.todaysdietitian.com
Periodical published 12 times per year.

Tufts University Health and Nutrition Letter

http://www.healthletter.tufts.edu
Newsletter published 12 times per year; abstracts available online.

UC Berkeley Wellness Letter

http://www.berkeleywellness.com
Eight-page newsletter published 12 times per year.

Books and Online Manual

Kellogg M. *Counseling Tips for Nutrition Therapists, Practice Workbook, Volume 1*. Philadelphia, PA: Kg Press; 2006.
Kellogg M. *Counseling Tips for Nutrition Therapists, Practice Workbook, Volume 2*. Philadelphia, PA: Kg Press; 2009.
Nutrition Care Manual (online). Chicago, IL: American Dietetic Association; annual. For subscription information, go to http://nutritioncaremanual.org or http://www.eatright.org.

Business Resources

Marketing

AllBusiness.com

http://www.allbusiness.com
Provides numerous products and services, such as sample forms, contracts, and business plans, to small businesses.

BarbaraStanny.com

http://www.barbarastanny.com/secrets-of-six-figure-women.html
Resources to increase your earning potential.

Consumer Trends Forum International

http://www.consumerexpert.org
Nonprofit organization which, through newsletters and seminars, offers members information on consumer trends, networking resources, and perspectives into business solutions.

Food Marketing Institute Report

http://www.FMI.org
Annual research study that tracks consumer behavior and attitudes on a wide range of issues that are important to understand the grocery shopper.

Marketresearch.com

http://www.marketresearch.com
Compiles and sells market research reports by industry, market research publisher, and geographic area.

Trendwatching.com

http://www.trendwatching.com
Focuses on consumer insights and behavioral trends and the hands-on marketing/business opportunities they present. Provides a free monthly newsletter.

Business Templates and Tools

Bplans.com

http://www.bplans.com
Provides articles and links for creating successful business plans.

Business Card Design, Marketing, and Printing Tips

http://www.businesscarddesign.com
Includes links to templates, resources, and printers of business cards.

CCH Business Owner's Toolkit

http://www.toolkit.cch.com
Provides information on starting, financing, and marketing your business.

Intuit QuickBooks

http://www.intuit.com
Information on the popular accounting software QuickBooks and additional services for the small business.

Nebs.com

http://www.nebs.com
Source for personalized forms, invoices, and products for small businesses.

Startup Journal

http://www.startupjournal.com
Includes articles and templates for creating business plans.

General Business Support

Chamber of Commerce

http://www.2Chambers.com
Nearly every town has a Chamber of Commerce. They can be helpful to small businesses in their communities.

COBRA Health Plan Advice for Individuals and Small Business

http://www.cobrahealth.com
Links and articles on health insurance for individuals and small businesses.

Entrepreneur.com

http://www.entrepreneur.com
Business resources, with a link to WomenEntrepreneur.com.

FastTrac

http://www.FastTrac.org
Offers classes nationwide in starting and running small businesses.

Insurance.com

http://www.insurance.com
Provides quotes on insurance.

My Own Business

http://www.MyOwnBusiness.com
Free online courses on starting a business.

Office of Small Business Development Centers (SBDC)

http://www.sba.gov/aboutsba/sbaprograms/sbdc/index.html
Sponsored by the SBA, the SBDC is a joint effort of private sector and various levels of government to help and guide you with all aspects of your small business.

The National Association for the Self-Employed (NASE)

http://www.nase.org
Provides many benefits and services, including insurance and resources, to make small businesses or "microbusinesses" successful.

Service Corps of Retired Executives (SCORE)

http://www.score.org
A resource partner with the SBA that provides small business counseling from volunteers who were successful in business.

US Small Business Association (SBA)

http://www.sba.gov
The SBA is a wealth of information for small businesses, providing assistance to help individuals start, run, and grow their businesses. Local SBAs may offer classes on specific topics.

Government Resources

Health Finder
http://www.healthfinder.gov

Internal Revenue Service
Home page: http://www.irs.gov
For tax forms: http://www.irs.gov/formspubs/index.html
For specific information on small businesses: http://www.irs.gov/business/small

National Center for Health Statistics
http://www.cdc.gov/nchs

National Health Information Center
http://www.health.gov/nhic

US Department of Health and Human Services
http://www.hhs.gov

HIPAA Resources

HIPAA Guidelines

Office for Civil Rights—HIPAA
US Dept of Health and Human Services
http://www.hhs.gov/ocr/hipaa

HIPAA Regulations for Covered Entities
American Dietetic Association
http://www.eatright.org/coverage (ADA members only)

HIPAA Obligations for Covered Entities
American Dietetic Association
http://www.eatright.org/Members/content.aspx?id=7504 (ADA members only)

Sample HIPAA Forms

Model HIPAA Notice of Privacy Practice

Sample Patient Written Acknowledgment Confirming Receipt of Privacy Notice
American Dietetic Association
http://www.eatright.org/Members/content.aspx?id=7511 (ADA members only)

Medical Nutrition Therapy and Medicare Resources

American Dietetic Association Publications

The ADA sells Medical Nutrition Therapy Evidence-Based Guides for Practice and Evidence-based Toolkits on topics including adult weight management, chronic kidney disease, disorders of lipid metabolism, gestational diabetes mellitus, and type 1 and type 2 diabetes. ADA also publishes *The Medicare MNT Provider* newsletter. For ordering information on these products, go to http://www.eatright.org/shop and choose "Medical Nutrition Therapy" in the left navigation menu.

Online Information

American Dietetic Association: Coding Coverage and Compliance
http://www.eatright.org/coverage (ADA members only)

American Dietetic Association: Medicare MNT Links and Resources
http://www.eatright.org/mnt (ADA members only)

Centers for Medicare & Medicaid Services
http://www.cms.hhs.gov

ICD-9-CM and ICD-10 Databases

EcodingNow ICD-9-CM and ICD-10-CM Search Results BETA
http://www.ecodingnow.com/OnlineCodes/codes.html

ICD9data Web Site
http://www.icd9data.com

ICD9.Chrisrendres Web Site
http://icd9.chrisendres.com

Book

Hodorowicz MA. *Money Matter$ in Medical Nutrition Therapy and Diabetes Self-Management Training: Increa$ing REimbur$ement Succe$$ in All Practice Setting$: The Complete Guide.* 4th ed. 2008. Available for purchase from: http://www.maryannhodorowicz.com

E-Marketing and Social Media Resources

ConstantContact.com Web site. http://www.constantcontact.com. Online resource for e-mail marketing, online surveys, and event marketing.

Mashable.com: The Social Media Guide. http://www.mashable.com. Social media news and Web tips.

Vaynerchuk G. *Crush It—Why Now Is the Time to Cash In on Your Passion*. New York, NY: Harper Collins; 2009.

Resources for Speakers

National Speakers Association (NSA)

http://www.nsaspeaker.org
Resources and education to advance the skills for those who speak professionally.

Toastmasters International Clubs

http://www.toastmasters.org
A program that teaches individuals how to communicate effectively.

Writing Resources

Books

Beyer J. *You Can Write A Book*. Auburn, MI: NutraConsults; 2009.
Poynter D. *Self-Publishing Manual: How to Write, Print and Sell Your Own Book*. Santa Barbara, CA: Para Publishing; 2007.

Online Resources

Authors Specialty Group of Nutrition Entrepreneurs Dietetic Practice Group

http://www.nedpg.org

Writer's Digest

http://www.writersdigest.com

Index

Page number followed by *b indicates* box; *f,* figure; *t,* table.